IN DEFENSE OF MENTALISM

IN DEFENSE OF MENTALISM:
a Critical Review of the Philosophy of Mind

René Marres
University of Amsterdam

AMSTERDAM 1989

CIP-GEGEVENS KONINKLIJKE BIBLIOTHEEK, DEN HAAG

Marres, René

In defense of mentalism : a critical review of the
philosophy of mind / René Marres; [transl. from the
Dutch by Marleen Rozemond and Philip Clark]. —
Amsterdam : Rodopi
Vert. van: Filosofie van de geest : een kritisch
overzicht. — Muiderberg : Coutinho, 1985. — Met
bibliogr., index.
ISBN 90-5183-071-8
SISO 413 UDC 159.922:13
Trefw.: bewustzijn.
©Editions Rodopi B.V., Amsterdam 1989
Printed in The Netherlands

CONTENTS

PREFACE to the Second Edition

This book is meant to be a review and to establish a point of view. As a review it is not complete. This would hardly be possible, considering the many different aspects of the subject. For instance, the book lacks a special chapter on language and thought. This matter would require a whole book, especially at the moment when it is arousing so much interest. I have decided to pay a lot of attention to various schools of thought.

For this translation - by Marleen Rozemond and Philip Clark - the text has been revised. This has led to what I hope will be an improvement in construction and clarity. A few additions have been made. I thank Juliette Shoenberg-Marres for her assistance.

Chapters 1, 3 and 4 have been somewhat altered and expanded, in order to explain and defend my idea of mentalism in greater detail. In chapter 1 the privacy of mental states and the status of the distinction between being and seeming have been brought into sharper focus. In chapter 3 the theory about one's knowledge of one's own mental states has been strenghtened by a couple of additions. The next chapter on introspection and the unconscious now also deals with a phenomenon such as hypnosis, which indicates a possible split between consciousness and reflexive consciousness.

In the chapter about knowledge of other minds I deal with—and criticise—Strawson's objections to reasoning by analogy. In the discussion on materialism special attention is paid to the points of view of Armstrong and Davidson, and on functionalism Dennett's ideas are given wider coverage.

Finally, when I illustrate the text with examples and talk about 'he', this should usually be read as 'he or she'. It would have been too irritating to write down both words every time.

Dr. René Marres

INTRODUCTION

The philosophy of mind was once practiced under the description 'doctrine of the soul.' The word 'soul' is no longer much used in philosophy because it suggests something that can exist by itself, and because it is strongly associated with immortality. Contemporary philosophy does not want to commit itself to the view that the soul or mind is a substance or immortal and for this reason it chooses more neutral terms such as 'mind', 'the mental' or 'consciousness'. The mind is not necessarily an entity or thing like the body. Maybe 'mind' is only a term for a complex of states or processes. For this reason I will usually not speak of 'the mind' but 'the mental'.

The term 'mental' is usually understood to refer to activities that are specific to human beings, such as thought, volition, and emotion insofar as it involves thought. In contemporary philosophy 'mind' includes everything psychological, even sensory states such as the perception of colors and the sensation of pain, that is, all phenomena which are thought to be non-physical except by materialists. This use of the term 'mind' has been around since Descartes and Locke, and the reasons for it will be discussed extensively. At this point I want to mention just one widely accepted criterion for the mental, namely the idea that mental states are accessible only to their subjects and not to others, which also seems to apply to sensations such as pain.

At first sight it may seem strange to call sensations or emotions mental. This philosophical use of the term can be traced back to Descartes, who used the Latin word for thought 'cogitare' when he meant consciousness. So the philosophy of mind is concerned with phenomena that presuppose consciousness, such as sensation, emotion, thinking, willing, dreaming and remembering.

The philosophy of mind is sometimes also called philosophical psychology, but it is better to distinguish the two. Philosophical psychology is the study of particular mental concepts, while philosophy of mind is concerned with the nature and function of consciousness in general. The latter is the subject of this book.

The following questions will be the focus of attention. Is the mental something distinct which cannot be reduced to anything else? Does it have characteristics that distinguish it from the physical? The mental has been identified with behavior (behaviorism), with physiological processes, in particular processes in the brain (materialistic identity theories) and with functional role (functionalism). These views will receive critical discussion. I will devote special attention to the views of the later Wittgenstein and Ryle.

If the mental is something special, as I will argue, then how do we acquire knowledge of our own mental states? We can acquire such knowledge by means of introspection, but even without introspection we often know what we think or feel. This point leads to a discussion of what in philosophy is called 'reflection', a capacity that is related to introspection.

The unconscious would seem, by definition, not to belong to consciousness. If it lends itself to introspection, however, it seems after all to belong to consciousness in some as yet unclear sense. Exploring the unconscious is important to the study of consciousness, because it is part of an effort to identify its limits.

The next question concerns knowledge of other minds. If we can only observe another person's behavior, and if his mind is something other than his behavior, then how can we know his mind? We can't perceive it, but perhaps we can know it indirectly. In that case the question is whether indirect methods can yield certainty.

The final question is how the mental and the physical are related. One view is that the mental and the physical don't interact, either because they are two aspects of the same thing or because mental and physical processes run parallel to each other. Another view is that the mental and the physical interact causally. But the question is how such interaction is possible. According to the dualism of Descartes the mental can exist by itself, independently of the physical, and can cause movement of the body. Others think that while the mental is distinct from the body, it is only a side effect (epiphenomenon) of the corporeal, and cannot cause anything corporeal. After a discussion of these views I will defend the thesis that the mental is a cause affecting the physical, but only because it is accompanied by corporeal processes.

To what extent is philosophy of mind possible? Science, in particular psychology, studies behavior and consciousness, so what is the task of philosophy? Natural philosophy is no longer practiced and has been replaced by philosophy of natural science. Shouldn't we acknowledge that philosophy of mind also is outdated and cannot claim to achieve knowledge as science does?

Philosophy of mind results in no factual knowledge. It examines concepts and tries to determine which concepts best capture the subject matter and how these concepts should be related. For this reason one might want to identify philosophy of mind with philosophy of psychology. I want to point out, however, that many branches of psychology are no longer concerned with the problems I want to discuss, so that in fact they are almost exclusively part of philosophy. During the nineteenth century they were still discussed in psychological handbooks. Philosophy of mind, like all philosophy, should not be in conflict with what has been established scientifically, but psychology, unlike natural science, lacks a generally accepted conceptual apparatus. For that reason philosophy of mind has more freedom than other branches of philosophy.

What is the place of philosophy of mind in philosophy as a whole? It is related to many other areas, in particular metaphysics, epistemology and ethics. The status of the mental is of great importance in metaphysics; even if one's views about it are not metaphysical in the traditional sense, they will have metaphysical implications. What a philosopher thinks about the mental is often closely connected with his epistemological views, as will become sufficiently clear. The connection with ethics depends on the idea that freedom, which is usually ascribed to consciousness, makes us responsible for our actions. So what one thinks about consciousness has consequences for one's views about ethical questions.

My approach is systematic, not historical. Views from the earlier periods of modern philosophy, which begins with Descartes, will be discussed when they are relevant. Philosophers from the classical period will be omitted not of course out of disdain, but on the ground that since Descartes the discussion has been determined by his conceptualization of the issues. For Plato the distinction between body and soul was strongly conditioned by ethical values, but not so for Descartes. Descartes regarded the physical as identical with what is extended in space and is studied by science, and the mental as identical with consciousness, including sensations such as pleasure and pain. Since he formulated his position, views about the mental have consisted in reactions to it. They either confirm it and elaborate on it or deviate from it and deny it.

The reader will notice that I focus on English and American philosophy. This is a limitation, but most points of view are represented in this literature. I have also considered some German and French literature.

My discussions are analytical in nature. Analysis makes it possible to evaluate the force of arguments and counterarguments before taking a point of view. A.J. Ayer does this particularly well in his writings. I do not object to synthesis. It is necessary and unavoidable. But if synthesis is broad, it usually says little, and if it leads only to the formulation of the point of view of the writer it often looks like preaching to the converted. I have wanted to avoid the latter, but in a book like this one this is possible only to a limited extent, because one needs certain presuppositions in order to get anywhere. Examination of every assumption is an important task, but limitations of size make it incompatible with the purpose of this book.

1. CONSCIOUSNESS

As I mentioned before I will not focus just on the higher mental faculties, such as thinking, willing and feeling. I will be concerned with consciousness in a wider sense that includes sensations, such as those of pain and heat. Consciousness is something so fundamental that it is difficult to give a definition of it that is not circular, that is, a definition whose definiens does not include terms that already implicitly presuppose consciousness. This is not a very serious problem since we are familiar with consciousness and know roughly what we mean by the term. A definition often serves to inform someone who is not yet familiar with the matter in question. Such a definition would be pointless here (Evans, 1970, p. 47). It is possible to indicate what the term 'consciousness' stands for by saying that it is what one has under particular circumstances. We have it when we are awake and not when we are asleep, except when we dream. We recover it when we come out of a coma and it accompanies our actions. It is something we human beings have, and also to some extent the higher animals, but not stones and plants. This does not say much, but it does indicate what we are talking about, which is sufficient at this point.

It is hard to determine where in nature consciousness occurs and where it does not. As one descends the evolutionary scale it is progressively less certain whether particular organisms have consciousness. It may be asked whether certain organisms can, for instance, feel pain. Consciousness probably characterizes only organisms that are capable of locomotion. Such creatures need it in order to find food or escape their enemies. Organisms that can't move have no use for consciousness. But it is also no easy task to determine whether a creature has the capacity of locomotion. Animals do, but there are creatures on the borderline between animal and plant, about which it is not certain whether they have this capacity.

So we can draw no sharp boundary to indicate which beings have consciousness and which don't. Some philosophers, like Schopenhauer and Teilhard de Chardin, have used this fact to shift the boundary -- which nevertheless does exist and roughly falls between plant and animal -- so that everything including inanimate matter has consciousness, or at least an inner life. For Schopenhauer the essence of this inner life is the will which can act unconsciously. This position, which was also held by Spinoza is called panpsychism. Other philosophers have concluded that nothing has consciousness (extreme behaviorists), not even human beings, or rather, that a complete description of human beings does not require terms like 'consciousness' and related expressions.

Such a line of reasoning is not convincing, whatever its results may be. The boundary between the colors red, orange and yellow is also vague, but that is not a good reason for concluding that only red exists, and not orange or yellow. Some shades of color are clearly red, others are clearly yellow (Shaffer, 1968, p. 9). Similarly it is clear that human beings have consciousness but stones don't, since they never give any sign of it. One might say that the atoms of a stone have potential consciousness, since evolution shows that consciousness is potentially contained in inanimate matter, but what does this mean? What is merely potential does not yet exist in reality.

Is consciousness an all or nothing matter or does it admit of degrees? Certainly someone's consciousness may be more or less intense just as a lamp can emit more or less light. But it can be argued that even a low degree of consciousness is full-fledged and not merely partial consciousness. A lamp is on or off, and even a lamp that spreads very little light is definitely on. On this view no organism could occupy a borderline between consciousness and lack of consciousness. Viewed this way consciousness would differ from life, since there are transitional stages between life and non-life (McGinn, 1982, pp. 13-14).

A lamp is so constructed that it is either on or off, but is this the case for consciousness? Our own consciousness can be faint. In retrospect we would say that even then there was consciousness, be it ever so little. But one could doubt the reliability of such a recollection. Borderline cases of consciousness probably don't lend themselves to recollection.

What is the situation for lower organisms? The problem here is that, as we have seen, sometimes it cannot be determined whether an organism has consciousness. Furthermore our power of imagination runs out here. At most it can be said that given evolution it is not probable that consciousness came about suddenly without any transitional stage. For these reasons, then, the issue of consciousness for lower organisms is very hard to decide.

The term consciousness can vary in meaning, which is not surprising for such a general term. The following characteristics pertain to the wide sense of consciousness.

a) In the first place there is consciousness in the sense in which it belongs

to human beings and animals and not to inanimate objects. Consciousness can be clear and intense or very faint, as in automatic or habitual
actions. Habitual actions require some consciousness, but not much, and
in such cases we say that we acted without being conscious of what we
were doing, that is, without thinking about it. Yet in another sense we
were conscious, for we were not asleep or unconscious, otherwise we
would not have been able to do what we did.

b) A clear awareness of what we are doing can be promoted by thinking
about our activity. So there is also consciousness in the more specific
sense of reflection. The possibility of reflection on one's inner life has
been regarded as essential for consciousness, for instance by John Locke.
I will discuss this view.

c) 'Consciousness' can also refer to that of which we can become
conscious, even if we are not conscious of it at all times. This is the
potentially conscious, which is kept in our cognitive storage space. In
depth psychology it is called the preconscious, in contrast with the
unconscious, of which we cannot easily become aware. But the question
is whether the preconscious should be regarded as a storage space:
belonging to consciousness in this sense merely indicates a disposition,
namely the capacity to become conscious.

By definition, the unconscious does not belong to consciousness. We
may wonder then whether an unconscious emotion counts as mental.
Suppose that someone is jealous. This state will lead to certain behavior,
but it is also a mental phenomenon, because the jealous person will be in
a particular mood at certain times of the day. Now is the jealousy no
longer mental if it is unconscious? It depends on how 'unconscious' is
understood in this context. If the term must be taken literally, the
question arises in what sense the jealousy does exist. On a different interpretation the jealousy is experienced in such a case, but the subject does
not know about it, because he has not reflected on it. The jealousy is part
of his consciousness, but he is not reflexively conscious of it. On that view
we can call a phenomenon mental although it is also said to be
unconscious. I will devote a separate chapter to this controversial issue.

The question what consciousness is can be answered by pointing to
conscious states such as emotions and sensations. We know of these
states because we are or have been conscious of them. We can be
conscious both of things which do and things which do not belong to our
consciousness. Something of which we are conscious is at that moment an
object of our consciousness. But our consciousness of that thing is not
itself an object of consciousness, although it may become such an object
if we consider it in turn. Thus we can distinguish between consciousness

as given, as an object of contemplation and knowledge, and consciousness as a state or activity in which something appears and in which what appears is known. About the latter we may ask whether it is a single entity, like what used to be called the soul, or an activity that changes continuously and for which we don't need to assume a mental subject like the soul.

The view that rational argument can show that there is a soul which is the subject of conscious states was undermined by Kant (1781, p. 338ff). According to him all thought is accompanied by the judgment "I think". This is a non-empirical, transcendental condition for all thought. While thoughts are included in consciousness by virtue of this judgement, it cannot be used to deduce rationally that there is a simple substance which thinks it and remains the same over time. After Kant's critique of the rationalist doctrine of the soul only consciousness in general was left, which is the subjective side of the world known by thought, and about which nothing empirical can be said. For if we try to talk about it we refer not to the soul as subject but to the soul as object. About this sense of consciousness William James said that it is nothing and can be abolished (1912, ch. 1).

I will not deal with the question of the mental subject. I will be concerned primarily with consciousness as a phenomenon that is known because it is given.

One curious characteristic of consciousness as a subject of knowledge is that it seems to be a void. When we are conscious of something, it appears to us, but when we wonder what this consciousness itself is, the only content we can provide consists in the object of which we are conscious. Consciousness itself is transparent, like a window through which we can see but which otherwise evades us (see Moore, G.E. 1922, p. 25). It can be more or less vivid, but this is known only by the way in which objects of consciousness appear to us. When we are vividly aware of something, we notice facts about it which escape us when we are barely conscious of it.

Sartre (1943) claims that when a human being is in a certain state of consciousness such as pain or sadness, he is always aware that he is not identical with this state. For Sartre consciousness is that by which and to which sadness appears. It is different from the sadness itself. Consciousness is, as it were, transparent and indeterminate. For this reason consciousness is supposed to be a void, a nothing, to which no positive properties can be attributed. Sartre believes that by virtue of this nothing we are removed from the pain or sadness, and that thus freedom constitutes the essence of our being.

This view does match our experience to some extent, but it is not compelling. It may be objected that the distance in question comes about because consciousness is not strongly tied to its content. We might say that when we are sad, our consciousness usually does not coincide with that state, not because our consciousness is a void, but because it can be turned away from the sadness, and because it can contain other things besides it, such as other emotions or traffic noise. It is true that consciousness can be detached from any particular object, and that it is in a sense removed from its primary object, since it is not completely absorbed by it. But these observations do not require that we posit that consciousness is a void.

Various kinds of contents of consciousness can be distinguished. There are thoughts and emotions, but our consciousness also adds to and interprets what is perceived. For instance, when we see a writing pad and pen, our consciousness sees these material objects which have particular shapes and colors as these utensils. A pet also sees these objects, but not as a writing pad and pen.

What should be regarded as contents of consciousness depends on the question to what extent we perceive reality as it is. Since Locke a distinction has been made between primary and secondary qualities of the material world. Impenetrability or solidity, extension and shape are primary qualities. Properties such as color and sound are secondary, that is, they depend on sensory perception and are to a certain extent created by it. On this view colors are contents of consciousness, not only in the sense that we can be conscious of them, but in the sense that they are part of consciousness. This may seem strange, but it is not unusual to regard pain, heat or cold as contents of consciousness, since these properties depend on perception by the senses.

The question now is how this knowing, supposedly empty consciousness is related to its contents. When we are in a particular state of consciousness, we are conscious, but are we always also conscious of the content of the state in question, in the sense that this content is present to our mind? I will argue that we are not.

DESCARTES AND RYLE

The modern distinction between consciousness and the physical comes from Descartes. Before him thought, judgment and volition were regarded as characteristic of the mind as opposed to nature. Sensations such as of heat and cold were regarded as connected to the body and thus as not properly mental. In the *Méditations* Descartes included these phenomena among thoughts, so that 'thought' became synonymous with consciousness, although he claimed that sensations such as hunger and pain are confused, that is impure, forms of thought, which involve the body (1641, p. 492).

Corporeal nature is characterized by extension, unlike thought or consciousness. For Descartes and for those philosophers who adopted this distinction the question arose how the extended physical world and unextended consciousness could interact. Furthermore Descartes thought that we could make errors about the physical world, but that consciousness could be known with certainty, or at least more easily than the physical world. Even if what we think about the world is wrong, we can be certain *that* we think it. These Cartesian views have continued to be influential. On the other hand, Descartes's conclusion that consciousness can exist without a body and is immortal has been rejected by many as a religiously inspired speculation.

It is possible to extract from Cartesianism the minimal position that consciousness has a special nature, and is not identical with behavior or with anything physical, such as processes in the brain or its functional role. I call this minimal thesis mentalism, and I will argue in favour of it. This view raises the question of the relationship between the mental and the physical, which I will address in the last chapter.

Since the term mentalism is not common, more needs to be said about it. According to Fodor's definition everyone who rejects philosophical or logical behaviorism is a mentalist. This definition leaves open the possibility that a mentalist accepts a version of materialism according to which mental states are identical with brain processes (1968, pp. 55-57). This definition is useful because the contrast between behaviorism and mentalism is so great. However, I prefer to define mentalism so as to exclude materialism, since a mentalist who accepts materialism regards his mentalism merely as a provisional position that is opposed to behaviorism, but does not express his fundamental view. According to my definition mentalism entails that the mental cannot be reduced to anything else, in particular not to behavior or brain processes. The brain physiologist Sperry uses the term in this way. He adopts mentalism while rejecting dualism, and distinguishes this mentalism from the kind of materialism that reduces the mental to a brain process (1983, p. 99ff).

The distinction between the physical and consciousness was rejected in the twentieth century by philosophical behaviorism, of which the main representative was Gilbert Ryle. In *The Concept of Mind* Ryle claimed that dualism relies on a category mistake, that is, that it makes a logical mistake about the nature of mental states. He illustrates his claim by means of a variety of examples. When someone who wants to get to know a university is shown the various departments, libraries and museums, he should not in addition ask to be shown the university, because he has already seen it in seeing its libraries and other institutions. The university is not an additional member of the set that contains these various institutions. It consists in the set itself, organized in a particular manner (1949, p. 18). This visitor makes a conceptual error. According to Ryle a dualist arrives at his view by virtue of a similar category mistake. This view is also adopted by Rorty (1980, p. 31).

This analysis is misguided, however. For Ryle a word like 'university' is the name of a set of connected institutions and buildings. This claim expresses Ryle's nominalism (Addis, 1965, p. 24). Apart from the question whether this nominalism is correct, it is compatible with certain forms of dualism. It is not so clearly compatible with the dualism of Descartes, since he thought that the word 'soul' referred to a single entity. But in general it can be claimed that even if terms like thought, volition and sensation are names of sets, they can be names of sets of *mental* phenomena. This view will be accepted by a dualistic nominalist. As a nominalist he will claim that a general notion like 'thought' is not an additional member of a set of concrete mental phenomena such as 'solving a particular problem x'. Philosophers like Locke and Hume, who held more or less dualistic views, certainly did not have the kind of Platonistic view of concepts that Ryle regards as a category mistake. It is a mistake to identify dualism with a non-nominalistic view about concepts (cf. H.D. Lewis, 1969, p. 36ff). I will discuss Ryle's plea for behaviorism in the relevant chapter.

Cultural Objects

In addition to the physical and the mental, which he describes as two different worlds, Popper adopted a third world, the domain of language, social institutions, works of art, theories and such, in short, cultural objects (1977, ch. 2). Popper regards this world as real, because through its influence on people it causes changes in the material world. He regards it as autonomous, because it is not invented, but discovered, just like an as yet unknown planet. A number system, for instance, begins as a human invention, but once it exists it leads a life of its own, exercises influence on people, and raises problems that have an objective, independent existence (ibid., p. 40). A work of art exercises influence by stimulating the creation of others.

This view, he acknowledges, is related to Plato's conception of the realm of forms. This similarity becomes especially apparent when Popper claims that objects of world 3 can exist independently from the material world, as well as from human recollections and intentions. Unlike Plato he does emphasize the fallibility of human attempts at discovering this third world.

This distinction is useful, but not fundamental to my project. On my view this world of cultural objects is not as autonomous as Popper suggests. It only exists for the human mind. A work of art is made as an expression of the artist's view; someone else experiences it and if he sees it as a work of art and if he is creative, it evokes other emotions and thoughts in him, which lead to another work of art. A work of art does not exercise influence by itself but only as experienced by human beings. The mind of one person influences the mind of another through material things such as shapes, sounds and colors.

The impression of autonomy and objectivity arises when people think alike to a very high degree, as is the case in mathematics. A numerical system seems to raise objectively determined questions, because they present themselves inescapably to anyone who understands the system and the questions. An answer is invented, like the whole system, but seems to be a discovery, because it is the only answer we see. But these questions and answers exist only for the mind of a number of individuals. This is quite clear in the case of art, where mental attitudes are far more diverse. A sculpture is a physical thing that is a work of art for, and by virtue of, the minds of human beings. A work of art from the past is lacking in one respect for one person, in another for another person, and for this reason the problems that it raises and the 'solutions' that are found vary with the individuals who want to develop art. If particular concepts which once were part of a dead language no longer exist for anyone, they no longer exist at all.

Since a cultural object as such only exists by virtue of the mental attitudes of people I will confine myself to the categories of the mental and the physical.

Attempts to determine the nature of consciousness have emphasized different aspects of the phenomenon. It is clear that consciousness encompasses more than rationality and the ability to use symbols. These two characteristics may be typical of the human mind, but consciousness is a broader notion. Furthermore I will usually speak of the mental, rather than consciousness, and use this term to refer to consciousness insofar as it is given and known. We will have to make an effort to determine the nature of the mental more specifically. The result will have implications for our views on a variety of issues. If the mental has properties that distinguish it from the physical, we will have to face the question of the relationship between the mental and the physical. If it turns out to be identical with behavior or with physiological processes, then we can avoid this problem. On the other hand, such an identification can be equally problematic in other ways.

THE PHYSICAL

Before we can start an analysis of the mental, we have to consider the question of the nature of the physical or material. When we discuss the question whether the mental is something physical, it must be clear what is understood by 'the physical'. Over time various definitions have been provided. According to one, the physical consists of those objects or processes that can be described by means of the concepts of a language that has an intersubjective observational basis (Feigl, 1967, p. 54). The problem with this definition is that it is too broad, for colors and flavors satisfy it reasonably well, whereas color and flavor impressions can not be regarded as physical, apart from the wave lengths of light and the chemical composition of the things we taste. But even if we regard flavors and colors as physical, the objection remains that the definition is much too vague because of the word 'intersubjective.' A large part of the philosophy of mind is concerned with the question what can or must be called intersubjective.

According to another definition the physical is what is described by the concepts of science, which are spatial, temporal, and quantitative. This definition is more substantial, but we would like to know what is described in this way. An obvious answer is: the mass and/or energy of particles. The mass of a body is the constant relationship between the force that works on the body and the acceleration caused by that force. As is known mass can be transformed into energy and vice versa. The particles of energy have a determinate mass or charge. They have magnitude and a determinate place in space. Thus electricity, for instance, consists in particles of atoms, electrons, which have a determinate size and speed.

Whether or not motion is essential to the notion of mass, the capacity for motion is essential to the notion of energy. Furthermore mass is potential energy, so the capacity for motion is essential to the notion of the physical.

How do we arrive at the notions of 'mass' and 'particle'? The concept of mass is arrived at by abstracting from gravity, which varies with place. The sensory basis for the concept of gravity is the muscular force that we feel -- by means of a special sense -- when obstructing the fall of a body or setting one in motion. Next the relative weight of bodies can be determined by means of scales. Finally one arrives at the definition of mass by abstracting from the weight that a body has at a particular place.

Whereas mass and energy together are constant, the size of an object is not. Thus the notion of mass seems to be fundamental. Any entity has a certain mass, but for the smallest particles of energy size is no longer relevant. Nevertheless Descartes's conception of matter as what is spatially extended need not be entirely abandoned.

The notion of particle depends on the notion of size or magnitude. An object of a particular size occupies space and can be perceived by the sense of touch in the skin (in short: it can be felt) and offers resistance to the pressure (motion) of our muscles. Furthermore it can be seen if it is not too small. The fact that something has magnitude is determined on the basis of the tactile and kinesthetic sensations resulting from motion of (usually) the hands or the fingers of a hand. The form of a thing is determined on the basis of changes in the direction of such motion which are remembered. Probably an object's ability to be touched and to offer resistance to our muscular motion is originally the ground for regarding it as physical, and the continuation of such sensations while the hands are in motion is the basis of the conclusion that a thing has size. Sight leads to the conclusion that there is something that has these properties, but it is not necessary, since for the blind material objects fully exist.

For John Locke, who was inspired by natural science, solidity or impenetrability was a criterion for the physical (1690, Bk II, ch. IV). It is clear that this idea is connected to the resistance that a physical object offers to muscles or to a tool that is used by the hand, that is, it is connected to the sensory data that led to the notion of mass. But the term impenetrability is not very apt, since some objects that seem to have it are in fact penetrable, such as certain solid substances that can be penetrated by certain gases. It could be replied that matter is impenetrable only if there is no space between its particles, but as it turns out there is always such space. As a result Locke already formulated the criterion as the principle that the space that is occupied by a particle cannot at the same time be occupied by another particle. But then the question arises whether this formulation amounts to more than saying that a particle occupies space --that is, that it has a particular size, which may decrease, but which never disappears entirely. For when two particles occupy the same space, there are not two of them, but only one. It is not necessary to discuss this issue here. I merely want to point out that the notion of solidity seems to depend on a combination of two properties which I have discussed, namely mass and size.

Science has expanded our conception of the physical. It has been discovered that there are particles that are too small to be seen or touched, such as the mixture of oxygen and nitrogen that surrounds us. We can, however, feel the resistance of this mixture, as we realize when the wind is blowing, and it can be condensed to a liquid or solid state, which allows us to touch it and feel its resistance to our muscles, and eventually see it.

Since science has studied very small particles which can only be seen --or of which we can only see effects-- visibility has become a sufficient ground for regarding something as physical, provided the object has mass. Although the connection with tactile and kinesthetic sensations has become more indirect, it still exists. A molecule cannot be felt by touch, but a set of molecules, such as a table, can. Bacteria cannot be touched, but results of their activity, such as lumps in the skin, can be. As long as something has a certain size, however small, some quantity of it can be touched. These examples, however, represent matter as inert, whereas in modern science matter is regarded as potential energy. Energy cannot be touched, but it can affect us. Small particles of radiation can come into contact with our skin and change it. Particles of electricity can pass through us and give us an electrical shock.

Finally the physical could be described as what can in principle be perceived by tactile and kinesthetic sensations, or has consequences that can be perceived in this way. But such a definition is problematic and not in accord with the modern scientific notion of matter. I have only wanted to point to the basis in sensory perception of our notion of the physical, which is formed in thought, but which would have no content if that basis were removed. For our purposes -- our concern with the physical is limited to the contrast with the mental -- it is sufficient to say that the physical is what has a particular mass or charge, size and capacity for motion. For my present purpose these short notes will have to suffice.

CHARACTERISTICS OF THE MENTAL

When specifying the characteristics of the mental we have to assume that mentalism is basically correct, since there are philosophers who deny that the mental is different from behavior or the physical. Later on I will discuss their arguments extensively. At this point I will only mention some of them. Thus the present discussion is provisional in nature, but it is necessary for the formulation of a starting point.

Negative Characterization

An obvious approach consists in describing the mental negatively. In contrast to the physical, the mental has no mass, and no spatial extension. It is extended in time, but occupies no particular place. It is possible to locate the electro-chemical processes which (probably) accompany thought in the brain, but thoughts themselves cannot be so located. A mental process does not take place either outside the body or inside it. Of course this point has been denied by materialists. Feigl (1969, p. 39) says that feelings, such as motherly love, have no spatial location, because they are abstract notions, which of course are never spatial. The problem with this view is that such notions are based on the occurrence of feelings in individual cases. If such an instance of feeling were physical, it would qualify for spatial location, which is not possible since such feelings have no mass or spatial extension.

Although the mental is not extended, we may doubt whether it is non-spatial in every respect. Sensations such as pain can sometimes be located in space. Since pain does not occupy space in the way in which physical entities do, the location of a pain cannot be exactly specified, but we can say that someone has a pain in his hand or his foot. But if it is discovered that someone has no foot, we will have to modify our statement and say that it feels as if he has pain in his foot (pain in a so-called 'phantom-limb'). Apparently the pain is not literally in the foot. Yet even if it has no spatial location, it is still regarded as real (see Quinton, 1968, p. 209).

It could be claimed that someone's sensations and thoughts are where he or she is on the following ground. If a person's mental states were not where he himself was, it would not be possible to distinguish them from qualitatively indistinguishable mental states that belonged to other people. Suppose that someone is in pain and that another person has a qualitatively identical pain; then we say that there are two instances of pain. This is possible because the two persons are spatially distinct and as a result the instances of pain are spatially distinct as well. The fact that mental states can only be identified as states of spatially located persons has been used to argue that it makes no sense to talk about mental states as non-spatial (Rorty, 1980, p. 21). But there is sufficient reason to talk this way, for it makes no sense to want to determine the weight or size of a mental state, whereas this is possible for physical entities. The idea that certain thoughts are 'heavy' or 'big' is metaphorical. No one will take it literally. Thus it seems that the mental has certain spatial features in some unclear sense, but it is not spatial in the precise sense of being extended, and it is distinguished from the physical in that it has no mass or diameter.

Dualists who think that the mental exercises causal influence on the physical accept that the mental has the capacity for motion, which is another characteristic of the physical. It is not, however, regarded as an essential feature of the mental.

INTENTIONALITY

Next we need to consider what the positive characteristics of the mental are. In *Psychologie vom empirischen Standpunkt* (Psychology from the Empirical Point of View) Brentano claimed that being-directed-at-something, or intentionality, is the defining characteristic of the mental. According to him the psychical -- which term he used rather than 'mental' -- consists in representations and phenomena that are grounded in representations. When we represent, judge, love, hate and desire there is always some object at which the mental state is directed (1874, p. 112, 125). This view may be correct about the higher mental activities, but it does not ring true for sensations such as pain or dizziness. In what representation is pain grounded, at what is it directed? Brentano has two answers (ibid., p. 116-117).

In the first place he points to the location of the pain. But it is doubtful that we always have a representation of it —we sometimes wake up in pain without realizing immediately where the pain is located. Furthermore someone who is in pain may turn to the place of the pain to do something about it, but the pain itself is certainly not directed at this place. Another solution suggested by Brentano is that pain is grounded in the representation of what causes the pain, for instance cutting or burning. It is possible, however, to be in pain without having such a representation. Even if we know that we cut ourselves, the representation of this event may disappear during, and as a result of, the pain. The pain is also not directed at the representation of the cutting: this representation is not its object. A desire without an object is no desire but only a sensation, but pain without representation of cutting or burning is still pain.

Moreover it is doubtful that moods are always directed at something (cf. Heidelberger, 1965, pp. 530ff). Someone can be sad about something, but we can also be cheerful or depressed about nothing in particular (Searle, 1983, p. 2). Is such a mood then perhaps directed at everything, is everything approached cheerfully? This does not seem te be true either, for cheerfulness is not directed at disasters, such as the collapse of the house where we live. According to behaviorists such a mood should be regarded as the disposition to act in a certain way. If action is always intentional, in the sense of being directed at something, then cheerfulness can be regarded as intentional after all (Quinton, 1968, p. 221). But the question remains whether a mood is nothing more than such a disposition. On my view this must be denied. A mood is something by itself, apart from action, as I will argue, and the typical mental component of a mood is not made intentional by its connection with actions.

Another way out would be to say that a person who is in a certain mood is conscious of this mood, and that the mood is itself the intentional object. But even apart from the question whether there are unconscious moods, this suggestion does not help, since the question was whether the mood itself was directed at something in the sense in which desire, love and hate are (cf. Trigg, 1970, p. 10ff). If moods are not directed at anything, they are not mental, according to Brentano's definition. But moods certainly should be regarded as mental.

Being directed at an object is not a necessary condition of the mental, but it is a sufficient condition. Although the mental is not always intentional, the intentional is always mental. Different strategies have been employed to deny the mental status of the intentional. We can't explore them here, so the following observations will have to suffice.

The ascription of directedness to physical processes is dubious, because it relies on the projection of our intentions onto the physical. Brentano pointed out that the mind can be directed at things that don't exist. It is possible to desire or fear something that only exists in one's mind. This does not happen in the physical world. A machine that is constructed to make things that did not exist before works according to specific principles which have particular consequences. The machine is directed at them only for the human mind, which wants these products. The machine has no representation of what does not yet exist. Directedness to what does not exist thus seems to indicate the presence of the mental.

The mental status of the intentional has been denied on the ground of the Wittgensteinian view that the intentional character of the meaning of typographical -- or other -- signs does not consist in some additional immaterial property, but in their relationship to other signs. The meaning of a symbol is supposed to derive from its place in the context of the total system of symbols (Rorty, 1980, p. 25-26). It is true that the meaning of a linguistic symbol is influenced by the other symbols in combination with which it is used. (Cf. "I go to the bank to get money" and "I was sitting on the bank of the river"). Usually the basic unit of use in a language is the sentence and not isolated words. But the meaning of a word is not created by context. When a language has not yet been deciphered, its entire system of symbols may be known, but not yet its meaning. Such a system stands for something, and is symbolic for something other than itself. It can only have meaning by virtue of its signs -- or at least most of them -- being connected to ideas, that is, to something additional that is mental, as has been explained by John Locke. Without mental, inner intentions sounds and lines on paper have no meaning (Searle, 1983, ch. 6 and 8).

Thus intentionality is important in distinguishing the mental, but we should consider the possibility that there are other positive characteristics of the mental, which do not apply only to the higher mental faculties.

PRIVACY

A person's mental states are private because they can be experienced and known directly only by that person, whereas the physical can be observed by everyone and is publicly accessible. A dentist can observe a patient's infected tooth and know indirectly that he is in pain, but only the patient himself can experience the pain and know it in that way. Since Descartes privacy has taken the place of rationality as the defining characteristic of the mental (Kenny, 1968, p. 360). For this reason I will discuss this privacy more extensively.

Some philosophers take 'direct knowledge' to mean that nothing stands between the object of knowledge and the faculty of knowledge, and that for this reason the object is known infallibly. I will not accept this construal of direct knowledge, and will contest the supposed infallibility. I take 'direct knowledge' to mean that the mental is known by introspection and reflection, where reflection is something like introspection that requires no special attention or effort. The directness consists in the contrast with the knowledge that others have of our mental states, since they can know our states only indirectly. In his essay 'Privacy' Ayer claims that introspection does not always take place. According to him direct knowledge of the mental is the ability to report our mental states without having to rely on evidence or provide evidence to others (1973, p. 62-64). It is of course true that we do not always introspect, but reports about a mental state do require that we establish that it exists, which requires some reflection. Noticing that the state exists is the justification of our report. Perhaps 'evidence' is not the right term here, because it suggests indirect indications in a certain direction, but what matters is that a subject has certain empirical data about his mental life that others don't have.

This aspect of the knowledge of the mental results from the fact that the subject alone, and no one else, has his conscious experiences. Another person can have no direct knowledge of the mental states of a subject, because this other person does not have these states. Another person can have states that are qualitatively identical with my mental states, for instance the same kind of pain, but he cannot have my pain, since his pain is different from mine by virtue of the fact that he is not identical with me.

Some philosophers believe that the fact that one person cannot have another person's experiences is merely a matter of logic (cf. Wittgenstein, 1953, § 248). Person A cannot have person B's experience because if person A had this experience, it would no longer be B's experience, for the same reason A cannot knit B's brow. If he did, it would no longer be B's brow but his own (Ryle, 1949, p. 199). This is only partly true. There is also a factual inability, since one can imagine a situation in which A and B's nervous systems are connected, so that A feels B's pain. In that case A has B's pain.

Apart from this point even from a Rylean perspective the fact that I can't feel someone else's pain is not merely a matter of logic. It is true that my pain exists separately and is different from another person's qualitatively identical pain because I am not identical with him. But the fact that there are different individuals with different experiences is an empirical fact, and not a logical one.

But does the fact that I am the only one who can experience my own pain sufficiently distinguish the mental from the physical? For I am also the only one who can knit my brow and experience my doing so. Another person can no more do these things than he can experience my pain, yet knitting my brow does not seem to be a mental event and it does seem to be public (Ayer, 1973, p. 80). But knitting one's brow has a mental component, namely the kinesthetic activity and my experience of it, as well as a physical, public component -- the motion of my brow. Another person cannot perform or experience my kinesthetic activity, but he can move my brow from the outside in the way in which it moves when I knit it. The fact that he cannot experience the mental component of my knitting my brow, but can bring about and experience the physical component is thus in accordance with the view that privacy is a defining characteristic of the mental.

We can conclude that the privacy of the mental consists in this: that a person can know his own mental states in at least one way in which others cannot know them. According to Ayer, however, this characteristic does not distinguish the mental from the physical, since we also know many processes in our own body in a way in which others cannot know them, namely via the kinesthetic sensations that accompany them. In this way we know, for instance, that we knit our brow. Others can know this as well, but not in the same way (1973, p. 53, 79). My reply to this point is that we know that we produce a certain physical movement when we have certain kinesthetic sensations because we have seen that movement and associated it with the kinesthetic sensation. Those movements that others only know by sight, we ourselves know only in that way too. Through a process of learning, kinesthetic sensations become signs for us that we have performed certain movements. In this way we can know that we produce a movement but we are acquainted with such movements only in the way in which others know them, whereas we are acquainted with the kinesthetic sensations in a way in which others are not. For this reason the aforementioned sense of privacy can still be regarded as characteristic of the mental.

According to some, direct knowledge of the mental is infallible. Others say this goes too far, and maintain that we can claim only epistemic authority about our own mental states, which means that the subject of a mental state has the most right to speak about it. I will defend the latter view in the chapter about mentalism.

A Distinction of Degree

The above distinction between the mental and the physical does not apply to all mental phenomena to the same degree. According to negative characteristic (1), colors (including shades of gray), sounds, and smells are mental, because they have no mass, even though colors do seem to be extended. These sensory data, however, are more or less publicly accessible. The same color and the same sound can be perceived by different people. It could be objected that colorblindness or deafness prevent their perception; but someone whose muscles are completely paralyzed cannot perceive matter, which is regarded as the prime example of what is publicly accessible, or in any case, its most important aspect, its weight. For people whose senses work, sense data like light and sounds are publicly accessible. Even if they are less accessible than matter, they are, on the common sense view, more accessible than impressions like pain, dizziness and tiredness, which we believe to be personal.

But the situation is more complicated than these remarks would suggest. Unlike smells, flavors seem to be private; when someone tastes something, he is the only one who perceives the flavor. If someone says there is an odor of gas, others can check this, but in the case of a flavor only the person who tastes it can make judgments about it. The fact that this distinction is a matter of degree is clear when we consider that both in the case of flavor and of smell person A and person B are in contact with different particles. So in the case of smell too, each smells something different. On the other hand, in the case of a flavor each can in a sense taste the same thing, just as we say that each can sense the same smell. When there is salt on the table, its flavor is publicly accessible. We can check what another person tastes as long as the supply lasts. The difference is that in the case of a flavor one must administer the stuff to oneself in order to bring about the sensory impression.

This line of reasoning shows that the distinction between public accessibility and privacy is relative and a matter of degree. It would be incorrect to say that perhaps flavor is publicly accessible, but pain is not at all. Pain is more private than flavor, but it is not absolutely private. In the first place, the sensation of pain requires a sensory faculty that works for almost everybody. There are more people who are unable to hear or smell than people who are unable to feel pain, which may be because without the ability to feel pain we can't survive for very long. In the second place, a person often knows more or less from his own experience what kind of pain another person is feeling in the case of a particular kind of injury, because he has been afflicted by such an injury, for instance a cut. Whereas in the case of flavors it is necessary to taste some of the same substance in order to check what another person tastes, such an approach is not required in the case of pain, since in most cases we have already had the kind of experience in question.

Couldn't we say, however, that salt exists independently of its flavor and is publicly accessible for that reason, but that pain is private because it only exists when it is felt? The answer is no, because although NaCl exists independently from our tasting it, this is not true of the flavor of salt, which is at issue here. It exists only when the salt is tasted. And the objects that cause pain also exist independently from our capacity for feeling pain. Both impressions, flavor and pain, are dependent on a specific sensory faculty.

Yet there are reasons that justify regarding pain as more private than flavor. If two people feel pain because they cut themselves with the same knife, it could be argued that through that sensation they both perceive the sharp side of the knife. But that would be rather strained, and in many cases of pain the term 'perception' --of the world-- does not apply. Pain is a --personal-- sensation. Pain can come about even if others perceive no external cause, for which reason it is very hard or impossible for others to form judgments about the presence or degree of a person's internal pain. It is true that when someone is in a lot of pain, he will behave accordingly, but self-control and the desire to exercise it vary among people. If someone says he has a headache, we cannot know whether that is true. This is an important reason why pain is regarded as private. In addition the degree of pain can be influenced by a variety of psychological factors. In fact the possibility of 'imaginary' pain is quite widely admitted. For its subject such a pain is indistinguishable from a real pain, but no physician can find anything to explain it.

In this way the degree of privacy can be determined for different kinds of sensations. In the case of pain there can be external causes. Fatigue, on the other hand, depends not only on a person's activities, but also on his way of living and constitution. As a result it is hard to make judgments about its occurrence in another person, and even more difficult to estimate its degree.

Where mental images, rather than sensations, are concerned, it is usually impossible to decide what is going on in another person's mind, except in simple, emotionally charged situations that we can assume have the same impact on people with similar psychological constitutions. Mental images are private, but like sensations, they are private in varying degrees.

Although the privacy of the mental is relative, the mental is so much more private than the physical that privacy can be used to distinguish the mental from the physical. As has been pointed out, the sensations on which the notion of the physical relies, are tactile and kinesthetic. Russell, who also thought that public access to sensations is a matter of degree, regarded touch as less general than sight or hearing, because the same object of touch — that is the same place on the same thing — can only be touched successively by different people (1971, p. 118). But he forgot that — as I noted before — in the case of sight and hearing two people do not perceive the same thing since different particles (from the same source) affect their sense organs. Moreover — and Russell himself admits this — although two people can hear or see something simultaneously, they do so from different perspectives. Tactile and kinesthetic sensations are more essential to selfpreservation, but in addition they are more general, because the same thing can be perceived by different people. They are not, however, completely public, because the temporal difference makes it the case that the second person may touch something different. These sensory impressions, which by themselves are already quite public, are usually accompanied by visual impressions. Although for different people these impressions are brought about by different rays of light, these rays are reflected by the object in a fairly systematic way, and people who see something from different perspectives can subsequently take the same point of view. The impressions on which the idea of the material are founded are thus public to a high degree.

The fact that the difference between privacy and public accessibility is relative does not mean that it is not real. It is a conceptual distinction with a foundation in reality. Most concepts are relative in this sense, yet such concepts can still be said to apply to some things and not to others. The borderlines between red, orange and yellow are also vague. One shade of red is more red, that is, closer to the paradigm of red than another, which is closer to orange, while there are also shades that lie in between red and orange. Nevertheless there are shades that are indisputably red. Another example: one game more clearly satisfies the definition of 'game' than another, which looks more like work. Yet there are activities that are clearly games and not work. In the same way we can say the mental is private and the physical is public, even though the degree of privacy of the mental varies.

Anyone who would deny the distinction between the private and the public because it is relative might as well say everything is private or everything is public. The arguments that can be used to ascribe privacy to one thing after another can also be used to show that everything is publicly accessible. For instance, the arguments for ascribing privacy not only to flavors but also to smells, can also be used to show that not only smells but also flavors are publicly accessible. Saying that everything is private results in Berkeleyan idealism, according to which 'to be' is the same as 'to be perceived', which amounts to 'being private'. The opposite approach results in absolute realism, according to which everything belongs to the public world and nothing belongs to the perceiving mind. American philosophers have adopted this point of view (Morris, 1932, p. 118ff). But such verbally opposite monistic views say nothing because they amount to the same thing. On my view it makes therefore more sense to maintain the distinction between the private and the public.

In conclusion I want to make the following point. The main reason for regarding colors and sounds as mental is that they are not material. On the other hand they are intersubjective to a high degree, and are part of the world around us. I regard them as occupying a position between the material and the mental, and when I speak of the mental I do not have them in mind, unless I indicate otherwise.

BEING AND SEEMING

Descartes claimed that if it seems to someone that he is warm, he is warm, even if the room only seems to be warm, but isn't (1641, p. 422). It makes no sense to tell this person that it only seems to him that he is warm. But if he says on the basis of his sensations that the temperature in the room is 30 degrees Celsius, then he can be mistaken and others can correct him. A person can start out saying that the room is warm and maintain, after someone has pointed out that the thermometer indicates that it is only 16 degrees, that he, in any case, is warm. As long as he confines himself to the mental he is supposed to have certainty.

This view has exercised great influence up to the present day. Mental contents appear to us exactly as they are, and they are as they appear to us, David Hume said in *A Treatise of Human Nature* (1738, I, Pt IV, section 2, p. 185). The mental is as it appears to the perceiving subject. It is neither more than nor different from the way it appears (C.I. Lewis, 1941, p. 333). For the mental, in Berkeley's terms, esse is percipi -- to be is to be perceived. This view is often formulated in such a way that it seems to follow that knowledge of the mental is assured. It is then claimed that for the mental being and seeming coincide (cf. Penelhum, 1964, p. 242).

But is this claim correct? 'It seems to him that he is warm' does express doubt about his noticing the impression, and thus suggests the possibility of a difference between reality and his noticing it. If 'it seems to him that he is warm' is intended to convey that he thinks that he is warm and reports that thought, then he can, in principle, be mistaken. This will almost never happen, but I will explain in chapter 3 that it is in principle possible to make mistakes in this way. If it seems to someone that he feels jealous -- or not jealous --, he can certainly be mistaken. If the statement 'it seems to him that he is warm' is supposed to mean 'he feels warm', it is almost certain that he is warm, but that is only because 'to feel warm' and 'to be warm' if not always, at least usually mean the same.

Let us drop the notion of 'seeming' or 'appearing', which is confusing in this context, and formulate the thesis as follows: what a person feels determines what mental states he has. When a physician hears from a patient that he feels no pain and he believes the patient, he will normally assume that the patient is not in pain. If a patient tells him that he does feel pain, and he believes the patient, he will assume that his patient is in pain, even if he can find no cause for the pain. In some cases the physician may think that the patient imagines his pain, but he will allow that for the patient this amounts to the same as actually having the pain.

The example of imaginary pain makes it doubtful, however, that feeling a sensation and having it are the same thing. If this expression is ever used appropriately -- and this seems likely given for instance cases of hysteria (about which more in the chapter about the unconscious) --, the implication is that even in sensation illusion is possible. And if it is possible to imagine pain, then it is also possible while in pain to imagine not being in pain. In such a case a subject would feel no pain but have pain nevertheless.

For this question the following familiar phenomenon is relevant. Sometimes a person feels pain over an extended period of time, but does not feel it, as Palmer put it (1975), for a short period, because he is distracted by something else. Once the distraction is over, he feels it again. Let us assume that the cause of the pain is still present while he feels no pain, or, in any case, notices none. The question is whether he has the pain even while he does not feel or notice it. If we categorically deny that he has pain, then we run into the following problem: after the distraction the subject can often remember that he felt pain, although he did not feel it at the time. (Just as when someone does not hear a clock, but when it stops remembers that he did hear it before it stopped.) So it seems that while at the time the person felt no pain, afterwards he does remember feeling it. This recollection is credible, since the cause of the pain remains present. Furthermore the subject will generally feel the pain when another, tactless person asks whether he now feels any pain. In that case he again becomes reflexively conscious of it.

To escape from this dilemma I would like to reformulate the above using the following distinction; during the distraction the sensation is *felt*, but not *noticed*. Although the subject remembers that he felt pain or that he heard the clock, he did not notice the sensation at the time -- he was not reflexively conscious of it.

Thus we cannot say that feeling pain is the same as noticing it. Feeling pain only leads to noticing it when we are paying attention to it. Thus for sensations 'to be' is not the same as 'to be perceived' in the sense of 'to be perceived reflexively, to be noticed'. But it is still true that feeling pain is the same as being in pain, and not feeling pain is not being in pain. (The distinction I have made could also be made in a verbally different way, by saying, for instance, that a person can have a pain without feeling it, i.e. without noticing it. Then having a pain and feeling it would be different.)

How should we now understand imaginary pain? If the subject really feels pain, even if there is no cause in the sense organ, it should be regarded as real. (Probably there is some cause in the brain.) If someone thinks he notices pain, although he does not feel any, it is imaginary. If someone feels pain although he does not notice it, he imagines that he is not in pain. For a normal person this can happen for a short time, and in unusual cases it can happen for a long time.

What should we now say about this feature of the mental? If we think we know certain things about the external world on the basis of our mental experiences, which turn out to be misleading, and if we identify and label these experiences correctly, we can still maintain that the experiences exist. It seems to be warm in the room. That is mere appearance, but for me it is and remains warm.

Warmth that appears to me is warmth and not a mere appearance. This position can be maintained, with the qualification that, as we discussed, imaginary phenomena in this realm can't be completely ruled out. Nevertheless since certainty requires thought, it cannot be claimed that we have certainty about our mental states on the ground that feeling pain and being in pain are the same. It is possible for me to think falsely that I am not warm if I feel warm without noticing that I do. In the case of such simple sensations this sort of error is of course uncommon among people who are mentally healthy, but it is not impossible. In the case of more complicated feelings such errors are not unusual. In chapter three we will see, moreover, that other mistakes can be made in the identification of these internal data and in the choice of words to describe them.

According to Rorty (1980, p. 30) the danger of the view that the nature of the mental is exhausted by the way in which it appears, is that it leads to Cartesian dualism. For it involves ascribing a special feature to the mental. If pain is identified with feeling pain the property pain becomes a subject of predication, a special kind of particular, for which being and seeming are the same. According to Rorty this approach would mean that we speak no longer of 'properties' of people — the fact that someone feels pain, which is all right — but of entities that exist by themselves, pains, which must consist in 'mind-stuff' of a Cartesian variety.

Rorty does not directly attack my view, but his arguments do bear on it. It does not matter what dangers attach to the recognition of facts. (The view that a particular conception and arguments for it constitute a danger is in philosophy a sure sign of dogmatic partisanship.) To say that mental properties have some special feature that distinguishes them from physical properties does not mean we must cease speaking about mental properties of people. Generally speaking, if something is a subject of predicates, this does not mean that it is an entity that exists by itself. If we say that feeling pain has certain features we don't thereby imply that pain is an entity that can exist independently from a human being. In the present case a particular kind of feature is at issue — that pain is the way we feel it is — which seems rather to connect it to a person.

Rorty wants to reject any characterization of the mental, for fear that it will become clear that it is something distinct from the physical. Being a materialist he only wants to acknowledge that there is a convention of reporting the mental and the physical in different ways (ibid., p. 32). But this practice, as it turns out, is based on the fact that the mental is different from the physical, and we can determine in what way it is different. Rorty rejects the so-called convention by means of arguments, which depend on his own arbitrary philosophical conventions.

2. BEHAVIORISM

Among theories about consciousness behaviorism is very influential, although lately it has been overtaken by functionalism. But it plays a prominent part in some versions of functionalism. Because behaviorism has implications for many aspects of the philosophy of mind I will discuss it extensively. It stands opposed to Cartesian metaphysical dualism, and to the kind of mentalism I want to defend. According to metaphysical dualism there are two different kinds of 'things' in the world, bodies and minds, which can exist without each other. As I suggested mentalism is less radical. It is the position that there are mental states and processes which are not physical in nature. According to dualism mental phenomema belong to a mind which is their subject. Mentalism on the other hand does not exclude the possibility that they must be ascribed to certain organisms (cf. Fodor, 1968, pp. 55-57). According to philosophical behaviorism the mental is identical with behavior. This view is also known as logical behaviorism, because its adherents claim that statements about the mental *mean* the same as statements about behavior.

Philosophical behaviorism must be distinguished from methodological behaviorism. The latter is a view in psychology according to which scientific study of human beings must be confined to their behavior because research about whatever other aspects of human beings there might be cannot be checked in accordance with scientific method (Watson, Skinner). A behaviorist in the methodological sense does not have to be one in the philosophical sense. But for a methodological behaviorist the question might arise whether some important aspect of human beings is lacking in his research, and this might lead him to adopt a form of philosophical behaviorism. Watson hesitated between philosophical and methodological behaviorism. Skinner's position is generally behavioristic in the philosophical sense (1964), though he sometimes makes the epiphenomalistic claim that the mental is something different and will be dealt with in the future (1972).

I will only discuss philosophical behaviorism. There is variation among the views of the different philosophical behaviorists, but I can only consider the most important differences. A striking proponent of radical behaviorism is Gilbert Ryle, whose book *The Concept of Mind* (1949) has been very influential. The views of the later Wittgenstein as embodied in *Philosophical Investigations* (1953) and other publications can be characterized as a form of linguistic behaviorism. We will see in a later chapter what this means. I will first discuss Ryle's view, since it is more traditional and easier to survey than Wittgenstein's. We saw that according to mentalism the mental is more or less private. We acquire knowledge of mental phenomena from ourselves, by having them ourselves. Behaviorism denies this. According to it we acquire knowledge of the mental because we perceive the behavior of others—and possibly also our own. A philosophical behaviorist holds that we know by someone's behavior that he is conscious. Someone who carries on a conversation is conscious, and someone who is conscious can and will carry on conversations or display other behavior that shows that he is conscious. Someone who lacks consciousness or has lost it temporarily does not react to certain stimuli. Consciousness is accompanied by behavior, and the absence of consciousness leads to the absence of behavior. A behaviorist tries to define consciousness and its phenomena in terms of, and thus to identify them with, behavior.

What does 'behavior' stand for? Ryle takes it to refer to the actions of human beings, which is the way the term is used in ordinary language. According to classical behaviorism it refers to the movements a person makes when acting. Like the movements of something physical, these movements are supposed to be describable in terms of space and time alone. One could extend this conception of behavior to include *all* movements, even involuntary ones like reflexes. Physiological changes in the body are not included, however. That would constitute materialism rather than behaviorism.

Radical philosophical behaviorism means that there is nothing but behavior in this sense, which, barring practical problems, can be observed by anyone. According to Ryle, existing terms for the mental indicate complexes of behavior. Thus, for instance, 'having team-spirit' is nothing but passing the ball to each other when this is good for the team, and other such behavior. The 'spirit' in question is nothing separate, but the manner, observable by all, in which the actions of the game are executed (Ryle, 1949, p. 18). 'Politeness' consists in passing the salt when asked and similar behavior. Ryle's philosophical behaviorism is logical or conceptual. That is, he thinks that terms for the mental mean the same as the terms for behavior into which they are translated by means of analysis. The idea is not to deny the existence of what is called mental in every day language: yet there is nothing other than behavior, because the terms for the mental refer to behavior, and to the way in which this behavior is executed, which is also behavior.

Now it is possible to say about a person who is sitting behind a desk that he has team-spirit, and the question is what such a statement means in that case. The behavioristic answer is that this person has a disposition to display behavior. This means not that he has a mental inclination to this behavior, but only that under certain circumstances he would probably display it. Similarly the fact that glass is brittle—an example of a disposition that is not human—is nothing other than the fact that it will probably break if it is hit by a stone. Thus 'he has team-spirit' can refer to a person's passing the ball, but also to the fact that he will probably do so in the future.

These examples lend themselves fairly well to behavioristic interpretation. To a certain extent this is true for character traits and abilities generally, especially habits that do not require much mental activity. It is characteristic of these kinds of states that their subjects are not better qualified than others to determine whether they are present. Team-spirit may involve certain feelings or thoughts, but ultimately the subject's behavior, which others can observe, determines whether he has it. Behaviorists rely on this argument (Ryle, 1949, p. 85, 88). Consequently, however, behaviorism runs into trouble over those mental properties for which the subject himself is in the best position to know whether he has them.

The question arises with what behavioral tendencies a mental phenomenon can be identified. In general a behaviorist is not able to answer this question exactly and exhaustively. Thus, for instance, 'being emotional' is displaying certain kinds of behavior under certain circumstances. But the number of different kinds of circumstances and behavior is too great to be specified in a definition. This fact does not count against behaviorism, however. Its proponents can rightly point out that human dispositions are too complex for such definitions, and that the circumstances in which they are actualized in behavior are not completely predictable. Secondly it can be replied that the mentalist too is unable to give an exhaustive definition of mental concepts, or to enumerate the mental phenomena that fall under a mental term like thought or feeling. But there are other, more well-founded objections.

CRITICAL CONSIDERATION

It is a condition of behaviorism that whenever a mental phenomenon occurs, there is behavior with which it can be identified. This condition is not always satisfied. Sensations, mental images, some feelings, and forms of thought such as understanding do not lend themselves to behavioristic analysis. It is possible to be in pain without showing it, or to have an itch without scratching. A person can remain immobile while having all kinds of images before 'the mind's eye,' images of which others have no knowledge.

For instance, a person may know a language—which is an intellectual capacity—but decide never to speak or read it out of dislike for the country. Such a person still understands the language, whether he wants to or not, when he hears it spoken. But understanding is not behavior. It is purely mental. Hearing the language may cause this person to leave, but leaving is not the same as understanding the language. When understanding a piece of information a person may notice that it does not concern him, and immediately forget it. A mentalist will say such a person draws a certain conclusion and then decides that he need not react. These are mental acts. But the behaviorist cannot point to anything that on his view is an action. He can draw attention to the fact that we can be mistaken when we think we understand something, and that this can be reflected in behavior. But this does not mean that nothing mental has taken place. Misunderstanding something is a mental event as well. The behavior that manifests our understanding, or misunderstanding as the case may be, only provides others with a test of our understanding. It is not the understanding itself, because that can exist without the behavior.

Ryle argues at length that insight is not acquired in one moment, but rather emerges slowly (1949, pp. 281-282). It is understandable that he emphasizes this point, because when we have a sudden insight the mental phenomenon is the most striking aspect of the event. The idea of his argument is that there is no mental seeing of an implication—a mental insight which can be located in time. But even if it is true that in a complicated case complete insight comes only gradually, it is possible that during research various elements of the whole are seen suddenly, and that such partial insights are datable (C.A. Campbell, 1969, p. 308).

A behaviorist who identifies behavior with movements may concede that there need be no overt behavior, but say there is bodily behavior that is hidden from the observer. It is quite possible that when someone is in pain but does not show it there is, say, a change in muscle tension. But that is no reason to identify pain with muscle tension. When a person is administered a drug that paralyses the muscles, and so shows no reaction during an operation, this person is not thereby anesthetized (after Dennett, 1981, p. 209). When someone who has an itch scratches himself, the scratching is not identical with the itch but a reaction to it. Behaviorists like Watson have supposed that when someone thinks while seeming not to move, there is behavior that is not noticed, either because it is too unobtrusive or because it takes place within the body. Thinking is supposed to be speaking subvocally, with slight motions of the lips, throat and/or vocal cords. This hypothesis is refuted, however, by various data. If these organs are paralyzed thought continues, for a patient with such a paralysis can still follow the train of thought in what he reads. Furthermore subvocal speaking slows down reading. Many people can read much faster than such movements would allow (Blanshard, 1939, pp. 324-326).

Even if it were discovered that movements of the lips and vocal cords accompany and facilitate thought, one could not claim that thought is identical with such movements. Having a certain thought is different from the movements that accompany it. What kind of behavior do we display when reading French? We sit more or less still, our eyes move back and forth, and we turn pages. This behavior is not identical with understanding the French sentences. We would display the same behavior while reading a novel written in a different language, though we would then have a different understanding. If behavior were the same as understanding then understanding something different would consist in different behavior. Furthermore, mental images are not accompanied by any particular kind of behavior. We daydream while sitting, lying or walking. This implies that our mental activity can not be identified with our behavior.

Dispositions to Behave

As we saw earlier, to get around the problem of hidden mental states, the behaviorist has recourse to future behavior. A person may hide his pain from those present, but this pain is supposed to be identical with the behavior that he will display when he is alone. It can happen, however, that the pain passes before he is alone. In that case there is no pain behavior. Thus the pain is different from the behavior. A person's having a certain thought or mental image is supposed to be a disposition to behave in a particular way in the future. In many cases, however, it is impossible to say what behavior is supposed to result from some mental state. In the case of understanding a novel the behaviorist will have to appeal to future behavior, but it remains unclear what kind of behavior. Not all understanding of a novel has to lead to behavior. I have already given the example of undisplayed understanding. 'Understanding' may be a matter of 'knowing how', of competence, as Ryle has argued (1949, p. 53 ff.), but this competence is not always exercised; often one does no more than consider exercising the capacity.

But what if there is behavior that is connected to a mental state? That someone does something with understanding or attention may become clear from what he does later. 'Paying attention to something' is an important notion because it is consciousness in a concentrated form. Ryle identifies this attention with subsequent actions. He applies the same kind of reductionist analysis to much of the mental, including agitations and inclinations. Statements like 'he pays attention to his task' or 'he enjoys it' do not, according to Ryle, refer to mental states of attention or pleasure that exist at the moment. Furthermore they do not imply that there is a difference in behavior between someone who acts with attention or pleasure and someone who does not, for such a difference is often not noticeable. Such statements mean only that the person a) is performing a task and b) will display certain behavior in the future. If someone acts attentively he will be able to execute the rest of the task better. If someone does something with pleasure, he will display irritation when interrupted. As Ryle says: the mind is not the topic of untestable categorical propositions—that is, propositions about private mental contents—, but the place of testable (semi-)hypothetical propositions (ibid. pp. 46 and passim). This position pervades his entire book (cf. pp. 27, 33, 93-94, 103-105, 120, 131, 162). The attention or pleasure with which we act are not supposed to be states or events. Their existence as something mental is thus denied. They consist in the disposition to react in a certain way later. For Ryle a disposition is not an actual state, let alone a mental one, but consists merely in the fact that in the future a person will probably display a certain kind of behavior.

So Ryle identifies behavior that allows others to determine later on whether a person paid attention or enjoyed something with these mental states. This approach is related to the old neo-positivist position that the meaning of propositions consists in the way in which they can be verified publicly (Hampshire, 1971, p. 100; cf. for instance Carnap, 1932).

This position is very weak. According to Ryle the only actual item that the proposition 'he pays attention to his task' stands for is the execution of the task. 'Paying attention' stands only for something dispositional and hypothetical. For this reason Ryle claims it is better to say 'he performed his task attentively.' The fact that 'paying attention to something' is a verb suggesting an activity is explained by Ryle by means of the execution of the task to which the subject pays attention. But then it is impossible to watch something attentively while not performing any task. In that case the only activity that the subject performs consists in the mental activity of paying attention. Ryle cannot say that the watching is the activity because according to him watching is a form of paying attention (Place, 1964, p. 217). If the activity consists in watching—and I think it does, since it is a mental activity—then it also consists in paying attention.

A more fundamental problem is that, as we saw, no further relevant behavior need occur. The task may be interrupted. If 'he does it attentively' meant the same as 'he will be able to adapt well to the rest of the task' it would be impossible to do something with attention without later behaving in a way that would make this clear to observers. But that is not right. Consciousness is a necessary but not sufficient condition for adequate reaction. Paying attention does not imply that we will better perform our task. It is possible that we are not equal to the task or that we are too tense. In fact paying attention requires no behavior whatsoever. If the pistol is broken, the runner listening for the starting shot will show no reaction that results from his attention. All the same he does pay attention for a while.

Furthermore we know that there is a mental difference between on one hand doing something attentively or with pleasure and on the other hand doing it automatically or with indifference. Anyone can know this about himself on the basis of some reflection. Often others cannot know—or cannot know well—whether we are doing something attentively or with pleasure. They must inquire, or derive it from later behavior; but we ourselves do know it.

When we attend to something or enjoy ourselves, others can also ask what it is like, what kind of impression it makes, just as we might ask about an actual state of affairs or event. It is not possible to inquire in this way about dispositions, such as capacities or habits. As long as they are not manifested they are not at all actual. Our *awareness* of a disposition can be something actual, but otherwise a capacity that is not presently exercised belongs only to the past and the future, and can only be talked about as such. We can talk about paying attention and enjoyment as something of the present moment. That suggests that paying attention is an actual activity or state, and more than just a disposition with respect to the future. We can describe our attention or consciousness by means of adjectives such as 'clear' or 'dim' (cf. Place, 1964, p. 222; Penelhum, 1964, pp. 241-243).

SENSATIONS AND MENTAL IMAGES

Thus far I have shown that certain standard behaviorist strategies fail for mental phenomena like enjoyment and paying attention. Consequently these strategies, which do seem plausible for some cases, are inadequate as a foundation for a behavioristic philosophy. There are other arguments, however. At this point I want to discuss some of these.

Ryle has two arguments about sensations (1949, pp. 195-199). The first is that sensations are not mental in the higher sense of being conditions of intelligence; deafness and colorblindness are not forms of stupidity. This is true, but it does not preclude that sensations are mental in the broader sense also used by Ryle.

The second argument is directed against the view that sensations are private. It is true that the dentist cannot observe his patient's pain, Ryle says, but neither can the patient himself, because sensations are not observable in the way external objects are. For only what exists independently from us can be observed, and sensations are not independent. Whatever one may think about this argument, it is hard to see how it shows sensations are not private. Ryle admits that the subject of a sensation can notice it and pay attention to it (1949, p. 197). Now the dentist cannot notice the pain in the way in which his patient can. The patient can notice it directly, because he has the sensation; the dentist can only know about the pain indirectly by noticing the infected tooth and the patient's behavior. Thus sensations are still private, and to that extent mental. Ryle emphasizes that sensations are not observable *objects*. If on the basis of a sensation something seems to be green, this does not mean that the sensation is a green object. But even if it is not right to call it an object, it is yet a private *event* or *state*, and its subject has privileged access to it, a privileged source of information (Quinton, 1971, p. 112; Ayer, 1971, p. 61).

A Case of Imagining?

In Ryle's view we should say not that someone has a mental image of his home, for instance, but that he imagines that he sees a house in front of him. It is a matter of 'make-believe' or 'pretending' (ibid., p. 242). There is the activity of imagining, but there are not supposed to be any special mental images.

A child that pretends that his doll smiles, however, does not necessarily have any mental image of his smiling doll. It is also possible to have a mental image but not be imagining anything (Shorter, 1971, p. 139). If someone imagines that he sees or hears something that is not there, he has a hallucination. In that case there are mental images—which Ryle does not want to admit—of the strongest kind. That mental images do not really exist is supposed to be clear from the fact that they cannot compete with or replace reality (Ryle, ibid., p. 239). But as we know hallucinations and visions can do these things. Apart from these unusual cases, people are sometimes unable to distinguish their mental images from weak real images produced by a projector (Matthews, 1971, p. 163), which shows that mental images are on a footing with real ones. Then there is the striking and well studied phenomenon of eidetic, that is photographic, visual memory. Eidetics, many of whom are children, can inspect images as we inspect photographs (cf. Kosslyn, 1980, ch. 7; Wright, 1983). This fits with the fact that it is possible to produce exact mental replicas of previously experienced scenes by electric stimulation of the brain (Penfield, 1975, ch. 6).

Of course mental images are not real images. Only the latter are seen. That is why we speak of *mental* images; but they do make approximately the same impression. Ryle says that dreaming is not being present at a private screening of a film (ibid., p. 241), but this comparison is in fact quite apt for hallucinations and strongly visual dreams.[1]

Skinner also appeals to imagining in his attempt to fit mental images into his behavioristic view. He begins by claiming that seeing is behavior. Then he argues that seeing does not imply that something is seen, since it is possible to say that we've seen someone and be mistaken. That is a case of imagination. Next he concludes that dreaming consists in the behavior of seeing, without anything's being seen (1964, pp. 87-89).

Both of these premises are incorrect. It is all right for Skinner to say that seeing is a form of action rather than a reproduction of the world, but seeing is perceiving that can also take place without behavior. It is possible to move one's eyes without seeing. It is also possible to see without moving one's eyes, although after a while an artificially stabilized image will disappear. The eye needs change. Rapid involuntary movements of the eyes are a condition of *continuous* sight, but not more than that.

Secondly seeing does imply that something is seen. This explains why we revoke our claim to have seen someone if it turns out there was no one. Although it is possible to be mistaken in thinking we see something, seeing is certainly not the same as 'thinking that one sees.' Also, having mental images is generally not the same as 'thinking that one sees.' In the case of memory images and daydreaming we know very well that we are not seeing anything, and in dreams we usually have no thoughts about whether we are seeing; we have visual images without having an opinion about this issue.

So the argument that dreams consist in behavior does not work. Apart from that it is impossible to see in what way dreaming could consist in behavior. Skinner does not claim that the rapid eye movements that accompany some dreams constitute dreaming. He says only that these movements are consistent with his interpretation, because it is unlikely that the dreamer really watches the dream behind his eyelids. We can grant that these movements are no problem for his thesis, but they do not support his position either. The eye movements in question—the only behavior that could be identified with the dreams—are different from them, and also from seeing. Finally, dreaming often occurs during deep sleep without these eye movements (Oswald, 1972, p. 72).

Behavior is Neither Sufficient nor Necessary

The fact that certain mental phenomena sometimes occur without behavior implies that behavior is not a necessary condition for the mental (cf. Putnam, 1982, ch. 16). Also, pain and other feelings can sometimes be simulated via behavior. Thus behavior is also not sufficient for the presence of these mental phenomena.

Attempts have been made to avoid this problem by including the cause of a sensation in its definition, as we will see in our discussion of functionalism. Pain is then understood to be the behavior that is produced by certain causes, such as burning oneself. On this strategy simulation is excluded, and cause and behavior together constitute the sufficient condition for sensation. (Notice that this amounts only to a condition and falls short of an identification!) It is a mistake, however, to include the cause in the definition of the mental, for this makes it contradictory to say of a sensation that it has no cause. Although there probably always is some specific cause, it is not a contradiction in terms to speak of a sensation without a cause.

Many mental phenomena are such that their subject knows best that he has them. Often other persons, even under optimal conditions of observation, can only suspect that the subject has them. If the mental were equivalent to behavior this would not be the case.

Ryle claims it is not essential to mental states that they are sometimes not noticeable to others, as for instance when someone thinks in silence. Thought ordinarily takes place through speaking out loud; we have to learn to do it silently (1949, p. 28). It is true that thought is learned from others because they speak out loud, but the fact that it can take place in silence is not accidental. The behavior—speaking out loud—is necessary for learning to think, but not for thinking once it has been learned. When we have thoughts, we have them whether or not we communicate their contents. The expression of a thought is not essential to it. It is essential to thought that it can be hidden from others, even if they use all the means for discovering what is publicly accessible (Teichman, 1974, p. 54). Again, if one adduces the public aspects of some mental activities in favor of behaviorism, one must take into account that the hidden nature of others goes against it.

Let me summarize the results so far. In the first place mental states sometimes occur without behavior, or at least without behavior that is specific to them, so that no behavior can be connected with such mental states. Secondly, behavior or so-called behavior (change in the tension of the muscles when in pain) that does occur cannot be identified with the mental states it accompanies. Pain can occur when the muscles are paralyzed, but even if the two phenomena always occurred together, they would be different events. Thirdly, mental states cannot be identified with future behavior, since no behavior specific to these states need follow. When connected behavior does occur, it is evidence of, and not identical with, the mental states.

Many philosophers think that philosophical behaviorism is at least partly incorrect, in particular for sensations and mental images. Nevertheless, in order to provide a solid foundation for the next chapter it was necessary to see why behaviorism is inadequate, even if this required making points that are obvious to many.

FEELINGS

The question whether feelings can be accounted for behavioristically is more controversial. Feelings were once generally regarded as mental experiences, but nowadays many philosophers are inclined to adopt the behavioristic view at least in part. It is worth exploring to what extent behaviorism is successful in this area, where it seems to have a better chance than with respect to the phenomena considered so far.

Ryle divides feelings into four categories. The general term he uses is not 'feelings' but 'emotions', and they include a) inclinations or motives, such as team-spirit or being interested, b) moods, such as cheerfulness or depression, c) agitations such as joy or anger (which are usually called emotions), and finally d) feelings, which include brief sensations such as a twinge of remorse or a shudder of fright. Only feelings in this narrow sense are events according to Ryle. The other three kinds of emotions are dispositions. When a person is said to be cheerful or depressed, this is supposed to mean nothing other than that he has displayed, and will probably display, certain kinds of behavior to which these adjectives apply. There is no mental state over and above the behavior (1949, pp. 93-95).

In the chapter about emotions Ryle does not discuss the question how feelings should be classified behavioristically. What he says about the classification of sensations should also apply to these kinds of feelings, since for him the difference between feeling and sensation consists primarily in their causes: a shudder is a sensation if it is caused by cold, and a feeling if caused by fright. Consequently my earlier treatment of sensations, and the conclusion that they are private mental events, also applies to these feelings.

Not surprisingly, Ryle argues extensively that inclinations, moods and agitations are not feelings in the narrow sense. For Ryle this implies that they are not events and thus not mental events. A mentalist can admit that inclinations and moods are not feelings in the narrow sense, even if such feelings do pertain to them. But a mentalist will maintain that moods and agitations are feelings in the broad sense, mental events of longer duration, which occur and disappear. Ryle's arguments have no force against this position.

He seems to think it goes without saying that because agitations and moods are not feelings in the narrow sense, they are not feelings at all. But this simply does not follow. Ryle's point of view makes more sense when one considers William James's theory in his *The Principles of Psychology*. James thinks that agitations consist entirely in the mental experience of physical processes that occur, such as a lump in one's throat, a change in heart beat, water running from one's eyes etc. (1890, II, pp. 449ff.). These are feelings in Ryle's narrow sense. If one assumes that during an agitation or a mood nothing mental occurs but these phenomena, and furthermore, as Ryle does, that agitations and moods do not consist in these phenomena, then they cannot be anything mental.

James's thesis is incorrect, however. In psychology it has been criticized by Cannon in particular (Strongman, 1973, p. 44ff). Although the experience of peripheral physical processes plays a role in emotion, it is not the whole of it. If sadness merely consisted in the experience of the flowing of one's tears, then one could not distinguish between tears of sadness and tears of joy. A feeling of fear is different from the feelings of trembling hands and heart palpitations. We sometimes have these feelings without feeling scared, for instance when doing unusually strenuous physical labor. We also sometimes feel a little scared without having these sensations. According to James if in thinking about anger one leaves out the so-called physical sensations, nothing remains but the purely intellectual judgment that someone deserves punishment (1890, II, p. 452). This is incorrect. What remains is emotionally charged thoughts and mental images, through which we do feel something, as we know from situations in which we control our anger. The absence of feelings in Ryle's narrow sense may mean that we experience no emotions, no *strong* feelings, but it does not mean that we have no feelings at all. The force of the feeling does seem to depend on behavior, but not its existence. But even if a feeling did not occur without a certain kind of behavior, it would still be different from the behavior. If we never got angry without raising our voice or waving our arms the feeling of anger would still be something different, namely the emotionally charged awareness that something in our environment bothers us and deserves to be attacked.

Feeling is Essential

Mental feelings are essential to the presence of a mood or agitation. A person can be called depressed or angry only if he or she *feels* that way. If a person only displays the behavior of an angry person, we cannot say that he *is* angry, but only that he pretends to be angry. It is a well-known fact that intentionally adopting a certain expression can influence our feelings, but this influence tends to be moderate. Furthermore some people are able to display the behavior appropriate to a certain mood or emotion they do not feel. As James mentions (ibid., II, p. 464), some actors can do this. I think this ability is generally shared by people who are good at observing and imitating others. This fact counts strongly against identifying a feeling with the behavior that tends to accompany it.

In defense of behaviorism it has been argued that there is a limit to pretending. If a person destroys furniture and attacks someone else, then he *is* angry, whether or not he admits it. Thus behavior is after all supposed to be the criterion for when someone is angry (Bedford, 1964, pp. 81-82). But in the first place it must be admitted that for a moderate display of anger *feeling* is decisive and not behavior, which may be pretense. Furthermore it is possible that a person who acts extremely angry is merely pretending. Whether we interpret a person's behavior in this way depends on the situation and on the reasons he may have for such behavior. A person can go very far to create a certain impression if the success of his pretending is important to him (Austin, 1976, p. 225). Whether a person *is* angry is ultimately a matter of his *feeling* angry.

For Ryle a criterion for feelings in the narrow sense, which count as events, is that it makes sense to ask questions about their duration, frequency and where we feel them (ibid., p. 85). The fact that it also makes sense to ask such questions about moods and agitations indicates that they are events as well. Of course some questions are not possible here. For instance, it makes no sense to ask *where* in the body a mood or agitation is located, because these states are not located. On the other hand, some so-called bodily sensations, such as feeling energetic or feeling ill cannot be located either. Ryle claims that these kinds of feelings are not feelings in the narrow sense either (ibid., pp. 97-98). This is consistent with his view about feelings in the narrow sense, because the kinds of feelings at issue usually last longer than a twinge or shudder. But given his view his denial implies that these bodily sensations are mere dispositions and not feelings at all, which is quite implausible. This kind of bodily feeling shows that mental states do not have to be located or be of short duration to be feelings. These feelings can be compared to moods that pervade the entire human being, at a different level, and in some cases they can hardly be distinguished from these moods.

Furthermore what Penelhum claims about 'enjoying' applies to agitations and moods as well (1964, p. 241). They are private events and not dispositions, because we can know directly, without relying on behavioral evidence, whether we have them. In order to determine whether a person has a certain disposition, such as politeness, we have to observe his behavior, and the same applies to ourselves. In order to know whether we are polite or intelligent, we must know whether we have the relevant sorts of reactions or could solve certain problems. But we know directly whether we are angry or depressed or enjoying something. We ourselves are in the best position to know this. Expressions of genuine agitation are usually recognized by others; but when we pretend, others are often taken in. Moods are harder to determine for others, but for ourselves it is usually not difficult. It does happen that we notice our mood because of something we do, but the mood that we notice is distinct from the behavior that makes us notice it.

INCLINATIONS

In contrast to moods, inclinations are not prime examples of feelings. Thus it is understandable that Ryle defends his behavioristic position primarily on the basis of inclinations. One reason why it is hard to determine to what extent inclinations are feelings is that they constitute such a heterogeneous category (Kenny, 1969, pp. 85ff.) Messiness, politeness and laziness are different kinds of inclinations from greed, ambition and interest. The latter three inclinations involve directedness, the former less so if at all.

Ryle's analysis applies fairly well to attitudes and habits, such as politeness or messiness. Other inclinations can become habits or attitudes, and when acting from habit we don't feel anything in particular. But Ryle's approach fails for inclinations in which directedness is the main component, such as ambition or interest. Such inclinations can be analyzed into the following components: a) thinking that something is desirable or undesirable and b) the consequent tendency to act in a certain way (Alston, 1972, p. 480; cf. White, 1968, p. 115). 'Thinking that something is (un)desirable' contains the feeling of being attracted or repelled. This feeling is certainly relevant to determining what someone's motive is. The question whether someone reads a book because he is interested in the subject or for other reasons can be decided by an honest answer from this person, because he knows best. Despite the possibility of repression or self-deception, the subject is at an advantage in determining whether he has a certain inclination. Furthermore we sometimes have inclinations of this kind that we hide. We can be attracted by something without doing anything to obtain it. Such a frustrated inclination is almost purely mental. We feel inclinations especially when we cannot or will not satisfy them. When we do satisfy our inclinations we feel pleasure.

Ryle thinks that taking strong interest in something does not consist in strong feelings, in his narrow sense, or impulses. If such impulses existed they would distract from the object of interest, since they require attention for themselves (ibid., pp. 85-86). This argument could be applied to any strong feeling of attraction. The argument does not work, however, because strong impulses distract from every activity but the object or activity at which the impulses are directed. Thus when we are very thirsty this sensation distracts from everything but drinking.

It is true that a person can do something out of interest without feeling interest at every moment. Does this show that we can do something from inclination without anything mental taking place? (ibid., p. 85). Not at all. We can say that someone acts out of interest when the feeling of interest occasionally makes him continue the project. This role of the feeling is essential to the inclination's really being present. Ryle denies that feelings can cause behavior. But he bases this at least in part on a doctrine I have discredited, namely the view that feelings are not events but merely dispositions to behave, which are never causes, according to Ryle. Feelings of interest may or may not occur. In the latter case we can continue to do what we started, but then it won't be out of interest that we do it.

In a similar vein, Skinner has objected that such a motive is not a real explanation, because interest *is* nothing over and above the kind of behavior we ordinarily describe as *expressing* interest. An explanation in terms of interest is supposed to be empty, because one and the same event—for instance, someone's reading a book out of interest—is referred to by two different terms. The mental term refers to the motive—interest—that is reconstructed from the behavior—reading the book—and the behavioral term refers to the result—reading the book (1965, pp. 29ff.).

This objection may be appropriate in specific cases of misuse of terms, but in general it does not work for two reasons. The first is that it is possible to have an inclination which we cannot follow because of the circumstances, and which therefore exists independently of the relevant behavior and *could* function as a motive. Second, we can do something for reasons other than interest, for instance because it is part of our job. Since there are several different sorts of motives, saying an action is done from interest can be both informative and explanatory (Scriven, 1956, pp. 121ff).[2]

A serious objection against the identification of inclinations and behavior is that at least some inclinations have no connection with any specific form of behavior. MacIntyre gives the example of resentment (1971, pp. 231ff). Any behavior can be an expression of resentment. Consider crossing the street (to avoid a colleague), buying something rare (that a colleague would like to purchase), and intercepting an invitation etc. Since there is no characteristic that an action must have in order to count as an expression of resentment, it looks as if any action can be an expression of resentment. Thus the relationship between inclination and behavior is contingent, and not conceptual, and the inclination is something other than the behavior that results from it. I doubt that this view applies to all feelings, as MacIntyre thinks, but it is certainly true for some inclinations.

VOLITION

I have emphasized repeatedly that feelings do not have to result in behavior, and that when they do the physical movements are distinct from the sensation or feeling that accompanies them. Ryle assumes that his form of behaviorism is justified if he can show that a feeling implies behavior, because he rejects the analysis of behavior as a composite of movement and mental states. To show that this kind of analysis makes no sense, he gives the following argument, which he applies to both volition and thought. The main idea of the argument is that the dualistic assumption of something mental makes no sense, because it leads to an infinite regress. I will discuss the application to volition.

According to many dualists and mentalists, an action is a movement that is willed. Volition distinguishes actions from reflexes. Some mentalists add that it is because of this mental cause that actions can be free and hence susceptible to moral judgment. Ryle claims that mental actions, such as thinking and fantasizing, can be judged morally as well, and so by the same reasoning must also result from volitions. The question now arises whether these volitions themselves are voluntary or involuntary. Ryle thinks that either answer leads to absurdity. If a volition is involuntary it cannot make an action voluntary. If a volition is voluntary, it can be so only due to a preceding volition, which can be voluntary only due to a volition preceding it and so on to infinity (ibid., pp. 65-66).

One could reply that volitions are the only acts that do not require a preceding volition in order to be free. As Passmore has explained the force of such an infinite regress depends on the question whether some specific category of statements or units can be given some special status (1970, pp. 28ff.). It is reasonable to demand a special position for volitions in this case. According to some dualists volitions are free, because we can want something or not, and if that is so, then volitions can make the movements they cause free without themselves requiring further preceding volitions to make them free. I am not concerned with defending this sense of freedom. My point is rather that it is possible to hold, in the face of Ryle's argument, that movements constitute actions because they are an exercise of will. A volition is by definition an exercise of the will and it of course requires no preceding volition in order to be a volition. Thus it is still possible to see an action as consisting in a movement and a mental state.

The fact that we can't say how many volitions we've had between twelve and one o'clock (Ryle, ibid., p. 63) does not count against their existence either. For neither can we say how many perceptions we have had in an hour, or how many actions we've performed. In all these cases the problem is how to individuate the items at issue. Without an answer to that question counting is impossible (H.D. Lewis, 1969, pp. 60-61).

Nevertheless it would be rather strange to say that every action comes about as a result of a volition. That heavy term only applies in daily life if there is a real decision that follows some deliberation or internal conflict. All day long we do things that we more or less will to do, and many of which we do semi-automatically. If we usually have breakfast, we don't have to decide to do so on a particular morning. If we have a habit of doing something, a decision is required only for not doing it. Consequently it is better to see willing, like perception, as a continuing experience that varies in strength, and in which occasionally the weight of a volition can be distinguished (cf. Whiteley, 1973, pp. 52-52).

Contrary to what Ryle thinks (ibid., p. 63) we can describe this willing by means of predicates like 'strong', 'weak', 'difficult' or 'easy'. Of course we will be inclined to do so only if something special is going on.

All in all not much is left of the behavioristic position with respect to the mental phenomena we have discussed.

TALKING ABOUT THE MENTAL: THE 'AVOWAL THEORY'

I have argued that we do not come to know our own mental states from our behavior. We can make statements about the mental because we know it directly, that is, not indirectly via behavior. We establish that we have pain or a mental image not on the basis of a behavioral manifestation, but by noticing the pain or the image itself. Similarly when we are depressed we notice that we don't feel like doing anything. In order to notice this we don't have to observe first that we haven't done anything all day. It is enough to notice the feeling at the beginning of the day.

A behaviorist cannot acknowledge that it is possible to report mental states that are known only, or in the first instance, by their subject. He must give a different status to utterances like 'I am in pain' or 'I am depressed.' He does this by means of the 'avowal theory'. According to this theory such utterances are not descriptive of mental states. They are just bits of behavior on a par with moaning or yawning. Saying that we are depressed is not a description of a fact, but one of the forms of behavior that constitute the depression. The rudiments of such a view can be found in Wittgenstein: such an utterance is supposed to be an acquired form of behavior that replaces natural behavior (1953, § 244; see also § 404, pp. 187, 189). I discuss primarily Ryle's version of the theory, because his presentation is the clearest and least hesitant (1949, pp. 98-99). Ryle holds, in keeping with the general strategy, that statements like 'I am depressed' are neither true nor false. They can be described only as sincere or insincere.

It is true that such utterances about the mental often have a strong expressive component, but this point does not support the avowal theory. Emotional force makes no difference to the informative character of an utterance. That depends on the utterance's linguistic structure. Even utterances which clearly have factual content, such as scientific claims, can be very emotionally charged. Such utterances fulfill two functions; they state information and express feelings.

Ryle's theory is untenable for the following reasons.

a) When a person says that he has a headache or that he is having a good time at a party, he may be uttering a falsehood. The fact that one can speak the truth or lie indicates that an utterance is a statement of a fact.

b) If a person responds to the question why he listens poorly by saying 'I am in pain,' he gives a reason. Giving a reason is also stating a fact.

c) The fact that reports are at issue is made clear by denials such as 'I am not in pain,' and utterances in tenses other than the present tense, which usually contain little or no emotional charge, such as 'I was in pain last month' or 'under those circumstances I will be in pain.' Utterances in the present and future tense cannot be part of pain behavior, because the subject is not in pain at the moment of utterance. Furthermore when we say that we have been or are going to be in pain there is no natural pain behavior for which this statement could be a substitute. This point counts against Wittgenstein's view that statements about one's own pain are substitutes for pain behavior (cf. Geach, 1971, p. 122).

On Ryle's view the utterance 'I am not in pain' should be behavior that is partly constitutive of the absence of pain. If that were right then one's pain could be lessened just by denying one had it. It would be nice if this were true, but it is not. It is this kind of utterance in particular that shows utterances about pain are as much reports as are utterances about public objects.

Finally on this theory a peculiar contrast arises between talk about oneself and talk about others. Utterances about others continue to be regarded as statements of fact because they refer to a person's behavior, including what that person says about himself. When a nurse says about a patient 'he is in pain' this is supposed to say something about him. But the patient's own utterance 'I am in pain', on which her statement is based, is not. However, the statement 'I am in pain' when made by John Smith, and the statement 'he is in pain' made about this same John Smith contain the same information. That is why 'he is in pain' can be confirmed or denied by John Smith by saying 'I am (not) in pain'. The difference is only in how the statements are verified: the nurse has to rely on John Smith's statements and/or behavior, whereas John Smith does not have to rely on his own utterances or behavior. He can notice the pain itself (Hampshire, 1971, p. 105).

So the 'avowal theory' is untenable for more than one reason. Whereas Ryle espouses this theory, he leaves open the possibility that such utterances about ourselves are reports if based on our noticing our own behavior. For him yawning and the utterance 'I am bored' are both partial contituents of boredom. But if we have noticed this behavior and say on the basis of it 'I am bored,' this utterance is supposed to be a report (Ryle, ibid., p. 99). Thus the same utterance is supposed to be a reaction like yawning in one case and a report in another case. The question whether someone's utterance is a report depends, however, on its linguistic structure, not on the way in which a speaker discovers its content.

As I said earlier, it does sometimes happen that someone notices his own mood because he is struck by his own behavior. But when he verbalizes his mood he does not intend to talk about that behavior.

Furthermore, when a person realizes that he is bored or tired, because he has yawned, he usually knows which of the two states he is in, whereas an observer who only notices his behavior cannot decide this question. On the other hand the statement that we are in pain is almost never provoked by the perception of our own behavior. The main point is that the statement concerns the inner state, whether or not it is prompted by behavior.

The conclusion of this chapter, then, is that mental phenomena are different from publicly observable behavior, and that their subjects can report them.

Notes

1. Elsewhere Ryle does speak of an 'internal cinematograph-show of visual imagery' (ibid., p. 28). For a discussion of his inconsistencies and ambivalence on this point see Ayer (1971).

2. Moreover intellectual mental acts can explain that an action is more or less intelligent. The intelligence of a move in chess consists in certain characteristics of the move, but the fact that the move has these characteristics normally results from preceding mental acts of the player (cf. Fodor, 1975, pp. 29).

3. MENTALISM

In our discussion of behaviorism we saw that at least some mental phenomena, for instance sensations and mental images, cannot be described in terms of behavior. I have argued that this is also true for one form of thought, namely understanding, and for most kinds of feelings. In this way I have laid the foundation for mentalism. I will now discuss this view and defend a version of it. I will only discuss the more important of the many different forms of mentalism. When I speak about mentalism without specifying a particular version of it, it should be assumed that the views at issue are held by most or at least many mentalists.

A defense of mentalism involves a continuous confrontation with behaviorism, presently its most important alternative. So far I have not considered 'linguistic behaviorism', the view held by the later Wittgenstein and his followers. This view does not deny the existence of mental phenomena, but holds that they play no role in communication between people. If this were true, then the fact that some mental phenomena cannot be accounted for by behaviorism would not by itself count in favor of mentalism. For in that case talk about the mental could be accounted for by linguistic behaviorism, and so mentalism would not be true. In this chapter I begin a discussion of the confrontation between mentalism and linguistic behaviorism, which will be the sole subject of the chapter about Wittgenstein and mentalism.

To a reader who is not yet familiar with modern behaviorism some mentalistic views will seem hardly surprising. It should be kept in mind that in philosophy almost everything that seems to go without saying is questioned, as will become clear in what follows.

THE MEANING OF NAMES FOR SENSATIONS

Consciousness in its different forms is an inner given and behavior is a manifestation of it. We know what pain is only from our own consciousness. The mind notices its own operations and thus acquires ideas of them, as John Locke claimed in *An Essay Concerning Human Understanding* (1690, Bk II,p. 124).

The question is how we can talk about something that we know only from our own consciousness, and how we learn to talk about it. We can learn to use expressions for pain because it has certain known causes and results in specific behavior that allows adults to know that a child is in pain. Consequently they are able to use the appropriate words to refer to the child's state while the child is present, and in this way it learns them. It is not necessary that the adults always be right. It is enough if they usually use the terms appropriately. Once the child has learned the term he can use it even when no cause or behavior indicating pain is visible to others. In that case others cannot know that the child is in pain, unless he says so. So publicly observable causes and effects allow the development of language—which is also something public—that refers to private events.

When a person says that he is in pain he refers to something that he alone experiences and notices directly at that time, while others know what he talks about because they themselves have experienced the same thing on other occasions. If a person could feel no pain—which is very rare—he would not know what the word means. Colorblindness is more common, and a colorblind person does not know what the names for colors mean. He can acquire all kinds of knowledge about the physical nature of colors and also which names for colors apply to which objects. As a result he may know that the sky is blue when it is clear, but the core of the meaning of 'blue' must escape him.[1]

Wittgenstein used the following well-known argument against the view that a mental image or idea is necessary to give a word meaning. Although a person who is ordered to get a red flower from a meadow may draw a comparison with a mental image of the color when executing the order, this is not necessary. He may execute the order without appealing to anything like an image. This possibility is demonstrated, according to Wittgenstein, by a person following the command: 'imagine a red spot'. There is no temptation to think that before he executes this command, the person must produce an image of red in order to serve as a model for the red spot that he is supposed to imagine (1958, p. 3). If someone can imagine red without comparing it to an image of red, why could he not identify a red object without making such a comparison?

The answer to this question lies in a difference between the two kinds of commands. The order to identify something implies recognition and that requires a comparison, but the command to imagine something does not have this implication. If in a case of identification no comparison can be made with an example of red that is at hand, a comparison must be made with an image in the mind. Wittgenstein's argument does not establish the intended conclusion. In both cases the subject must have a mental image of red, but in the case of getting a flower he must in addition use this image for identification. When given the command 'imagine a red spot' he is asked to imagine what constitutes the meaning of the word 'red'—apart from the word 'spot'. But in the case of the other command he must in addition apply this meaning, which is why in that case the mental image, which constitutes the meaning, is indispensible.

Furthermore it is easy to see why we don't realize, when we see a red object and recognize it as such, that we do so via a memory image. When told to find something red we will not first produce an image, since it is easily available to us. The red object that we see makes a stronger impression than the mental image, which is pushed aside by the new impression and, as it were, covered by it. It is useful to call up the mental image first only if we are not very familiar with the color in question.

According to Malcolm, a follower of Wittgenstein, there is something to be said for the view that a blind person does not know fully what the meanings of color terms are, because he cannot attribute the correct color terms to objects by seeing them. But Malcolm thinks that someone who cannot feel pain could know what the word pain means, including what it would mean in his own case. Such a person, whom we will call FNP (for 'feels no pain') could learn to simulate pain behavior, for instance in a play, and then say at the right moment that he is in pain. Also when a doctor is treating him in order to get him to know the sensation of pain for his own good, he will be able to say that he still feels no pain. Malcolm thinks that FNP understands the meaning of this sentence and thus also the meaning of 'I feel pain', even if he can never utter the latter sentence truthfully. It follows, Malcolm argues, that he understands the meaning of the word 'pain', even if he never feels any (1972, pp. 46-49).

Malcolm assumes that understanding a concept is the same as being able to use the word for it correctly. Consequently he thinks that FNP's correct use of the word 'pain' shows that he understands what 'pain' means. But this conclusion does not follow even if we accept Malcolm's assumption about what it is to understand a concept. Suppose FNP suddenly feels slight pain which is due to internal causes and which does not lead to characteristic pain behavior. In that case he will not know that he feels pain. If his first pain is so severe that it makes him scream, he can know that it is a case of pain, provided he has been told beforehand that pain—and only pain—has this result. But without such a symptom he will not know that he is in pain, because he has no idea what pain is.

If FNP tells his doctor that he still feels no pain, he means that he still feels nothing special, nothing new; on this ground he concludes that he still feels no pain. His statement 'I still feel no pain' means to him 'I feel nothing new'. This point and the fact that he does not understand what he says are made clear by the following observations. Suppose that he has also never felt an itch and that this fact has gone unnoticed. Suppose furthermore that his doctor's therapy results in his having an itch. This sensation will be new to him and so he will say that he now feels pain. For he cannot recognize this feeling. He will call a new sensation pain, because his doctor's efforts make him expect it to be pain. So he does not know what 'pain' means.

The above example is less farfetched than it may seem. In the medical literature there is a case of a woman who was genetically insensitive to pain. She thought she started to feel pain, because she became better at preventing injuries. The rest of her behavior suggested, however, that she felt no pain. It seemed more likely that she had improved her ability to identify possible causes of injury in her environment (Trigg, 1970, p. 170). Such a mistake is understandable in someone who has never had pain and is only able to guess about the content of the term.

I will return to linguistic behaviorism later, but first it is necessary to discuss the issue of knowledge of one's own mind. We have seen that the use of a concept that covers mental experiences depends on an idea of such experiences, which is remembered. If we did not have such an idea, we would not recognize the experience when it came back. When the idea has become too weak, we start to make mistakes or lose the ability to recognize the experience altogether.

This view has been criticized on the ground that it implies that the use of a concept requires that we have the experience again. Thus we should have an aversion to using words like 'pain' or 'sadness', because the ideas which are replicas of pain and sadness would evoke these unwelcome experiences. Geach claims that this is not so and that the present view is therefore incorrect (1971, p. 108). But such a reliving of an experience is certainly possible to some degree, especially if we recently had the kind of experience in question. Hence the Arabic saying that in the house of the hanged one should not talk about the noose. But if a word is quite common in ordinary usage, we loose our sensibility to its evocative force. Furthermore reliving an experience is not necessary since the idea is something other than the experience itself, and insofar as it resembles the experience, it is much weaker.

According to another objection this view implies that some people are hardly or not at all able to recognize mental experiences, because they have not had them at all, not frequently enough or were unable to learn to distinguish them. But, so the objection goes, no one is blind to emotions such as fear or anger in the way in which some people are color-blind (Geach, ibid., 109-110). It is true that almost anyone can recognize pure forms of anger and fear, which are basic and very common experiences. But people vary widely with respect to their ability to identify mental experiences that are less common and harder to recognize. The objection overlooks the fact that some people are quite bad at distinguishing their mental states. Thus one person may only be able to say that he thinks something is pleasant or unpleasant, whereas another person could provide a detailed description of his feelings. In this respect our ability to analyze our mental states resembles our ability to identify colors: some people only know the meaning of a few color terms, others know the meaning of and can apply dozens of them.

REFLECTION AND INTROSPECTION

REFLECTION

Introspection yields information about the mental that would remain unknown to us if we paid no more than ordinary attention to our mental states. We can know much about the mental without any special effort, however, for instance that we are warm or cold, cheerful or depressed. Introspection is a concentration of our ordinary capacity to know our inner states. I will first discuss this capacity, which a number of philosophers have called the capacity for reflection.

According to some, consciousness of our mental states and processes is the same as knowledge of them. Others think that knowledge of our mental states requires reflective consciousness. I accept the second of these views. Ryle objects that both of these views involve abuse of the logic and even grammar of the word 'to know'. He points out that we must distinguish between 'knowing' as used in 'I know that type of state' and 'knowing that', as in 'I know that something is the case'. Ryle claims that it makes no sense to speak of knowing a thunderbolt or a stab of pain. According to him 'to know' is 'to know that something is the case' (1949, p. 155). It is true that it is odd to speak of knowing a thunderbolt or a stab of pain because there is not much to know in these items. But it clearly does make sense to speak of knowing a *kind* of thing, for instance a kind of bird or a kind of feeling. It also makes sense to say that we know a particular thing if it is relatively complex, such as a machine or a thought. It seems odd to say about a particular simple thought that we know it, but it does not seem odd if it is said about a *kind* of simple thought or about a particular line of reasoning. Thus Ryle's objection to the idea that reflection yields knowledge of the mental does not have much of a foundation. The following two arguments he gives are aimed at the view that consciousness is 'self-luminous', that is, the view that it knows itself automatically. I agree with Ryle that this view is unacceptable, but it does not follow that mental states and processes cannot be known by reflection.

What is reflection? Often we make statements about what we think or feel without thinking about it. We do not have to examine anything, but can say something immediately. The question has been raised how we can maintain that such statements express knowledge. Ayer struggles with this question and proposes that knowing what our thoughts and feelings are consists in the ability to make true reports about them. He rightly rejects the idea that doing so always requires introspection, but does not discuss reflection or any other mental capacity. He thinks that these kinds of statements do not require evidence, and that this is why the kind of knowledge at issue is often called direct. The question how we can make these true reports simply does not arise and does not have to be answered. Thus the conclusion is really that we 'just' or 'simply' do it (Ayer, 1973, pp. 62-63). Along the same lines Shoemaker has claimed that statements in the first person about one's own experience (for instance, 'I see a tree' or 'I have a headache') are special in that their truth alone gives someone the right to make them, and not the observation that they are true or evidence that they are true (1970, p. 122).

Nevertheless since these statements can be false the question remains how a person knows that they are true when they are. So this view is unconvincing. Ayer claims that there is a difference between our ability to say truthfully what we think or feel and our ability to make other true statements, because in the case of other statements we must always be able to provide supporting statements that contain evidence for our initial statement. This claim is not quite accurate, however, since for a certain kind of observational statement no supporting statements can be made but nevertheless there is a sense in which there is evidence. Suppose a person stands in front of a meter and says: 'the needle is bouncing.' If this person is asked for his ground for this statement, he cannot say much more than: because it's bouncing and I see it. I am inclined to regard the bouncing itself as evidence for the statement that the needle is bouncing, but I do not want to commit myself to the term 'evidence'. My point is that there is an analogy between this kind of statement and statements about the mental. When someone asks us for our ground for a certain statement about our feelings or thoughts, we can't say much more than that the feeling or thought in question presents itself to us and we notice it. This is the same kind of 'evidence'—if one wants to use this term—as is available in the case of the statement about the meter. In both cases something needs to be noticed, and noticing is a mental activity.

I can express a thought because it presents itself to me and I notice it. Noticing or observing one's thoughts is a mental activity for which the existing term 'reflection' is appropriate. We can observe reflection in ourselves. Suppose we say something automatically because we assume we know it, for instance we say that we want something because we usually do. Now it can happen that a moment later we realize that in this case we do not want it. One moment of consideration is enough. No introspection or investigation is necessary. We just needed to allow our mental state to register with us so that we notice it. This is reflection. It seems to us as if we make many statements without any reflection, but this is because they are so easy to make or have become so through practice. When a person expounds thoughts which are very familiar to him, he can do so almost automatically, as in the case of a campaigning politician or a philosopher who describes a philosophical system which he has explained dozens of times. In such a case a person only needs to exercise mental supervision of what he says. So little reflection is needed that it seems absent. But when we say that none is needed, we mean that so little is needed in comparison with times at which we apparently reflect for a moment, that it is not worth mentioning.

So there is largely sufficient reason for speaking of reflection in addition to introspection. Reflection may not be a sense, but it can be regarded as a sort of 'inner sense', as Locke observed. For reflection resembles vision and hearing in the following respects (Mellor, 1978, pp. 98-99). a) We can decide what to look at, and similarly, we can decide, to a certain extent, what to reflect on. b) We cannot decide what to see when we look, and in the same way we usually cannot decide what convictions and feelings we will discover in ourselves. Our convictions are influenced by what we want to believe, but on the other hand, our prejudices also influence our perceptions. c) We can develop our reflective consciousness and improve our ability to recognize our sensations and our ability to say what we think and want. The following two similarities will be discussed elsewhere: d) there are aspects of what falls within our visual field that we cannot see or, in any case, that do not register in our consciousness. Similarly there are mental states of which we are not reflexively conscious. e) We can make mistakes in perception and also in our awareness of our inner states.

Reflection Contained in Consciousness?

According to some philosophers (Locke 1690, Bk. II, ch. I, section 19) in reflection a person is necessarily and automatically conscious of his own mental activities, without having to pay special attention to them.

Brentano defends the view that when a person has a representation of something, he perceives this representation at the same time ('nebenbei'), and the representation and its perception constitute only one act. The act of representation is supposed to include its perception (1874, Bnd I, pp. 176ff., 196). But how can one mental act be both a representation and the perception of this representation?

Is the subject of a sensation, feeling, desire or thought necessarily and automatically aware of the mental state in question? In the case of thought it is clear that there is consciousness of something, but is the subject unavoidably aware of the fact that he thinks? We may be inclined to answer in the affirmative, since in many cases we are aware of our thoughts, and since this reflective consciousness comes naturally and without effort. A person who is hot will usually be aware that he is hot, and this goes without saying for him, because he assumes that he has a certain minimal capacity for reflection. A normal conscious human being constantly takes a reflective stance, as is clear from phrases like 'I feel...', 'I want...', 'I think that...', which are used to convey not only the content of mental states, that is, *what* is felt, wanted or thought, but also to convey *that* something is felt, wanted or thought.

There are, however, conclusive objections to the view that reflection is built into conscious states. We are not automatically reflectively conscious of all such states. Consider, for instance, a feeling of jealousy or a particular belief. Furthermore Ryle has pointed out that this view has the following unacceptable consequence. If making an inference implies that the subject knows that he is making an inference, it is natural to assume that the subject knows that he knows that he is making an inference and so on. Consequently the subject must know an infinite sequence, which is impossible (1949, p. 156). So thinking something and thinking that we think it are different activities. When a subject has a certain thought, the only thing he is necessarily thinking is the content of that thought. Ryle concludes, incorrectly, from the fact that this particular view of reflection must be rejected, that there cannot be any reflection which could result in knowledge of the mental (cf. Addis, 1965, pp. 58-59).

A subject does not have to be conscious of his mental state. It is hard to see this point for simple sensations such as pain or heat. Nevertheless it does happen that we suddenly notice that we are hot and that we have been hot for a while without noticing that we were. Being aware that we are hot is different from feeling hot and requires something more. A subject may fail to be aware that he has a certain feeling or hope not only because he does not want to recognize it—a reason emphasized by depth psychology—but also because it simply did not occur to him. When we think about a very demanding problem, it is very hard to realize at the same time that we are thinking. When we play chess we are usually aware of doing so, but when thinking hard about a move we may lose that awareness.

It seems to go without saying that we can notice that we are hot, but very small children and animals, who also feel heat, probably can't. It is quite likely that animals have sensations like heat, hunger and thirst without being reflectively aware of them. It is possible for a child to think something, despite the fact that he is unable to know that he thinks because he lacks the notion of thought (Ayer, 1973, p. 63). Armstrong makes the interesting suggestion that sleep-walkers, who apparently perceive their environment, but do not realize that they do and do not remember it afterwards, lack reflective consciousness (Armstrong-Malcolm, 1984, p. 139). (I will discuss this point in the chapter about the Unconscious.)

So we are not necessarily 'conscious of' our mental processes in the sense of having them 'present to our mind'. Sensations, feelings and thoughts are forms of consciousness. But consciousness of them is a different form of consciousness in which the other forms become, in a sense, objects of consciousness, although not real objects which exist independently of our mental states. If someone is capable of reflection, then he *can* be conscious of these states. The fact that we are often aware of our mental states is an empirical, contingent fact (cf. D. Locke, 1971, ch. 2).

On the present view it is possible to be in pain or to feel hot without being reflectively conscious of these states. Many will admit this point for feelings but not for sensations like pain. It seems as if we are not in pain, if we are not conscious of pain. The reason is that it is very easy to be conscious of pain. I have already given an example that shows that a subject can realize that he has had such a sensation for some time without noticing it (cf. Palmer, 1975, p. 291). No doubt there is a difference between feelings and sensations in this respect; but it is a matter of degree.

Reflection should Not be Identified with Consciousness Tout Court

Reflective consciousness comes in many degrees. The question now is whether an adult always has *some* degree of consciousness *of* his mental states, be it ever so low. I think that during some dreams, for instance, there is no reflective consciousness at all, but only consciousness of the content of the dream. The conviction that there always is some degree of reflective consciousness has led some philosophers to say that we are always conscious *that* we have a sensation or feeling. But if we always had this kind of consciousness then it would sometimes be so rudimentary that we would not detect the experience in question, which amounts to not having this consciousness *of* our mental states.

Reflective consciousness is identified with consciousness *tout court* in John Locke's definition, according to which 'Consciousness is the perception of what passes in a man's own mind' (1690, Bk.II, ch.1, section 19). We were already introduced to the view that what is part of a person's consciousness is automatically perceived: Locke's definition makes this perception a condition for consciousness. This definition leads to an acute form of the problem that we signalled for this view, which was already raised by Leibniz (1765, II, 1, section 19). If consciousness requires perception—that is, consciousness—of this consciousness, then this perception can only be consciousness if it is itself perceived. The same point applies to this second perception and so on ad infinitum. Consequently consciousness requires an infinite number of perceptions of perceptions, but such infinite sequences do not occur. We can reflect on our last reflection when we want, but we will stop at some point because the process becomes pointless and we can't complete an infinite sequence.

In order to avoid this infinite regress it might be suggested that what happens in one's mind is consciousness only if it is perceived, but that this reflective consciousness does not need to be perceived in order to be consciousness. But it is not clear on what ground this distinction could be made. Why would what happens in our mind be consciousness only if it is perceived but this perception be consciousness even if it is not?

Our mental processes include sensations and perceptions of the world, and these are part of consciousness as is indicated by Locke's formulation 'what passes in a man's own mind'. A sensation of heat is part of consciousness and, as pointed out before, we can have that sensation without our being reflectively conscious of it. We know this from certain memory experiences.

A person's state of mind at a particular moment does not in general consist exclusively in what he primarily feels or thinks. Usually there is attention to something else, either to some other feeling or thought or to a reflective thought about one's feeling or thought. When we feel pain we can usually feel or think something else in addition and thus also have the thought that we are in pain. The stronger the pain the more it occupies consciousness and the more it tends to exclude other thoughts and feelings. Finally one is, so to speak, 'nothing but pain', although if Sartre is right (cf. chapter 1), our consciousness is never entirely one with the pain. It is hard to say whether consciousness ever is entirely taken up by a particular thought or feeling. I have suggested that our distance from a sensation decreases as the sensation becomes stronger. The question is whether this distance is ever entirely abolished. Do we have consciousness *of* a dream while having it? There is no distance until afterwards when we recapitulate the dream. During the dream we are not aware *that* we dream. Consciousness seems to be completely absorbed by the content of the dream.

NO INFALLIBILITY OF KNOWLEDGE OF THE MENTAL

The question of knowledge of the mental leads to consideration of the notion of introspection. The acquisition of such knowledge by introspection is a subject of much controversy. Many philosophers assume that experience of a mental state determines whether it exists. This view has led them to say that the mental can be known with certainty, or in any case more easily than the external world (cf. Russell, 1927, p. 134). Inner perception is supposed always to be correct, because mental phenomena are exactly as they appear to us (McGinn, 1983, ch. 4; cf. J. Wisdom, 1965, pp. 172-173). But we already saw at the end of the first chapter that not all mental states reach self-consciousness or reflective thought, and many are transformed in the process. And even if our mental states reached self-consciousness unchanged, our knowledge of our own mental states would still have defects.

If a mentalist claims that we cannot make mistakes about the mental, then he must accept that certain states which he regards as at least partly mental, such as love, dislike and jealousy, are not mental. For it is quite possible to have such feelings without knowing it, even if those feelings are reflected in one's behavior. The fact that self-knowledge is not at all automatic and is hard to attain has been adduced as a reason for denying that certain inclinations are mental at all. According to this line of reasoning if these inclinations were mental, then their subject could not so easily make mistakes about them (Ryle, 1949, ch. VI).

This argument can be countered with the help of Sartre's distinction between pre-reflexive and reflexive consciousness (1943, pp. 16-23). We experience our jealousy prereflexively—this consciousness consists in the experience of our jealousy—, but this does not mean that we think about this experience. When we don't do so, or do it inadequately, we may make mistakes.

Following Descartes many philosophers have claimed that knowledge of the mental is certain. Thus Brentano claims that the subject's experience of a mental state while it occurs cannot be deceptive and excludes all doubt (1874, Bk. I, ch. 2, section 3, p. 50). Descartes argued that we can doubt everything but not the fact that we doubt, so that only the existence of consciousness is certain. Even if I am mistaken when thinking that I see or hear something or that I feel warm, it is certain that I seem to have these sensations (1641, pp. 415, 422). This use of the word 'seem' has been criticized at the end of the first chapter.

I want to discuss this view of Descartes's, since two centuries of theory of knowledge and philosophy of mind are based on it. If all my perceptions of the world were illusory, and the world did not exist or were different from the way it seems to me, I would also have no certainty about the correctness of my concepts of the world. And the concepts we use to describe the mental are drawn from concepts we use to describe the world. As a result I would be as uncertain about my knowledge about the mental as about my knowledge about the world. I have learned these concepts from other people, but if I were continually deluded about the external world, I could never learn a concept such as 'warm'. For when others used the word 'warm' it would refer to states which for me would vary widely. When it was warm, for instance 25 degrees Celsius, I would sometimes be cold, and at other times be very hot or have no experience of temperature at all. If I did not know the concept I would also not *know* that I was warm. Even the certainty that I was not certain about anything and thus that I was conscious at least, would be lost. For the concept of '(un)certainty' would have no content.

Despite such fundamental problems, Descartes's view contains an element of truth. If we restrict the scope of a claim of knowledge to our mental states, then we cannot make a certain kind of error, namely errors about the world. (This is of course a trivial truth.) A claim about our mental states can, however, still be erroneous. This point can easily be overlooked because of the following kind of example: suppose someone says 'it is warm here' and then takes this claim back to make the more restricted claim 'I am warm'. This last claim is almost always true when made sincerely.

Perception of the world can go awry because events in the world take place in space and time. The mental occurs in time but not in space. Consequently errors can be made about mental states whose perception takes some time, such as moods and inclinations. We may fail to remember something or our memory may be deceptive.

But consider a mental state whose nature can be determined in one moment or in a very short time. Defendants of infallibility almost always rely on such examples. In such a case we sometimes need to let our experience register with us. Sometimes we are not sure of what we taste or feel, for instance. In introspection, by definition, we pay attention to our experience; but often in our daily experience we don't. As a result we can make mistakes about our experience because we have observed it only superficially (Austin, 1979, pp. 91ff.). If the experience can be repeated, we can correct our errors, but often we never realize we made a mistake. Sometimes fearful anticipation makes us think erroneously that we (already) feel pain. We think we notice pain, but we are not in pain, as we realize afterwards.

Even if a mental state is present to our mind entirely and accurately, this merely means that a necessary condition for knowledge of this state is fulfilled. Having a sensation is not the same as identifying it (cf. Armstrong, 1971, p. 106); its identification requires comparison with other sensations. We cannot determine the nature of a mental phenomenon until we observe that it sufficiently resembles other such phenomena and thus are able to classify it. Sensations without concepts are blind, as Kant said. Recognition and classification require concepts, which depend on memory and our memory is fallible. Sometimes we don't remember exactly what a certain shade of color is like and confuse it with another one, for instance, mauve with heliotrope.

Classification of mental phenomena is done by means of the concepts we learned for them and which are connected to words for them. We have the concept of pain which for speakers of English is connected to the word 'pain', but which in other languages is connected to different words.

Communication of our knowledge requires that we know the right word for a phenomenon that we have identified. This condition is easily lost sight of because it is normally taken for granted. When we are able to identify something we usually know the word for it; nevertheless it is possible that we know a mental phenomenon but cannot remember the word for it. This happens, for instance, when we have lived in a foreign country for some time, and no longer think in our native language but do not yet master the foreign language sufficiently. We have identified something and the relevant concept is present to us, but we can not think of the appropriate word in the foreign language. Such experiences allow us to realize that words are arbitrary signs for concepts.

We can conclude that description of the mental can go awry in more than one way (cf. Aune, 1967, pp. 31-38). We can choose the wrong concept for a mental state or the wrong word. The fact that in certain kinds of cases mistakes are hardly ever made does not mean that no mistakes can be made. The following is an example of a mistake that is easily made. Someone says in reply to the question what he is doing 'I am thinking, or rather, I am just day-dreaming'. Such a person realizes that what is going on in his mind resembles thought too little to deserve the name. He had not been sufficiently aware of what he was doing. Similarly, after an electrical shock a person may say first that it hurt and then take it back saying that it was a horrible experience, but not pain. Such a person classifies his experience incorrectly at first because he does not realize what the concept of 'pain' amounts to. Sometimes we classify correctly but absentmindedness causes us to choose the wrong word even for simple mental data. In the case of moods finding the right word is often difficult.

In some cases reflection or introspection is required to find out what kind of mistake has been made. Sometimes we realize that the concept we have used—for which we have chosen the right word—is after all not applicable. This is probably the most common kind of error. But there are cases in which we use the wrong word although we have the right concept in mind.

EPISTEMIC AUTHORITY

Although the subject's knowledge of his own mental states is fallible, he is in the best position to know what mental states he has, because he can notice them himself. We have 'epistemic authority' about our own mental states (cf. Baier, 1970, p. 98), even if this authority is not absolute. Similarly an eye-witness is in the best position to say what happened at a certain place and time, even if it is known that such witnesses make mistakes (Ayer, 1973, p. 72). It is true that others can be sure *that* a subject tends to have certain sensations and *sometimes* they can determine from his behavior and circumstances that he has a particular kind of sensation at that moment. Or so I will argue in the chapter about knowledge about other minds. Nevertheless the subject himself usually knows better than others when exactly he has a particular kind of experience. The subject himself has the last word. This also applies to mental images, thoughts, and intentions. Others recognize this in so far as they believe a subject is sincere. When they have doubts about his sincerity they will in some cases think that their knowledge overrides the subject's statements. But this fact does not alter their recognition that the subject does have the last word if he is sincere. For the most part others will have to say that they can't find out the truth if the subject is not willing to divulge it. This epistemic authority applies in the first place to everything that can be detected by reflection and does not require careful attention, that is, introspection.

Materialists like Armstrong (1971, pp. 107-108) and Rorty (1970, pp. 204ff.) have claimed that this kind of epistemic authority might disappear. Given enough physiological data a physiologist could make the following kind of claim about a person. According to the encephalogram he lies when he says that he is in pain, for it shows that his brain is not in the state required for pain, or, if he is not lying, he simply doesn't know what pain is and uses the word incorrectly.

We must admit that it is possible that this situation will occur and that consequently not every individual has epistemic authority for every statement about his mental states. He has this authority only when he can distinguish pain from other sensations and has learned the word for it. When a foreigner who does not speak English well, claims 'that hurts' when he wins a match, a native English speaker can correct him and say that he must mean 'I am happy about that'. No statement about one's own mental states is incorrigible in the sense that such a statement is always more justified than statements of others about them. For although a subject has privileged access to his mental states, it is always possible that he does not use it well. This fact is sometimes used to conclude that statements from subjects about their mental states are not necessary for a psycho-physiological theory (Bailey, 1979, pp. 144, 149).

These statements are necessary for such a theory, however. The subject has authority over the physiologist, though this authority does have its limits. The physiologist can do his job only if he can distinguish the phenomena and name them correctly. So it is unfair to contrast a competent physiologist with a person who cannot identify or name pain. In the same vein a mentalist could attack the physiologist's statements by assuming that he does not know how to do his job or does not master its vocabulary when he does not accept an admittedly sincere statement of a subject about his pain.

A more principled defense of the authority of the subject relies on the following consideration. In order to contradict a report about pain of one subject the physiologist must rely on the reports about pain of other subjects. For he can determine the state of the brain that generally accompanies pain only on the basis of information from people about their own mental states. In some cases he can rely on unmistakable pain-behavior (Bailey, ibid., p. 144), but he knows only from other people's reports that a person behaving in this way is in pain. Consequently when a physiologist contradicts a person's report about pain, he does so not only on the basis of his knowledge of the brain but also by accepting the epistemic authority of individuals about their mental states. This authority provides him with indispensible information. So the knowledge of the psycho-physiologist depends unavoidably on the primary knowledge of individuals about their own mental states, which is regarded as generally reliable. J.S. Mill pointed out to the positivist A. Comte—who rejected reflection and introspection and wanted to restrict psychology to research of the skull—, that for research about the correspondence of two things examination of only one of them is not sufficient (1865a, p. 65).

Bailey argues that if every single statement of a person about his mental states is in principle susceptible to refutation, then all the statements of this and other persons taken together can be refuted (ibid., ch. VI). This view is often assumed implicitly, but involves an unjustified generalization. The kind of refutation in question is not possible, since it would undermine the psycho-physical theory that is used to carry it out. If all or a considerable portion of statements about one's own mental states could be refuted on the basis of a theory, then the reliable data about the mental that such a theory needs would no longer be available.

This means that epistemic authority about mental states lies with their subjects. Ordinarily their statements, if sincere, are better justified than the statements of others.

Our epistemic authority is fallible, but usually we cannot be corrected by others. The notions of 'infallibility' and 'incorrigibility' are sometimes used interchangeably, but they are different (Bailey, 1979, p. 100ff.). Infallibility implies incorrigibility but not vice versa. Sometimes others suspect that our report about our mental states is erroneous. They may propose a correction, but in many cases they are unable to do so. This means that when we are in error about our mental states—for instance when reporting a dream—we make mistakes that no one can discover. Again the comparison with the report of an eye-witness is appropriate. If such a report is erroneous, it can sometimes be refuted on the basis of indirect evidence. Such evidence is not always available, however, and if it is not, then the truth will never be known.

If a mental state requires introspection in order to be known, epistemic authority about one's own mental states is more doubtful, because in introspection errors are quite common. As was mentioned before, sometimes it is clear to others from a person's behavior that he is in some at least partly mental state, such as love, dislike or jealousy, while this person himself does not realize that he has the mental state in question. He may even deny that he has it without being consciously dishonest. Furthermore we often do not see connections between mental contents very well and it is quite common for a person to think too favorably about himself. Selfknowledge is hard to achieve. Ryle claimed that an impartial, competent observer is a better judge of a person's inclinations and abilities than the person himself. He concluded that this observation counts against the idea that a subject has privileged access to his own mental states (ibid., p. 88).

External observers can be prejudiced as much as the person whose mental states are at issue, however, and lack discernment as a result. It is too quickly assumed that if a person does not know himself others do know him. Given equal powers of discernment and impartiality, a subject is in a better position to know his own inclinations than others, because he can observe both his mental life and his behavior. Reflexive processing of pre-reflexive experience requires a lot of attention and discernment. A person may not have what it takes and not know himself, but the material for self-knowledge is available to him. It is not so easy to observe one's own behavior; some habits strike others more than ourselves. We can learn to observe our own behavior, however. The ability to deduce another person's feelings or thoughts from his behavior is also susceptible of improvement, but it will always have certain insurmountable limits and be unproductive some of the time. If someone acts on a simple inclination for a long time, anyone can see that. But in the case of a complex inclination the knowledge that others have is restricted to suppositions that are derived indirectly by more or less adequate reasoning. Inclinations that result in very little or no behavior remain (almost) entirely hidden from observers. Whoever does not see this point will continue to be amazed under unusual circumstances by behavior of people he thought he knew.

INTROSPECTION

Introspection is a concentrated form of reflection. In it a person focuses on the 'perception' and representation of his own mental states and processes. When a subject knows without any effort what is going on in his mind we do not speak of introspection, since this implies special attention to the mental. Of course it is not perception in the ordinary sense. In introspection we try to make the mental known to *thought*.

According to Lyons introspection is a replay of perception. It is the use of our perceptual memory and imagination to find out about our motives, thoughts and the like by finding out about our published, revealed-in-speech-gesture-expression-and-behavior motives and thoughts (1986, ch. 7). But it is more than that. We are able to introspect feelings and thoughts which did not lead to behavior, e.g. a thought about an action which we did not perform. We can afterwards find words for what we felt without words or gestures. And imagination is not just perception in another mode (ibid., p. 129). It is something like thinking, based only partly on remembered perceptual images.

Given our discussion of reflection there is no need to elaborate on the fact that there is no philosophical reason for regarding introspection as infallible. There is no guarantee that all our mental states and processes are noticed and perfectly represented. We saw that errors can be made in reflection. This point applies *a fortiori* to introspection, because it is used only when acquiring knowledge of a particular mental item is hard. A person who is unable to report a clear after-image or violent pain correctly must be very confused. But the description of a thought-process requires concentration, a good memory, an open mind to what is going on, and the ability to describe the thought accurately.

James observed in *The Principles of Psychology* (1890, ch. 7) that introspection is as difficult as observation of the external world. When introspecting a person must classify and analyze his mental states and compare them with each other. For instance, it is not easy to determine the order of a rapid sequence of sensations, or to decide what images and thoughts accompany a particular mood. In general mental states that require longer observation are harder to decipher. Many people lack understanding of mental factors that determine their behavior and are unwilling to recognize that their behavior is partly determined by 'coincidences' (Nisbett & Wilson, 1977). I think that introspection is a good way of acquiring insight into this issue. But probably some people do not like to engage seriously in introspection because it is an interruption of ordinary life and of our natural focus on the world. Furthermore there are people who do not wish to recognize data that are in conflict with their conception of themselves as rational people with high moral standards.

So there are problems, but they can be overcome to some degree. Introspective reports are more reliable when verbalization is as much as possible synchronous with the activity (Ericsson & Simon, 1980). There is no better justification for rejecting introspection than for accepting its infallibility. In what follows I discuss primarily general, theoretical issues.

The first problem is that some mental processes, such as thought about a complicated matter, require so much attention that a person is hardly or not at all able to study the mental process while it is going on. If one tried to follow the process of thought while thinking about the solution of a problem, one would be distracted from the solution of the problem. So in such a case introspection will have to take place after the fact.

Ryle doubts that it is possible at all to study a mental process introspectively while it is going on. Even if such introspection were possible, he claims, some mental processes would still not be intro-spectible, since there is a limit to the number of mental processes that can take place at the same time. Consequently certain acts of introspection, namely the last ones, are not introspectible, for instance the act of introspection of the act of introspection of the act of introspection of the process of solving a problem (1949, p. 158). This claim is correct but it does not matter, because each act of introspection can be subjected to introspection after the fact.

A second problem is that introspection, when applied to a mental process while it is going on, sometimes influences that process. Introspection requires peace of mind and is for this reason not easily applied to a fit of anxiety or of anger, as Hume pointed out. If we tried to examine such an emotion while having it, its character would change. This is not always true. A simple identification of fairly simple mental data, such as ordinary moods, also has an introspective element, but does not modify, or hardly modifies, the state identified. On the other hand, suppose a person studies what images and thoughts occur to him when he is depressed. Then his effort will probably neutralize his mood somewhat, since it requires interest, which is something that is absent in depression.

In such cases it is preferable that introspection take place afterwards, as soon as possible after the mental process in question. Thus there are several indications that introspection often has to be retrospection, that is, thought about a past mental experience. Ryle argues for this conclusion and suggests that this kind of retrospection is not introspective and is not aimed at something that is hidden from others (ibid., p. 160). This suggestion is incorrect, however (Price, 1969b, p. 81). I can catch myself scratching as much as I can catch myself daydreaming, as Ryle observes. Others can catch me in the first of these activities, but they cannot detect my day-dreaming as I can; they can do no more than suspect it.

The preceding observations do not imply that retrospective introspection should replace simultaneous introspection completely. For the latter is more reliable than the former. Sometimes simultaneous introspection is quite feasible, for instance when we execute a task that is not particularly difficult. Moreover, 'retrospection' does not mean that a person reports only after a mental process is completely over. While the process is going on he can continually be describing what went through his mind the previous moment. That would be a case of retrospection with respect to the stages of the process. Such introspection may well be reliable.

We may wonder whether retrospection requires that at the moment of the occurrence of a mental event its subject is reflexively conscious of it. Probably not. Why would it be impossible to remember something of which one was not reflexively conscious at the moment of occurrence? The study of certain special kinds of cases suggests that this is quite possible. A person who is anesthetized can hear something without being reflexively conscious of it and without knowing it, but remember it afterwards (Oakley-Eames, 1985, pp. 223-224). In any case there is no serious problem here because most mental events are accompanied by reflexive consciousness—which is a preliminary stage for introspection. Simultaneous introspection is often difficult, since it requires full attention. But this difficulty does not arise to the same degree for spontaneous reflection.

The objection has been raised that introspection yields inconsistent data. That feature is not unique to introspection, however. It results from defects which plague others forms of research as well. In the first place, a researcher may criticize previous studies on the ground that they used different methods and that their subjects were influenced unintentionally (Valentine, 1978, p. 7). Secondly, mental processes may differ from one individual to another. One person may have many and very vivid mental images, another only few, which are quite dim. It would of course be incorrect to conclude that a particular mental phenomenon does not occur, or occurs only rarely, on the basis of the observation of oneself and a few other people. But unjustified generalization is not exclusive to claims based on introspection. In the third place, in the case of perception of events in the external world too there are differences among our interpretations and perceptions of the events. Consequently the occurrence of such differences in introspection does not count against it. Ryle wonders why certain theoretical questions about the activity of consciousness cannot be answered immediately if introspection is possible, for instance the question whether there are acts of the will (1949, p. 159). But it should not be surprising that data uncovered by introspection are susceptible to various theoretical interpretations and classifications. Such is the case for data about the rest of reality, especially concerning human beings.

In the course of the history of psychology various other objections have been raised against introspection. A common methodological objection is that the researcher cannot control data provided by a subject on the basis of introspection. This is not entirely true, since sometimes a certain amount of indirect control is possible as is shown in Nisbett and Wilson (1977). Nevertheless it is true that direct verification is impossible. But this situation is not all that unusual.

The situation can be compared to a trial in which the court has to rely on witnesses, who are, of course, not always completely reliable. There is a difference in that a psychologist is not limited to a certain number of witnesses and can, if necessary, use tests to choose ones who are in any case reliable witnesses about the external world. He can exclude witnesses on various grounds, such as indifference, a tendency to say what is expected, too much imagination or poor verbal skills. The Würzburger school (Külpe, Ach, Bühler et. al.) introduced introspection and used

68

educated subjects for its experiments to prevent certain methodological problems. A different method for avoiding possible unreliability is to demand that something be reported by a certain number of people before accepting it as significant.

There are plenty of problems, but they do not differ fundamentally from those of other scientific methods that depend on inference, and there are various ways to overcome them to some extent (Valentine, 1978, p. 19). If introspection were dropped as a method of research one would have to forego a lot of data about, for instance, the nature of thought and volition. For this reason introspection is used even today despite behavioristic objections. One of the most interesting studies is still *Thought and Choice in Chess* by A.D. de Groot, which contains a useful discussion about the method of introspection.

Is Introspection an Illusion?

According to the functionalist Dennett introspection is not a source of knowledge about our own mental states (1981, ch. 9). He thinks that we only have access to the *results* of our mental processes, thoughts 'that p,' and not to the processes themselves. In introspection, he says, we notice that we want to *say* all kinds of things about what is going on in us. This observation leads to theories about how we can do this. One of these theories is the common view that we perceive these events in us, and that this perception is the basis and explanation for our semantic intentions. Dennett proposes an alternative theory, according to which the mental images about which we want to say something are creatures of inference or extrapolation from what we want to say. When we make a stereometric figure revolve in our mind, we are not conscious of the revolving mental image, according to Dennett. Instead we are supposed to be conscious of propositional episodes, that is, various statements such as 'now it looks like this' or 'now it looks like that.' The movement that we think we perceive is merely an illusion, and the different positions of the image are mere extrapolations of what we want to say. Since we apparently want to say something we introduce as an explanation the idea that we perceive a mental image, or so Dennett claims (ibid., pp. 165-168). So introspective statements are not supposed to be statements about our own mental states and cannot teach us anything about them.

He uses a well-known example, from external reality, of illusory motion—film is another one. But such an example does not show anything about introspection. There is no reason to think that 'seeing' a mental image move when we rotate it is an illusion. Inconsistently with his own view, he appeals to introspection, claiming that close examination of our own experience shows that the image which is supposed to move in fact does not. Rather its position changes step by step. This is not true for me in any case. When I make a mental image of a car move, I do not see the position of the car change step by step. At any rate, this point is of secondary importance, because even if the impression of movement were an illusion, that would not show that the mental image is an illusion.

The following reasons show that Dennett's idea is a reversal of the real situation. Extrapolation of introspective contents from what we want to say requires that we have ready the sentence that we want to utter. Nothing can be deduced from the fact that we want to say something, if we don't know what we want to say. But often we have no sentence ready. Sometimes we don't find words to express what we see with our mental eye. At other times we try to verbalize with difficulty afterwards. And we may succeed only in part, as also happens sometimes when we see something in the external world. Moreover our description is never complete. If I say, for instance, 'I imagine a red palace with an eighteenth century park,' my mental image contains more and is more precise than this description. My report is compatible with a variety of images, whereas I only have, sometimes at any rate, one, definite, concrete image. This is the case even if my description is elaborate, because it is given in general terms. I could not deduce precisely from my report what I imagine, any more than another person could. This shows that we have the mental image first and that corresponding statements are reports about them and not the other way around.

Furthermore on Dennett's view animals and people without language, such as children and deaf-mutes who have not yet learned sign-language, could not introspect and would not have consciousness at all (ibid., p. 152). It has been suggested that this consequence can be avoided by assuming that such people store the information of their consciousness for later use in their future speech-center, although they don't yet have language (Lyons, 1986, p. 85). But this option is not available if, as Dennett claims, this information becomes available and even comes into being only as a consequence of language. For Dennett it is not information but an illusion. Deaf-mutes who have not yet learned a language thus have no 'inner' life, according to Dennett. This is highly improbable. There is no reason to think that children who cannot speak do not dream. Nor that deaf-mutes who describe what they felt, dreamt and thought before they learned sign-language, did not have any of these mental states. This consequence amounts to a reductio ad absurdum of Dennett's view.

Perception of the World and Introspection

Is there really any difference between perception of the world and introspection? I have assumed that there is because it follows from what I have said before about privileged access. But Ryle is not the only one who has tried to undermine the difference between the two or to argue that it is not significant. Other attempts in this direction can be found in psychology.

The main line of argument is then that both the observation of behavior and introspection are directed at the same thing, namely a person's actions. Mental processes like listening, looking at and thinking in silence are also actions. An observer can notice various things about them, although the subject performing them is usually most knowledgeable about them. Psychology is concerned with the activity of the human being as a whole. Introspection and observation of behavior complement each other by each providing information about different aspects of the total activity. This is the reason why the activity of a human being should not be characterized as 'external' or 'internal'. 'Internal' and 'external' only apply to the point of view of the observer, not to the activity itself. Therefore it is better to use the terms 'self-perception' and 'perception by others'.

It is a virtue of this position that it regards observation of behavior and introspection as complementing each other in providing data about the human being as a whole. Nevertheless I do not find this argumentation convincing.

One problem for this view is the fact that we have thoughts and feelings that suddenly occur to us and which cannot be called actions. Such mental phenomena are necessary for action because they are part of a situation in which action takes place and which exercises influence on us, but there are people who do little or nothing in such situations. Nor does the fact that something is part of a situation of action mean that it is an action itself. Furthermore a thought that occurs to us or a feeling that comes over us does not have to lead to action and cannot be observed by others.

The crucial question is whether the only difference between the thought 'I am wallpapering the room' and wallpapering the room consists in the difference between knowledge of the thought and knowledge of the activity of wallpapering. According to some psychologists both are actions. But even if we grant this on the ground that organized thought has an element of action, they are still different kinds of action. Wallpapering requires a lot of movements, the thought of wallpapering requires none. (This is why some people prefer the latter.) This difference can be indicated by calling them 'external' and 'internal' actions respectively. There are good reasons for making this distinction —I have discussed them earlier—and I see no reason why they should be disregarded.

Another point can serve as an introduction to a different problem that I want to discuss. Sometimes the mental is reintroduced as something separate because it is admitted that the perceptions of an external observer differ qualitatively from the experiences of the agent himself. But then it is argued that the nature of the subject's experience cannot be conveyed by means of introspective reports; it is ineffable, because it is impossible to describe something that is completely subjective, for which there is no concept in the language.

This last claim is correct, but it does not prove the point. For the qualities of subjective experience need not be unique, and there are often general concepts for them. Numerous examples could be used to refute the point, but I hope that one will suffice. Suppose on a sunny spring morning someone enters a garden where the flowers are out and says 'this bleak world seems to consist in stage sets illuminated by artificial light'. This person describes the subjective qualities of his experience by means of a general concept, 'bleak', and a comparison which also uses general concepts. If someone hears this statement he may be unable to share the feelings expressed by it, but he can understand it and it gives him information about the speaker's state of mind. Poets and novelists expend a lot of effort expressing the subjective qualities of our experience. Others do it as well, although usually with less originality.

The most important proponent in philosophy of the view that the mental is ineffable because private is Wittgenstein. I will discuss his arguments extensively in chapter 5.

How do introspective terms acquire their meaning? An illuminating discussion about this question can be found in Findlay (1969, pp. 346-349). To describe our mental states we use expressions which would be suitable to describe the world even if at the time they do not apply to anything in the world. Consider the following examples. It is as if I see someone in front of me, even though he is not there, that is, I have a vivid mental image of him. It seems to me as if everything around me is dead, although that is not true, that is, everything makes a dead impression on me. We can also characterize our experiences by means of implicit references to observable behavior that we could but do not currently display. For instance, someone claims to be very fond of something, that is, he makes a great effort to get it, but not at the moment. Or he would do much to get it—for instance, go to all the stores—if there were no important obstacle. Someone says that he is irritated by something, that is, if he could he would sweep it off the table, but since he can't, he is irritated. His state of mind is of the kind we are in when there is a bothersome fly that we strike at, but there is no fly for him to chase away.

Terms for the mental have come to be in this way, and we can create new ones by using such analogies with public situations. Then the analogy can be replaced by a phrase which no longer contains references to the world and to behavior.

Note

1. Similarly the meaning of color terms like 'infrared' and 'ultraviolet' escapes us. But since there are no human beings who can see such colors, although other organisms can, it seems more appropriate to say that for human beings these terms are not color names, and to define them in terms of radiation.

4. INTROSPECTION AND THE UNCONSCIOUS

The reader may wonder what the connection is between the philosophy of mind and the un- or preconcious. What does not belong to consciousness would seem by definition to fall outside the scope of the philosophy of mind. But the matter is not so simple, as is clear from statements like 'unconsciously I sensed that..., but I did not think of it at the moment.' When we sense something unconsciously, that state is part of consciousness, even if it is not a form of conscious *thought*. In the statement at issue the word 'unconsciously' is used with the meaning of the psychoanalytical term 'preconscious,' which has not entered the vernacular.

The question is whether what is called unconscious is unconscious in every respect, and thus inaccessible to introspection. The un- and preconscious are part of the mental only if they are accessible to introspection. I will first consider the unconscious.

The notion of the 'unconscious' was already common during the 19th century, even before Freud made it the cornerstone of psychoanalysis. It played an important role, for instance, in Schopenhauer's philosophy. But since the current meaning of the word is most strongly influenced by Freud's use of it, I will first explain roughly what it means for him.

In Freud's mature theory the core of the unconscious is something that has not yet been conscious. It is discovered by interpretation (Freud, 1900, ch. VII, F). The Oedipus complex is one of the best-known examples. According to J.O. Wisdom, Freud thinks a traumatic event that is not remembered at first, but is remembered later, belongs to the preconscious, although its influence is unconscious (1972, p. 190). This interpretation may go too far, but it is true that Freud does not regard such events as part of the core of the unconscious (cf. 1915, pp. 33-34, 154). In any case we are completely unconscious of, and ignorant of, our own unconscious. In his essay 'Das Unbewusste' ('The Unconscious') Freud says that we are related to our own unconscious states as we are to the mental states of another person. We know them only on the basis of observed behavior. A representation can be repressed in such a way that its subject is unable to notice it, even if he is told that he has it (1915, pp. 128, 134).[1]

A person does not have access to his own unconscious, because it is kept unconscious by repression. Only analysis by another person can give him access to his own unconscious. The repression takes place unconsciously and is not observable. It is unconscious at least in the sense that we don't notice it. It is not perfectly clear that repression is unconscious in every respect according to Freud, but the prevalent view is that he supposes both the unconscious and repression to be unobservable (MacIntyre, 1967, p. 70). Nevertheless something that is repressed can become conscious. A psychiatrist is needed to bring this about, but an analysis cannot be regarded as correct until the patient agrees with it. A representation can be completely unconscious (Freud, 1915, p. 137) so that the patient denies, perfectly sincerely, that he has it. Alternatively, he may after a time come to remember that he had it. The unconscious is completely inaccessible, that is unconscious in every respect, but after long treatment it can be made accessible by another person.

Why think there is an unconscious?

Freud thought the postulation of the unconscious was necessary because of gaps in the data of consciousness. Certain mental events cannot be explained just on the basis of what is conscious. In order to explain them it is necessary to assume that there are mental processes of which we have no knowledge, and which therefore must take place unconsciously (1915, pp. 125-126). In *The Unconscious* MacIntyre has objected that explanation of our mental lives does not require the notion of the unconscious. Freud's hypotheses about childhood events as causes of neurotic behavior can be formulated without reference to the unconscious. Its postulation as an inaccessible realm of inaccessible events, MacIntyre claims, does not contribute to the explanation of neuroses (cf. Flew, 1978, pp. 157-158).

But the unconscious is not so easily omitted from the Freudian system. Where human behavior is concerned, the question sometimes arises how it is *possible* that A causes B, because it is not at all clear how A results in B. An important function of the unconscious is to make it intelligible that cause A (an event in a person's childhood) leads to effect B (neurotic behavior by the adult).

Secondly, sometimes the same event A leads to different behavior in different people. This is explained by assuming that these people have digested A via different unconscious processes. According to psychoanalysis the causal efficacy of events depends to a high degree on postulated unconscious processes which are really supposed to take place.

In modern terms, the unconscious is a theoretical entity that is posited because of its explanatory value, and which is conceived of realistically.

The postulated processes are really supposed to take place. On the other hand, the unconscious can be made conscious, at least in part. At that point it is no longer a theoretical entity. I do not want to go into the question how these two aspects of the unconscious are related for Freud and whether they are compatible (Cf. Dilman, 1984, pp. 46-48). I will take both aspects into account. I hope this preliminary discussion of the notion of the unconscious will suffice as an introduction to a more systematic treatment.

CRITICAL DISCUSSION

An important objection to the notion of an unconscious is that it is inaccessible to the subject himself. As a result when we postulate an unconscious link between cause A and effect B, we can hypothesize various connections without being able to determine which is the real one. Insofar as the unconscious is a theoretical, postulated, entity there are no conscious data that could confirm our hypotheses. Consequently the question as to what the real connection is remains a matter of speculation. A Freudian example of forgetting as a result of repression can be used to show how different chains of connections can be construed, all of which seem equally plausible. The conclusion is that Freud's approach does not amount to reconstruction; his explanations are constructions that may or may not accurately reveal the real processes.

The practice of psychoanalytical theory illustrates this problem. After Freud, explanations in depth-psychology vary with different general theories or 'systems' (Adler, Jung, Horney etc.). It is impossible to determine which is the right view. The question arises to what extent these various views bear on a particular case that is to be explained. Assuming that only one kind of explanation is right, the other kinds are not more than constructions of the interpreter that do not apply to the case. But this question cannot be answered, since the subject does not have access to his unconscious. So the connection that is supposed to provide an explanation is in principle secret. This is unsatisfactory. If the unconscious is in principle inaccessible, a realistic interpretation of this theoretical entity can never be concretely filled out. Given this problem it is better to abandon a realistic conception of the unconscious. For the conviction that something unobservable really exists is mere faith. Once a realistic interpretation is dropped, the different psychoanalytic systems are no more than constructions of the psychologist that serve to make behavior intelligible, but which have no claim to being genuine explanations.

Another question is whether the notion of the unconscious is coherent. So far I have assumed that the unconscious is inaccessible. The view that the intervention of a psychiatrist can make it conscious raises a different problem.

We saw that the core of the unconscious has always been unconscious. The problem is then whether a patient can be certain that he really remembers having some unconscious representation, and that he is living through it again. It is impossible to remember a mental state which was entirely unconscious when it occurred. How can a patient know that the analysis of a supposedly unconscious state is correct if he cannot compare the result of this analysis to this unconscious state? Supposedly this state becomes conscious. But if this unconscious state is not an experience which can be noticed, then it is nothing, and the conscious state that comes to be is an entirely new state and not a conscious version of an unconscious one.

At first there was an unconscious representation, which means there was no representation, for in an unconscious representation a subject does not represent anything to himself. Afterwards, encouraged by another person, the subject thinks that he did have some unconscious representation. But for the subject too this can be no more than a supposition, since he cannot recognize what he did not have before. He cannot get a hold on the past, no matter how well his memory is refreshed. If something that was once unconscious becomes conscious, then it is impossible to be sure that it really did exist as something unconscious. So in this case the theoretical interpretation can no more be confirmed than in the case in which it is impossible for the unconscious to become conscious. There is just consciousness of something new where there used to be nothing mental to be observed, and no comparison is possible with former mental states. Consequently it is incomprehensible that there should be a feeling of recognition as in recollection. The Freudian notion of a mental process that is entirely unconscious is contradictory.

If a patient cannot notice a repressed representation, even if he is confronted with the claim that he has it, then it is not present, not even unconsciously. If it were present its subject could notice it, although he might not, as a result of internal resistance. An unconscious mental representation of which the subject cannot be conscious is as unthinkable as a round square.

Given the fact that the assumption of this kind of unconscious leads to very different constructions it is not surprising that scientists and philosophers of science have either rejected the unconscious or accepted it only as a model (cf. James, 1890, I, pp. 164ff.).

In addition it is doubtful that repression can be unconscious. Another important objection to the Freudian unconscious was raised by Sartre (1943, p. 91). The unconcious cannot be literally unconscious, so this objection goes, because the repression of feelings and representations requires some thought that they should not be acknowledged and thus some consciousness of their nature. In order to interrupt a budding sexual or agressive phantasy the subject must at least have some vague awareness of the nature of the phantasy and of the fact that he does not want it to be continued.

Repression seems to require consciousness of what a person does not wish to know. This consciousness may remain vague and dim, however, and it may consist in a presentiment. Sartre claims that the subject must have exact knowledge of the truth in order to hide it from himself (ibid., p. 87), but that is too strong. If the subject has precise knowledge, it is too late for a cover-up. Also exact knowledge is not necessary. A suspicion of what could reveal itself to be an unpleasant truth is enough. (This means that a person may repress something unnecessarily or repress more than is necessary, because a suspicion can be misleading.)

THE UNCONSCIOUS AS PART OF CONSCIOUSNESS

Given these inescapable problems with the notion of the unconscious we may wonder whether it is possible to understand the term 'unconscious' differently, not literally, and to give it an empirical basis. 'Unconsious' does not have to mean 'unconscious in every respect' (Wenzl, 1933, p. 76). The notion of the preconscious provides a starting-point for an alternative interpretation.

A preconscious state is a mental state of which the subject is not conscious, but of which he can become conscious by introspection. Freud includes the preconscious in consciousness because it can become conscious and has the same properties as consciousness. But as long as it remains preconscious it is unconscious in the descriptive sense (1915, pp. 131-132). Consequently it occupies an intermediate position.

Various kinds of mental contents may count as preconscious. To begin with the least interesting, there are many things that we can remember without any trouble, but which are not always present to our minds. Knowledge of a foreign language, and knowledge of historical facts are like this. When a person who knows French is in no way occupied with this language, it is not at all in his consciousness. For this time his knowledge of French is preconscious, since he can easily activate it. When we say he knows French, we ascribe a disposition to him. That is, we claim that on some occasion in the future he will understand French expressions or use them himself. It would be incorrect to say that this kind of preconscious is part of consciousness. While it is preconscious, it is not conscious. There is only a disposition to consciousness in the future. On the other hand, in ordinary life we would not describe such knowledge as unconscious.

In ordinary language the term 'unconscious' is used for something else, something that is not yet articulated, and that is preconscious in the Freudian system. We say for instance, 'I already sensed unconsciously that..., but at the time I did not think of it, I was not conscious of it.' As I pointed out before: when we sense something unconsciously, that feeling is part of consciousness, even if it is not part of conscious thought. It is a real content of consciousness, which the subject does not notice. A person may also say that an unconscious recollection played a role when he took a decision. Afterwards he remembers that he had the feeling or the recollection. If he does not remember afterwards he can at most suppose it was there and say: 'the feeling must have played a part unconsciously, but I don't know anything about it.' In such cases we mean by 'unconscious' that we were not reflexively conscious of the feeling or recollection. Sometimes a person is unaware of states he would be perfectly happy to acknowledge. A person may deny with perfect sincerity that he ever had a certain phantasy in his day-dreams and then remember it on further reflection. Or he may not remember it, but when he has the phantasy again it may suddenly strike him because he has been asked about it. *A fortiori* it is not surprising that a person is not reflexively conscious of things that he prefers not to remember, because for instance they do not agree with the image of himself that he wishes to have.

This kind of unconscious state is both experienced and part of consciousness. It is real and observable. We may wonder whether the unconscious, insofar as it is real, might be of this nature. Perhaps this conception of the unconscious can play the role of the Freudian unconscious at least in part. Several prominent depth-psychologists after Freud have proposed this kind of view. For instance, Stekel substituted for the idea of repression the theory that people turn a blind eye to certain things which they could bring to the surface but do not wish to see. Horney and Sullivan describe as unconscious inclinations that we notice vaguely without fully realizing their influence, and inclinations that we ignore as a result of selective inattention (Brown, 1976, pp. 42, 187).

Repression

It is contradictory to call something mental that is unconscious in such a way that the subject cannot notice it. It is not contradictory, however, to say that a person does not notice his dislike for someone, and consequently is not reflexively conscious of it. The person's repression of his feeling is a refusal even to realize that he has it, let alone think about it. When an agressive phantasy begins he will quickly think of something else. When he hears of a misfortune that befell the object of his dislike he may ascribe his feeling of satisfaction to the nice weather.

This sort of repression fits Fingarette's position that becoming explicitly and intellectually conscious of something is not an automatic process, but an activity (1969, pp. 39ff.). He calls this activity 'spelling out.' A person can abstain from this activity out of indifference or laziness or, of course, disinclination. Fingarette claims that it is noteworthy that certain things are made clearly conscious rather than that many things remain in the twilight of the so-called unconscious.

When a mental phenomenon imposes itself undeniably, a person can refuse to put it into words. What is not put into words is not acknowledged and can easily be forgotten. Someone may also try to stop the mental phenomenon by seeking distraction, for instance, by doing something that requires other thoughts. But when it becomes impossible to avoid something, a person can process it incorrectly. Thus he can fashion an interpretation that is favorable to himself, drawing on those mental states and actions of his that he cannot deny and on a selection of what best fits his own purposes. Such strategies are not only used when self-knowledge is at issue.

Repression depends on an unwillingness to face something, and thus partly on dishonesty. But if someone denies his unconscious dislike to a depth-psychologist, he is not necessarily dishonest in doing so. At the moment of his denial he may not have the feeling in question, and past feelings that were ignored can easily be forgotten. But once his feeling has been pointed out to him, he will hardly be able to deny it when it presents itself occasionally. If he continues to deny it he will be insincere. For a feeling that exists can be recognized, though perhaps only with difficulty, if it is weak or vague. It is noticed as soon as attention is made available for it.

Repression and what is repressed are phenomena of consciousness that are not, but can become, reflexively conscious. Consequently it makes sense to take the acknowledgment of the person analyzed as a criterion for the correctness of the analysis. In principle the patient can see that he has a certain feeling or remember having this feeling. There is still a question as to whether a person can reliably remember previous feelings on which he has never reflected. If Freud was right in claiming that patients can imagine that their phantasies are recollections (Ellenberger, 1970, p. 446), then how could they remember unarticulated past experiences correctly? But this problem does not arise for current mental states. An unconscious dislike can be recognized, and when a patient is sincere his confirmation or denial is decisive.

CONSCIOUSNESS AND SELF-AWARENESS

So far I have not taken into account the special phenomenon of hypnosis. The question arises whether hypnosis shows the existence of an unconscious. In hypnosis a person executes a previously given command without knowing why he does so. Another striking effect is that some subjects of hypnosis are less sensitive to certain pain-stimuli (Hilgard, 1986, ch. 8). Also it is possible to hypnotize oneself to a certain extent.

A difference with Freudian unconsciousness is, however, that no repression in the psychoanalytic sense is operative. For upon complete removal of the hypnosis the subject can remember the command he forgot and the pain he did not feel. Hypnosis has been described as 'dissociation'. Certain data of consciousness have become detached from the person. According to Hilgard loss of memory plays an important part in this process. A curious complication arises from the fact that a significant number of subjects seemed to have a 'hidden observer', who strongly resembled the normal, non-hypnotized person (pp. 209, 233). This means that during hypnosis another part of the person did know what was forgotten and experienced the pain which seemed not to be experienced: so these data were not erased but covered up. This fact is connected to cases of divided consciousness in ordinary life, when something does not reach our reflexive consciousness, but later appears to have been experienced nevertheless (p. 207).

What is the best explanation for this curious phenomenon? Assuming that there is dissociation, the question is what is dissociated from what? I want to say: between the states of consciousness that are not acknowledged and reflexive consciousness, that is, self-awareness. Those who feel less pain or no pain at all achieve this by directing their attention to something else (Hilgard, ibid., pp. 172ff.). This is reminiscent of the fact that we are sometimes not conscious of things to which we pay no attention. In hypnosis this state is induced intentionally and is maintained for a length of time. The 'hidden observer' is apparently dissociated from the hypnotized subject. The existence of the hidden observer indicates, however, that the dissociation of the states of consciousness from the person is not complete. For a part of the person does observe these states. The person and the hidden observer in him are also not always completely dissociated from each other: in some people the observer is not hidden, but constantly present in the background. On the other hand, he is entirely absent for others, because for them the hypnosis has succeeded completely in keeping out reality, as with the pain (ibid., p. 208).

I have said before that when a person wants to have access to his consciousness, and devotes all his attention to it, he will succeed. In the case of hypnosis, however, such access is barred. On the other hand, it must be kept in mind that hypnosis requires a cooperative attitude on the part of the subject (Hilgard, ibid., pp. 224, 230). The subject gives up his initiative and the exercise of his will (pp. 164-165, 229), including access to his consciousness if the hypnotist so desires. Following the suggestion of the hypnotist he turns his attention away from some of his states of consciousness. The hypnotist's statements are accepted without question (p. 231). So this phenomenon is not in conflict with my view, since the subject of hypnosis does not desire access to his consciousness. Still more striking phenomena occur in hysteria, especially in cases of so-called conversion-hysteria. In ordinary language the term 'hysteria' implies overdramatization. I am using it in its technical sense, however. In this sense a hysteric is someone who displays physical symptoms, for instance paralysis, that have a psychological cause, such as fear. Before Freud the French psychiatrist Piere Janet used hypnosis to bring back to consciousness what he regarded as separated complexes of traumatic ideas which a patient was unable to remember (Ellenberger, ibid., pp. 364ff.). The nature of these recollections was such that they probably evoked a lot of internal resistance. After hypnosis the patient sometimes forgot them again.

One might say that the patient's consciousness would be accessible to him if he wanted, but that he cannot want it; he wants the opposite. It is significant that for a long time the sincerity of hysterics was doubted. Finally it was concluded that they do not merely pretend. But that leaves open the possibility that they deceive themselves. There is no doubt that a subject of hypnosis or a hysterical person who claims that he cannot move his arm suffers from self-deception. For the inability is self-induced (Hilgard, ibid., pp. 118-119), but the subject is not reflexively conscious of this fact. Hypnosis indicates that a temporary barrier can be created between states of consciousness and self-awareness, but cases of hysteria show that the barrier can become longlasting. It comes about as a result of a kind of self-hypnosis (J. Breuer, according to Hilgard, p. 81;

Oakley-Eames, 1985, p. 243), that is, a split in a person's consciousness brought about by the person himself. This split can then be abolished by hypnosis induced by another person.

The idea that such 'forgotten' events were at one point conscious constitutes an essential difference between the present notion of the unconscious and Freud's. Janet called such events subconscious. In English the term 'coconscious' has sometimes been used, because these events turned out to be conscious for a certain separated part of the person. I would like to say that they belong to a separate part of consciousness but not to reflexive consciousness. There is no need to posit an unconscious.[2]

Conclusion

We can conclude that what is called the unconscious consists at least to some extent in experience, and that it is a part of consciousness. In special cases this part is split off. If this conception of the unconscious is rejected in favor of the view that unconscious processes are completely unconscious, then the unconscious must be regarded as a theoretical entity. As we have seen, the latter approach has serious disadvantages. The postulation of processes that are in every respect unconscious and which cannot be observed introspectively leads to widely varying results. Consequently the postulation of such processes resembles not so much a product of science as a creation of the unbridled imagination of a novelist.

It is impossible to determine whether in the Freudian system all unconcious processes consist of this kind of experience, and it is not necessary. It is enough that sometimes a person can conclude that he once had certain mental states of which he had no knowledge because he did not want to have this knowledge. This kind of realization truly is a case of becoming conscious of what up to that point had been—reflexively—unconscious.

Even if this kind of unconscious is taken into consideration, it is possible that some mental processes continue to display the kind of gaps which brought Freud to his notion of the unconsious. But I doubt that such gaps will make the assumption of a Freudian unconscious necessary.

Non-Freudians have taken recourse to the unconscious to explain that sometimes the solution to a problem on which we have worked unsuccessfully, occurs to us later while we are not thinking about it.[3] Supposedly the solution is worked out in the unconscious. But the impression that the right solution—and nothing else—occurs to us suddenly is usually inaccurate. Most often various solutions occur to us over time. Upon further examination all but one turn out to be incorrect. This indicates that we do not unconsciously carry out reasoning which leads to the solution. Nothing is worked out unconsciously. When the problem returns to the mind, it causes a new *possibility* to occur to us, which we had not yet explored, as happened before when we were working on the problem. Now we have the advantage of having rejected a number of blind alleys. But most people forget that several spurious solutions have occurred to them. They are so struck that one of them turned out to be the right one that they only remember it. A mathematician or physicist who hits upon a correct formula during a walk or even a dream remembers it as something special, but forgets the many spurious scientific phantasies produced by his dreams. (Similarly people remember the odd time when their presentiments prove to be correct and forget that unless based on clues such presentiments are mostly deceptive.)

Secondly, J.S. Mill (1865, p. 279) and W. James (1890, I, p. 166) already pointed out that the incorrect impression that links are missing can arise because we forget flashes of thought that preceded the solution of the problem. This is not a mere supposition on their part. For we can often retrieve these thoughts if we try. Consequently it is reasonable to assume that it also happens when we don't think about it.

In the case of thought processes and actions that have become habitual it is normal that steps of thought are skipped. In such cases various stages are connected not by an unconscious link but by association acquired through habit (Brentano, 1874, Bnd I, p. 154).

Furthermore the question whether there is a gap is determined by standards for rational thought. But mental processes are not always rational, and people differ on the question as to what constitutes sound reasoning.

Finally, consciousness is usually more or less discontinuous, and not only when there is repression. This is true for consciousness in general, which is interrupted, for instance, by dreamless sleep, but also for particular thought-processes. This discontinuity does not have to lead to the conclusion that unconscious processes take place during those apparent interruptions. Suppose a recollection comes back, which up to that moment belonged to the first kind of preconscious I have discussed, the kind that consists only in a disposition for the future. We do not have to assume that until then it existed as a mental state but as an unconscious one. It is a sufficient explanation for its return that a certain connected brain-process has become active again.

There are various degrees and layers of consciousness. Some of these we call unconscious. Sometimes the reason is that we have noticed a process but have not processed it in our thought, or have processed it incorrectly. At other times we have not noticed a process at all. Introspective reflection can uncover such mental items in principle, even if people who suffer from certain syndromes lack the necessary force of will.

Notes

1. This is generally regarded as Freud's view but sometimes he seems to have a different conception of the unconscious which does not so clearly exclude the view I will defend (1915, p. 160).
2. Cases of multiple personality can be dealt with in the same way insofar as the issue of the unconscious is concerned.
3. Chomsky thinks that the rules that determine the form and meaning of sentences are largely unconscious and cannot become conscious. Our knowledge of the language that we speak gives us no privileged access to these rules and we cannot determine them by reflection or introspection. This is supposed to apply in particular to the rules of the universal grammar that underlies all languages (1980, pp. 231, 237, 244). He thinks that we must postulate a universal grammar and innate knowledge of linguistic rules in order to explain how a child can acquire any language that is spoken in his environment. We are not conscious of such a grammar and knowledge. But it is doubtful they exist. The fact that a child can pick up the rules of various languages does not require these kinds of innate faculties. It can be explained by an innate capacity to grasp different kinds of rules instead of innate knowledge of a repertoire. Further, usually we have no reflexive consciousness of the rules of the language that we speak, but they are described by grammarians. This shows that we have access to these rules. They can be made fully conscious.

5. TALKING ABOUT THE MENTAL: WITTGENSTEIN AND MENTALISM

According to the mentalist we learn the meaning and reference of our mental terms from our own inner, mental experience. In learning a language we learn to connect the terms for the mental with that experience. This way of learning the meaning of words is called private ostensive definition. This is not a very appropriate term, for two reasons. In the first place definitions ordinarily rely on verbal explanation, and not on pointing or referring to something. Secondly, insofar as we learn the meaning of a term by hearing other people use it, this requires the observation of more than one utterance. Only in the case of proper names is one observation enough. For instance, the name for a color is learned on the basis of a number of observations. For a color term stands for a number of different shades of color. The basis for this process of learning is our own experience. A person who is color-blind cannot know what the names for colors mean, even if he is often able to apply them correctly. The same holds for other mental experiences. If someone only knows the behavior that often accompanies pain, he does not know what 'pain' means. We learn the meaning of 'pain' on the basis of experiences which are more or less private, that is, which are not generally accessible to others.

This view is contested by Wittgensteinians. They think that there are decisive arguments against what they call a private language. This is a language whose expressions refer to the speaker's immediately experienced private sensations, which are accessible only to him. Another person cannot understand such a language, according to Wittgenstein (1953, § 243). On my mentalistic view the language for the mental, which includes expressions for private sensations, is not private; others can also know these experiences and understand this language.

But Malcolm (1975) and others think that Wittgenstein's arguments are relevant to the existing language for the mental, in particular for sensations. They believe that on the mentalistic view the language for the mental must be private. Since in fact the language for the mental is not private it follows that mentalism would be untenable (cf. Locke, 1971, p. 82).

This interpretation of Wittgenstein's view finds support in a number of passages in the *Philosophical Investigations*. I will discuss the most important ones. According to mentalism the meanings of terms for the mental are derived from private experience. Wittgenstein thinks if this were right, we could not know what others meant when they used these terms. Consequently the language of the mental would be private, and could not describe or refer to the mental. Wittgenstein wants to get rid of the idea that mental states are private objects that we can talk about (ibid., §§ 290-294, p. 207).

On the other hand he thinks that in *some* contexts an utterance like 'I am scared' can be regarded as a description of a person's mental state (pp. 187-189). Consequently his arguments against mentalism should only bear on the non-descriptive utterances. This restriction is not apparent in his arguments, however. In any case they are directed against the mentalistic view that utterances like 'I am scared' are normally descriptions of mental, inner states.

So there is reason to consider the force of these arguments against mentalism. For an account of Wittgenstein's views, I am indebted to interpretations by other philosophers, in particular Malcolm, Pitcher (1964), Kenny (1976) and Fogelin (1980).

TERMS FOR THE MENTAL

Suppose on some occasion I have a sensation which I call 'S' and later I again call a sensation 'S'. How do I know what I mean by 'S'? According to Wittgenstein I cannot know this in a private language. This notion includes for him speaking about private objects such as our sensations. Suppose that an ostensive definition of the form 'this is S' has been given, and that a speaker of a private language says about a later sensation "This too is a S". Then we can ask him what he means by 'S'. He can give three answers, none of which Wittgenstein regards as satisfactory (Kenny, ibid., p. 193). I will argue that the second and third of these answers are adequate, and that both are necessary for an account of our ability to speak about private objects such as our sensations.

1. Meaning 'this'

The first answer is indeed unacceptable. If the speaker replies "By 'S' I mean this" referring to his own present sensation, it is clear that 'this is S' is not a genuine statement which can be true or false. If the speaker only refers to what there is *now*, he simply gives again a name to what he refers to, and he can name it as he wishes (Wittgenstein, 1953, § 258, p. 207).

2. *Giving Meaning to a Sign*

The second reply consists in the speaker's saying, in a private language "By 'S' I mean the sensation that I called 'S' in the past." Can he do this? Since he no longer has the past sensation, Wittgenstein argues, he must rely on his memory. He must recall a past occurrence of S and compare it with his present sensation to see whether they are the same. He must *correctly* represent the connection between 'S' and the past sensation. But he has no criterion for the correctness of his representation. We might say: whatever occurs to him is correct. He may have the wrong recollection without realizing it. Therefore he does not really know what he means by 'S'. It is pointless even for the speaker to say "Well, I *think* that this is sensation S again." For this belief is merely the impression that he believes it. If he does not know what 'S' means he can't even have the belief.

But is it not possible that he remembers the meaning correctly? Wittgenstein thinks that the correctness of his recollection of the meaning can be confirmed only by reference to a public object. A recollection cannot be confirmed by another recollection of the same thing (ibid., §§ 258-265).

The basis of Wittgenstein's argument is his view about rule following, which is applicable here because he regards the use of a word as a case of rule following. "() following a rule is a practice. *Thinking* that one is following a rule is not following the rule. One cannot follow a rule privately, for otherwise thinking that one follows the rule would be the same as following it" (ibid., § 202). We may add: if thinking that one follows a rule were the same as following it, then there would be no real rule following.

The second answer, which is presently under discussion, was that the speaker means by 'S' the sensation he has called 'S' in the past. This answer may not be acceptable in a private language. But it is certainly acceptable coming from a speaker of an ordinary language who is referring to a private sensation. This use of language is a case of a private language according to the Wittgensteinians. This last point is at issue here.

It is quite possible that the speaker has the wrong recollection when he tries to represent the meaning of 'S'. Nevertheless it does not follow that the speaker does not know what the meaning is. It merely follows that it is possible that he does not know it. It is equally possible that he has the right recollection and does know the meaning. The Wittgensteinian view about rule following, which includes rules for meaning, is not logically sound (Candlish, 1980, p. 91). It is true that thinking that one follows a rule when using a word is not the same as following the rule. This is true in the sense that it is *not necessarily* a case of following the rule, but can be one. It cannot be concluded, as Wittgenstein does, that there can be no rule following in a case of private rule following in which the subject thinks that he is following a rule but is not sure that he is doing so correctly. Even if he cannot verify it, he may be following the rule correctly, because he intends to and because he knows the rule. So it is possible to follow a rule privately, at least insofar as the application of familiar, acquired terms for sensations to our own sensations is concerned. (How we come to adopt those terms will be discussed at (3)).

Our speaker thinks he remembers that he used 'S' to refer to the kind of sensation that he feels now. He may be mistaken, and if he is often wrong we will say he does not know the meaning of 'S'. But what seems correct to him does not have to be correct, as he himself may realize.

First, he may be able to correct himself. It is sometimes possible to correct a casual recollection of a private experience by making a better effort to remember the experience. Although we may still be wrong, the distinction between appearance and reality is clearly present (cf. Castañeda, 1971, p. 148).

Second, a speaker learns the distinction between following and not following a rule via language about publicly accessible objects. He can then apply this distinction to his private sensations, although he cannot determine whether he does so correctly. But it is quite possible that he rarely makes mistakes, and uses a word reasonably consistently. In that case he knows its meaning. He cannot check whether he knows its meaning, but that does not imply that he does not know it (Donagan, 1968, pp. 339-340). Insofar as his memory has proven reliable for comparable tasks for which he could check it, he can assume that it is reliable here as well.

We must draw a distinction between using a sign 'S' with a certain meaning and verifying that this is done correctly. There is a connection between correct use and a sign having a meaning, since a sign that is used arbitrarily has no meaning. But a sign can be used correctly or not, even if this cannot be determined by any public standard.[1]

A speaker can say he thinks that his sensation is another S-sensation even if he is not certain that he uses 'S' correctly. It is not necessary to be certain of a concept one uses in order to doubt whether this concept applies to one's mental state. The doubt may be rooted in the lack of such certainty (which consists in part in the doubt as to whether the mental state falls under the concept.)

Furthermore a speaker does not have to be uncertain. When he learns the meaning of 'S' by several experiences in the morning and afternoon he need not be in doubt when he uses 'S' on the evening of the same day for another experience of the same kind.

Trust in Memory

If the speaker intends to apply 'S' to the same sensation each time, he must apply a rule for its meaning. For different examples of what is regarded as the same kind of sensation are not perfectly identical and are considered the same according to a rule. Wittgenstein claims that such rules are conceivable only in a public, social context. For we can speak of correct rule following only if there is a generally accessible criterion—that is independent of the subject's mental insight—and agreement about its application, that can be used to check whether the subject follows the rule correctly. Supposedly such a criterion can be provided only by others who can recognize the rule the subject is following from his actions and point out his mistakes.

No doubt reliance on our memory is not a very strong basis for determining whether we follow a rule correctly. It does not follow, however, that following a private rule makes no sense. For ultimately we do have to rely on our own memory for identifications even if others do have a chance to correct us. For how do we know that we recognize the words and gestures of another person, who corrects us, as what they mean and that we remember the correction accurately a second later? And that when we check our memory against a train schedule, which is a public standard, that we identify the figures correctly and remember them correctly afterwards? We have to trust our memory. If the notion of a private rule made no sense then the idea of following a rule in general would make no sense. It is true that it is more likely that we do it correctly if others can check us and correct us. But it does not follow that we cannot do it on our own in principle. For ultimately a person does in fact do it on his own, because he must rely on his memory (Ayer, 1973, pp. 41-42; Fogelin, 1980, pp. 162-163).

Wittgenstein points out that in order for it to make sense to give a name to something, various requirements must be met by the language. He thinks that these requirements are not met by a private language. For instance, we cannot simply say that 'S' is the sign for a sensation, for 'sensation' is an expression in our public language (§§ 257, 264). This observation is right, but it poses no problem here. For I am dealing with his arguments in relation to the language for our sensations, which develops while the language for public objects (mostly) already exists. If this assumption is not made, then Wittgenstein's point will not be relevant for the question whether mentalism is tenable. For of course a mentalist does not deny that language about sensations and other mental processes exists in the context of the language about public objects (cf. Donagan, 1968, p. 341-342).

It should be remembered that I am not defending the possibility of a private language, but the mentalistic conception of the language for sensations. The linguistic behaviorist thinks that mentalism makes this language private. While dealing with this opponent I sometimes adopt his terminology for convenience. So when I object to the linguisitic behaviorist's claim that private language is impossible, I merely mean to defend the view that the language for sensations is a language that can be used to talk about our private sensations.

On the view I defend someone can give a name to a sensation others have never had. Others will not know the sensation, unless its nature can be defined or at least clarified to some extent on the basis of experiences that are known to them (cf. § 257). If such an explanation is not possible, they will be unable to understand the core of the meaning of the term. For them the term will remain an empty sound. This condition is only contingent, however. For as soon as others have the sensation in question, they can also understand the term. This does nonetheless require the occurrence of some common public event, for instance, the same cause, behavior or symptom.

3. Communication of the Meaning via a Public Correlate

There is a third answer to the question "What do you mean by 'S'?" the speaker might give. This answer would refer to a publicly observable correlate of S. Suppose a person discovers that when he has a sensation he calls 'S' a meter indicates an increase in his blood-pressure. This person could say that by 'S' he means the sensation he has when his blood-pressure goes up. In that case he will be able to predict an increase in his blood-pressure without a meter, and that is a useful result (ibid., § 270). Wittgenstein rejects this answer as well. Since it is part of the mentalistic view, I want to spell it out some more.

In the context described 'S' does not function only as part of a private language. It can also acquire a meaning in the public language. The mentalist thinks words for sensations such as 'pain' acquire a generally valid meaning via public correlates such as external circumstances and behavior. Pain is the kind of sensation we have when we are hurt and display certain kinds of behavior. The meaning of 'S' can be made clear to others in the same way. 'S' can acquire a meaning for an interlocutor when his own blood-pressure rises and he has the same sensation. Until the interlocutor has the sensation in question, 'S' means no more for him than 'some sensation or other that the speaker has when his blood-pressure rises'. But when he experiences it himself, he gets to know the sensation that 'S' refers to. At that point 'S' can start to mean the same thing for both because the sensation is accompanied by the same external symptom, the manometer's indication of a rise in blood-pressure. It is of course doubtful that one such symptom is enough to determine a particular sensation, but the present example indicates in a rough way how expressions for the mental acquire public meanings.

When an increase in blood-pressure is predicted on the basis of the sensation, Wittgenstein claims, it does not matter whether the subject recognizes the sensation *correctly*. Consequently any hypothesis of error is mere show (ibid., § 270). Why does Wittgenstein make this claim? It would seem that it does matter. For suppose the subject thinks that a sensation is S but it is not, then he may say that his blood-pressure is rising whereas it is not. Wittgenstein's point is that it does not matter whether we identify the sensation correctly as long as the result, the prediction about the blood-pressure, is correct (Kenny, 1976, p. 195; Fogelin, 1980, p. 161). Section 271, which I will discuss in a moment, shows that this is his point. But let us first turn to a reply to it.

In general the prediction will be incorrect if the identification of the sensation is erroneous. If a person thinks mistakenly that the sensation occurs, he will predict a rise in blood-pressure, which will then not occur. A prediction will come out right by coincidence only in the case of two different kinds of errors which neutralize each other. This is the case when someone misidentifies a sensation—he thinks there is a S but there is none—, and in addition he has forgotten that S leads to a rise in blood-pressure. This combination of errors will result in a correct prediction that there will be no rise in blood-pressure. But this will rarely happen. Correct identification is important because usually the correctness of the prediction will depend on it.

Attempt to Eliminate the Private Object

A later section makes clear what Wittgenstein has in mind. He asks the reader to imagine someone who cannot remember what 'pain' means, and applies it to something different each time. Nevertheless this person uses the word in conformity with the usual symptoms and presuppositions about pain, that is, he uses it as we all do. He concludes: a wheel that can be turned without anything else moving with it does not belong to the mechanism (ibid., § 271). That is to say: something that can change without leading to any change in the use of the language plays no role in the language. His intention in asking the reader to imagine the kind of person in question comes out in the following exhortation: 'Always get rid of the idea of the private object in this way: assume that it constantly changes, but that you do not notice the change because your memory constantly deceives you' (ibid., p. 207).

It is true that something that can change without any consequences for the use of the language plays no role in its use. But the supposition about such a forgetfgul person is misleading, because it is claimed that such a person would use the word 'as we all do.' Someone who has forgotten to what sensation the word refers, but still uses it to fit the usual symptoms and presuppositions about pain, must have remembered the connection between the symptoms etc. with the word. Supposedly he uses the word on the basis of those connections, not only when he applies it to others, but also when he applies it to himself. This idea is unrealistic, for even if we display recognizable symptoms we do not say on the basis of those symptoms that we are in pain. Instead we go on our recognition of the sensation. But let us accept, for the sake of argument, that someone might describe his own mental states in this way.

Such a person will be quite limited in his ability to apply the term to himself. To do so he will need to display undeniable symptoms in what is clearly the right kind of situation, that is, he will require circumstances in which others are in an equally good position to say that he is in pain. In other cases, which are in fact quite common, he will not be able to apply the word to himself correctly. No one, not even this person himself, will be capable of recognizing when he makes a mistake. But we know he will make mistakes. For he has only his sensations to appeal to, and by hypothesis he identifies those incorrectly, applying 'pain' to something different each time. So if we were to take an interest in such a person, there would be no point in listening to him describe his 'pains.'

It is critically important that once words for sensations have been learned they are often used independently of common symptoms and circumstances (Feigl, 1969, p. 34). Others are unable to correct a person in such cases. But it is sometimes crucial, for instance in medical cases, to use a word correctly. We can do this only by identifying the sensation correctly and remembering the term for it accurately.

The basic idea of sections 270 and 271 is this: if we have to rely on external symptoms—or behavior—in order to apply terms for sensations, then what is the importance of the content or nature of the sensation? It does not matter for the use of language. I have briefly argued that it does make a crucial difference because often we cannot rely on external symptoms or behavior.

Terms for Sensations and Behavior

Wittgenstein's basic idea is nevertheless quite influential. Even Don Locke, who maintains a critical attitude with respect to the private language argument and rejects part of it, thinks that he has to accept this idea (1971, pp. 100-101). The acceptance of this Wittgensteinian point leads to a particular negative conception of the meaning of mental terms, when combined with various other ideas. One such idea is that it is not possible to identify a sensation and then give it a name which is valid for all. According to Wittgenstein, words for sensations cannot play a role in the common language if their meaning is learned only on the basis of one's own experience (§ 347) and if the existence of such experiences cannot be directly verified by others. If the way in which sensations are expressed is interpreted on the model of 'object and designation,' the object is supposed to drop out as irrelevant (§ 293). (This is a mistake because indirect verification of the existence of experiences of others is possible and sufficient. I will return to this point in a moment.)

Given that Wittgenstein holds these views it is understandable that he thinks that the sign 'S'—the sign for the sensation that accompanies a rise in blood-pressure—, if it means anything at all, means nothing more than something indefinite, and does not mean what the sensation in question is for its subject. Analogously 'pain' would mean: whatever we experience when we are injured and moan and scream.

But if this were the meaning of 'pain,' we could not say that we are in pain in a mild case in which typical pain-behavior is absent. Without specific pain-behavior a person would have no reason to call a sensation pain. There are many minor pains that come without such behavior. Secondly we would be unable to apply the word when we displayed pain-behavior that was different from the behavior observed when learning the word. Except in extreme cases, pain-behavior varies. A person might know he was in pain when he was screaming, because his mother had told him. But as an adult he would not recognize other behavior, such as moaning, as an expression of pain. Consequently he would seldom go to see a doctor, and such a visit would often be pointless.

The word could no longer function in communication with others. When a patient displays pain-behavior and is visibly injured, it will make no difference to a physician what the word means. He will initiate treatment whether or not the patient says he is in pain. But a patient who says he was in pain yesterday is in trouble if his doctor is a student of Wittgenstein. This doctor understands that his patient felt something or other that is felt in the case of a certain kind of behavior. He will have to ignore the content of yesterday's sensation because it is supposed to be irrelevant. He understands only that his patient had some sensation or other and really not even that much, for according to Wittgenstein it might be nothing (§ 304). So he will be unable to draw any conclusions from his patient's statements and he cannot undertake any treatment (cf. Trigg, 1970, p. 33). This is the absurd result of Wittgenstein's ill-considered position. (I argue in the section about the 'avowal theory' in chapter 2 and in the section 'linguistic behaviorism' in chapter 6 that Wittgenstein's meager beginnings of a positive view cannot replace the view I defend.)

This consequence is sufficient to refute the view that the nature of the sensation is not relevant to the meaning of the term for it. We can tell someone else about our mental states purely from communicativeness and the other person can listen out of interest. In reality we describe a definite state of affairs of mental character. The answer to the question about the relevance of the nature and content of sensations for language is thus disappointingly simple: we can report that we have a certain sensation and not another one, and this report is understood. Of course it is sometimes misunderstood, but that fact should be considered against the background of the understanding that does come about. Sometimes we don't know whether we've been understood, but that is consistent with the possibility of our being understood.

NAMES FOR PRIVATE EXPERIENCES

Wittgenstein holds that names for private states cannot be given generally valid meanings. He thinks it is essential to a private experience that no one knows whether another person has the same experience or some other one. Thus it would be possible to assume—though not to verify—that for some people a term corresponds to one kind of experience, for others to a different kind (§ 272). If sensations were private in this way, they could indeed play no role in the language.

But Wittgenstein does not stop here. He also thinks that words for sensations can play no role in the common language if their meaning is learned on the basis of one's own experience (§ 347)—which is the case according to mentalism—and if such experiences cannot be directly verified by others. He says: suppose that each person has a box containing a beetle, and that no one can ever look in another person's box. Each person says that he knows what a beetle is only from looking at his own beetle. In that case it is possible that each has a different kind of thing in his box, and that it changes all the time. If the word beetle has a function in the language, it is certainly not used to refer to anything. The thing in the box does not belong to the language game, not even as 'something,' for the box could be empty. The thing in the box is irrelevant. That is to say: when the way in which sensations are expressed is interpreted according to the model of 'object and designation,' the object drops out as irrelevant (§ 293). If a sensation were nothing, it would have the same function as if it were something about which we could say nothing (§ 304). (Wittgenstein uses the term 'Bezeichnung' which means 'designation' or 'reference.' He is a nominalist, that is, he thinks that what is called the meaning of a word consists in the reference to a set of different things, which amounts to what is usually called 'meaning.' I will use the latter term.)

As we saw, Wittgenstein's line of reasoning rests on the assumption that we cannot know the sensations of another person. Given this assumption his conclusions do indeed follow. Kenny (1968) thinks this assumption is present in Descartes's view, according to which a person is certain only of the contents of his own consciousness and not of those of another person's consciousness. If it is assumed, furthermore, that when someone is not certain of something, then he does not know it, it follows that he does not know another person's consciousness and that his own is private. Consequently he does not know what another person means by the terms for his mental states. If this is all true, Kenny is right. But we may wonder whether we can only be said to 'know' something when we have the kind of absolute, unshakable certainty that has been sought by many philosophers, and which in the Cartesian system is lacking for other minds.

A number of Cartesians and mentalists have doubted the possibility of knowledge of other minds. Often this doubt has taken the form of the claim that we can never be completely certain about the experiences of other people.

In some of his writings, Russell (cf. 1927, ch. 12, 13) claims that a person perceives his own sense data, rather than external objects. These sense data are no more than signs for external reality, which cannot be proven to exist. We cannot be certain of the content of the sense data of another person, because we do not perceive his percepts—the contents of his perceptions. If from this observation the conclusion is drawn that a person has no knowledge of the sense data of another person, it follows that he does not know what the other person means by his terms. Wittgenstein's criticism applies to this extreme position.

Many mentalists think, however, that we perceive a public world, and that in certain circumstances we have justifiable knowledge of other minds. I mentioned that Wittgenstein thinks it is essential to a private experience that no one knows whether another person has the same or a different experience. This claim is in any case not right for sensations, which are nevertheless private. As I will argue later, sometimes we know what mental experiences others have on the basis of their circumstances and behavior via analogy with ourselves even though we cannot directly verify this knowledge. If so Wittgenstein's argumentation does not apply.[3]

If we know the core of the meaning of terms for sensations on the basis of our own experience, Wittgenstein claims, these terms cannot have a meaning that is valid for everyone. This claim is incorrect, however. It often happens that one person's experience is the same as the experience of another person. This happens in particular when people display the same behavior under the same circumstances; consider for instance children who scream when injured. Given this fact different people can learn to associate the same meaning with a word. Doing so requires, to use Wittgenstein's image, that there is the same kind of thing in the boxes that belong to different individuals. It does not require in addition that one person can look into the box of another person. In order to know that one person assigns the same meaning to a word it is necessary to know that he has the same thing in his box. But this also does not require looking into his box. The requirement of direct verification is unwarranted, since indirect verification is possible and sufficient. People can know sometimes on the basis of behavior and circumstances that the mental states of others are the same as their own. Consequently they can know that the meaning of a term is the same for others.

The meaning of names for sensations is communicable even if it is derived from one's own experiences. This undermines Wittgenstein's view that behavior alone provides a basis for linguistic communication.

Taste

It is illumating to consider a different kind of sensation, taste, which is more varied than pain and which is not associated with specific behavioral reactions. The meaning of 'salt' can be learned by tasting kitchen-salt, sodium chloride. We come to connect the word 'salt' with a specific flavor. Afterwards we can notice, identify and name this flavor independently of our noticing the presence of NaCl. We can even notice NaCl and yet claim that we do not taste salt. A person does that on his own, trusting that he remembers correctly what 'salt' means. Usually others give credence to this private activity which concerns a private experience. The word activity may be too grand a term for the identification of such a simple flavor, but not for the blind recognition of rare, complicated flavors. In that kind of case a person also makes mistakes more easily.

Identification of a flavor does not rely on a criterion in Wittgenstein's sense. A flavor is identified on the basis of what it is. We identify a flavor not by means of the associated substance, kitchen-salt, that gave the flavor its name (Strawson, 1968, 45-46). When we say that something tastes salty, that is a statement that is true or false, although sometimes it cannot be verified. Someone may suspect an error, however, when others do not notice the flavor of something that tasted salty to him, or when the tasted stuff does not contain any substance that is known to taste salty. In the first case it is possible, however, that the person has a more sensitive sense of taste than the others. In the second case he may have an abnormal organ of taste.

Conclusion

My main point is, again, that once a person has learned (public) terms for the mental from others by virtue of connected causes, symptoms and behavior, he can then apply these terms to his own mental states, to which he has privileged access, without relying on associated causes, symptoms or behavior. He can distinguish various kinds of mental phenomena in himself—including his own mistakes about them—by introspection and without relying on others. The second and third answers to the question what a speaker means by 'S' are *both* needed to make it intelligible that someone can speak about his sensations. The third answer shows how a child can learn a term for a private sensation. Adults assume that the child has the sensation when certain causes, behavior or symptoms occur, and use the term on those occasions. This gives the child the chance to apply the term to the sensation himself. The second answer was: "By 'S' I mean the sensation that I called 'S' before." This answer shows how subsequently the child can apply the term to himself, even when he cannot rely on causes, behavior or symptoms.

STATEMENTS ABOUT THE MENTAL

The preceding discussion is of course relevant to the status of statements such as 'I am in pain.' These statements need further discussion, since Wittgenstein has other arguments to support his view about them.

He denies that statements in the first person singular in which the word pain occurs, are descriptions of my sensation, which I first identified. Not the sensation, but the statement that I am in pain is the beginning of the language game. He wonders rhetorically how one could intervene between the expression of pain and the pain itself by means of the language. 'I am in pain' is not a description of my state of mind in the sense that I read it off from my mental state (ibid., § 245, 290-294, p. 189). His point is that statements about another person's pain do not involve a comparison of a 'picture' of that person's pain, but with the criteria for his pain, that is, his behavior and utterances (§§ 297, 300-301).

This last claim is right, but in the case of statements about another person I must also know what 'pain' is. It is true that to determine the correctness of such a statement we look at the other person's behavior and the like. But to give such a statement meaning requires a 'picture' of pain, which I have experienced myself, which is of course not a visual image, but an idea that relies on memory. Furthermore in the case of statements about one's own experience one does compare one's experience with the idea of pain. This idea is acquired on the basis of one's own experiences, and the application of this idea to one's own experience determines whether one is in pain or not. As the reader may notice, I do not say anything original here. I am defending a view which has been common since John Locke.

The meaning of a description must be independent of the described, specific state to which it is compared if it is to be possible to determine its (in)correctness (cf. § 265). The statement 'I am in pain' satisfies this requirement. After the concept has gotten its meaning we can test to see whether the concept is applicable in a particular case by comparing it with current experience.

Knowing that One is in Pain

Wittgenstein thinks the mentalist's interpretation of talk about mental states has the consequence that we can say certain things which in fact make no sense. According to mentalism we must identify the sensation and can in principle make mistakes in doing so. Wittgenstein thinks that it should then be possible to say that we learn that we are in pain and that we know that we are in pain, that we do not know whether we are in pain and that we doubt that we are in pain (ibid., §§ 246, 288, 408, p. 221). Such utterances make no sense according to him, because the current language use—language game as he calls it—does not allow such statements (§ 246, 288) (cf. Pitcher, 1964, p. 290). The non-philosophical ordinary language user will probably agree with Wittgenstein that it is 'nonsense' to doubt one's own pain. He will, on the other hand, also regard as nonsense Wittgenstein's view that one cannot say someone knows that he is in pain. In both cases the non-philosopher is largely right. Let me make it clear that I do not wish to appeal to ordinary language. But if one uses ordinary language as an argument, one cannot reject it when it does not fit one's purposes without explanation.

Let me start with the statement 'I know that I am in pain.' Wittgenstein thinks that by this statement one cannot mean anything other than 'I am in pain.' Now an adult who is in pain generally knows it, but saying that someone is in pain is different from saying that he knows it. When an organism is in pain this does not imply by definition that it knows that it is in pain. 'Learning' is too strong to describe the perception that one is in pain, but there is a difference between being in pain and noticing that one is. Animals may be in pain without knowing it. Furthermore a child may say that he is in pain, but not yet have the concept of knowledge and thus be unable to say that he knows that he is in pain. We rarely say that we know that we are in pain, because it is usually superfluous (cf. Aune, 1965, pp. 48-49; Fogelin, 1980, p. 157). But when others doubt that we are in pain, we will claim that we know that we are. We might say, for instance, 'who would know better than I that I am in pain.' Saying that one knows that one is in pain is a genuine statement, although it is in most cases superfluous (Ayer, 1984, p. 154).

The same applies to simple statements about the world. Looking around a room we would say 'there is an ashtray on the table' and not 'I know that there is an ashtray on the table.' We say the latter only when there may be doubt about our knowledge, for instance because of poor eye-sight or because we speak about a room where we are not.

The fact that 'I know that I am in pain' is a statement that contains information is clear also from the fact that it can be a lie. Lying is saying something that we know to be false. So we can know whether we are in pain or not.

The following set of assumptions constitutes the background of Wittgenstein's view. Like some Cartesians, Wittgenstein thinks that 'I am in pain,' if sincere, is always true and cannot be false (ibid., §§ 288, 408). There is no distinction between its sincerity and its truth. Furthermore he thinks that statements that cannot go wrong are not statements about reality. Finally if 'I am in pain' is not a statement about reality, we cannot say that we know it, because there is nothing to know.

The first premise of this argument has the following problem. From the fact that we never or almost never go wrong, it does not follow that we cannot go wrong. It is true that sincere statements about pain in the first person are seldom false, because it is so easy to know for the subject whether they are true. Still even these statements are sometimes made erroneously. I think we can make mistakes when we expect something to hurt. In such cases we say too soon that we are in pain, and may realize afterwards that there is no pain (yet) and that we have imagined it. The possibility of errors in such statements is more obvious for cases of sensations that are less simple, frequent and important than pain, such as feelings and intentions.

Wittgenstein says that 'know' in the statement 'only you can know if you had that intention' means that an expression of uncertainty is senseless (§ 247). So here he recognizes a different function of the word 'know' when applied to one's own experiences (cf. Kenny, 1976, p. 201). Wittgenstein's claim is incorrect, however. Often we know exactly what intention we had, but sometimes we don't. We do make mistakes about this. The sentence 'only you can know if you had that intention' in fact means something like the following: if anyone knows it then it is you, because we certainly don't.

The fact that statements about certain sensations are almost always right is not so striking. When someone says sincerely that he breathes, or is sitting (rather than standing or lying), he is also almost always right, although these statements can in principle be false. The reason is the same as in the case of sensations, namely that it is so easy to ascertain whether such statements are true. Nevertheless they are statements about reality, in the case of breathing and sitting statements about the world, and also in the case of pain, namely about that part of the world that is our own consciousness.

We saw that Wittgenstein thinks it is a problem for mentalism that it is committed to the possibility of doubting whether one is in pain, or even of complete ignorance of one's own pain. We have already touched on my objection to this point. I think that doubt is not in principle excluded, but that it almost never occurs, because it is so easy to detect pain. For this reason it is in most cases 'senseless' to doubt that we are in pain. But when someone knows that he sits on a chair by a table, he almost never doubts this either. And yet a statement to this effect is an empirical report about matters that must be identified and named (cf. Kenny, 1976, pp. 213-214). The same applies to 'I am in pain.'

Notes

1.   The point has been made before that the private language argument depends on the logical positivists' view that the meaning of a term is its method of verification (Urmson, 1968, pp. 109ff.). The later Wittgenstein still adhered to this view (1953, § 353). The folllowing claim would be a variation on this untenable idea: a sign is a sortal name S in someone's language if and only if it is possibble to determine whether something is S (Thomson, 1971, p. 200). But the idea resulted in fact in the following view: a sign S is a sortal name in someone's language if it is possible to determine by means of a public standard whether S is used regularly enough to count as a sign (cf. Locke, 1971, pp. 94-95). In Wittgenstein the emphasis has shifted from a public standard to the public *use* of such standard.

In fact it is sufficient for a sign to be a sortal that it be used regularly enough to count as a sign. In principle no verification is necessary, certainly no public verification. A concept about empirical reality must of course be developed by means of this reality. But once the concept is there, it can be used independently of reality. It is desirable that the user of a sign can check occasionally whether he still follows the rule he accepts for the use of the sign. It is useful to be reminded of the rule so that one keeps on the right track. But this is merely a practical point which does not bear on the present issue.

2. Candlish (1980) thinks that Kenny's interpretation of Wittgenstein—which I follow here—is not correct on this point. He thinks that in the sections in question Wittgenstein's point is that the recollection of the correlation between the sensation and the sign S should concern something specific that exists independently of the recollection. Candlish wonders rhetorically how the recollection can show this. S's having a meaning requires such a correlation, but the recollection can not show that such a correlation exists independently of the recollection (p. 92). But the passages I referred to prove sufficiently that the interpretation rejected by Candlish is defensible. He relies on certain passages without showing how they support his view. This is not the place to discuss this interpretational matter, however.

He thinks that on his interpretation Wittgenstein's position is not susceptible to the arguments I have discussed. But on his interpretation this position also relies on the rejection of the possibility and usefulness of memory of private events. Consequently it is subject to my criticism. It is true that—in Candlish's terms—memory cannot prove that the necessary correlation exists. But if we remember something it may well be plausible or probable that there is in fact something that does or did exist independently of our recollection. Sometimes it is certain, for all intents and purposes. This probability, which sometimes amounts to certainty, is enough.

3. I will argue extensively in chapter 6 for the view that other minds are known by analogy. At this point I will not go beyond some suggestions. I urge the reader who has doubts about the argument from analogy to read the relevant passages in the next chapter. The correctness of the analogy view is an essential condition for the refutation of Wittgenstein's view. This would be a reason for dealing with knowledge of other minds before discussing him. I have not done so because the present issue, talking about the mental, is connected to the preceding chapters. From a mentalistic point of view, knowledge of one's own mental states comes first, but for a linguistic behaviorist statements about the mental states of others are primary.

6. KNOWLEDGE OF OTHER MINDS

Thus far I have focussed on knowledge of one's own mind. I now turn to the equally important question of knowledge of other minds.

If we know our own mind by reflection and introspection and observe only the behavior of others, the question arises how we know their mental states, assuming that we do sometimes have such knowledge. This is an important issue in the debate between behaviorists and mentalists. In this chapter I will complete my discussion of this debate.

I will first discuss the idea of analogy, which is associated with the view about the mental that I have defended. Then I will discuss behaviorism and linguistic behaviorism about knowledge of other minds.

KNOWLEDGE BY ANALOGY

In our own case we know not only our mental states but also the behavior that accompanies them, and often their external causes. We may assume that when others display the same behavior and undergo the same causes they have the same mental states as we do. So we infer their mental states from their behavior by analogy with our own case. The core of this theory can be found in J.S. Mill (1865, ch. 12, p. 191). Its basis can be rendered in Kant's words: 'Now I cannot obtain the least representation of a thinking being by means of external experience, but solely through self-consciousness. Such objects are consequently nothing more than the transference of this consciousness of mine to other things which can only thus be represented as thinking beings.'[1]

I cannot observe the mental state of another ensouled being directly, but I can ascribe to it the same kinds of mental states that I have.

In some cases our ascription is so well-founded that we achieve certainty. This can happen with pain. I will discuss later the problem of cases that are less clear. What is true for pain applies to other sensations and to all mental states. I will continue to use the example of pain, as is customary, and mention other kinds of mental states when they differ in relevant respects.

In principle, knowledge of the mental, inner states of others is a result of reasoning. But connections between behavior and the mental can be or become fixed data so that no more reasoning is necessary. Reasoning is implicit in our assumptions, however, as becomes clear when our interpretation is questioned, and we have to defend it. This is why we may say that we perceive that someone is in pain and that someone is sad when he is crying. But in reality we do not perceive the pain or the sadness. We only perceive the sad person's tears. An ascription of sadness amounts to an interpretation of another person's mental state.

An adult says to a child who is not yet able to speak, that he is in pain when he has hurt himself and is screaming. The adult reasons 'if this circumstance and this kind of behavior occur then the child is in pain.' 'Reasoning' may be too heavy a term, but it must be admitted that a conclusion is drawn about the presence of pain on the ground of things other than the pain. It is, at least, a case of drawing a conclusion. In less simple cases explicit reasoning may be necesary, for instance, when the question is whether a crying child is in pain, hungry or perhaps tired.

This view was presented, with much conviction, by the psychologist Humphrey (1984, pp. 6-8 and passim). A human being can use his privileged knowledge of his own mental states, acquired via introspection, as a model for knowledge of the mental states of others. We are better able to predict the behavior of others if we ascribe to them the kinds of mental states we know from our own case. This ability to predict the behavior of others had evolutionary survival value for human beings, and is still very useful.

This view is appealing, but the question is whether we can assume that others are the same as we are. With respect to a number of basic primary drives most people are probably roughly, but certainly not completely the same. Our attempts to understand others by analogy with our own case often fail. This problem requires a restriction on the idea of analogy.

Analogy Fundamental for Meaning

Knowing the mental states of others requires knowing the meanings of the terms for these states. These meanings are learned by analogy. Secondly we must know that a statement in which such a term occurs sometimes really applies to another person. This knowledge is not always acquired by analogy.

The common meaning of a term arises as follows. When a child is in pain, he hears from others that he 'is in pain,' which can happen only when it is clear to others that he is. Once the child has heard this several times he understands what the word refers to. At that point the term has acquired the same meaning for the child as it has for the adult. In the case of the meanings of other terms such as words for flavors, the cause will play a bigger role, because the tasting of flavors is less closely connected with a specific kind of behavior than is pain. This is the basis for the argument from analogy. I will defend the view that we can argue from our own case, even in complicated cases, in my discussion of the objections against the idea of analogy.

When the child has learned the meaning of the word he can say that he is in pain even when he is in circumstances that the adult has not experienced, or in which the adult did not suffer any pain. The adult can believe that the child is in pain under such circumstances, generalize it and use it in his assessment of other people. So the idea of analogy does not require that a person always bases his assessment of the pain of others on his own case, although many publications in favor of the view do give this impression. Arguing from one's own case is required only to establish the common meaning.

We assume that a common meaning exists for all who can feel pain. The question was how this common meaning arises. We now have an answer to this question.

The naive but partly correct assumption that others have the same mental states as we do should be replaced by the following: 'Another person's mental states are *like* mine and his motivation for behavior is *like* mine.' This makes it harder to understand others, but it also offers additional possibilities for explanation and prediction.

So far I have given no more than an outline that can be filled out in different ways. Our confidence in our method for ascribing sensations to others can be reinforced if we notice that others ascribe pain to us correctly on the basis of external data available to them (Hampshire, 1971, pp. 118ff.). Observing others' ascriptions of pain to us can of course also undermine this confidence; but in the case of pain this will not happen so easily. We can observe that others are usually right in situations which are apparently quite clear, and sometimes wrong in other, more complicated situations.

Another amendment is necessary. It must be admitted that we observe our own behavior in a different way from others and that in some situations we do not know our own behavior very well. When our mood is sadness or anger, we are usually not so clearly aware of what we are doing. Others will make more accurate observations. Nevertheless we do notice our behavior generally, and that is often enough. Furthermore when a child is learning the language he hears person A say to B that B is furious, and he observes B's behavior (cf. Whiteley, 1961, pp. 166-167). In this way he can see exactly what a display of anger is. What the child already knows about himself in outline is filled out by his observation of B's behavior. He may not immediately say that B is angry on the basis of his knowledge of his own behavior, but he hears it first from A. In this way his suspicion that B's behavior indicates anger is confirmed. He must make the connection between his own behavior when he is angry with B's behavior, but A's remark makes this easier. It is not uncommon for us to achieve a clear sense of how we behave by observing another person who behaves similarly. We don't know our own behavior very well in such a case, but well enough to recognize it in the behavior of others.

Facial Expressions

Our own perspective differs from the perspective of others in that they can, but we cannot see our own facial expression. Broad thinks this difference is very important and argues in *The Mind and its Place in Nature* that it is sufficient reason to reject the view that we know the mental states of others by inference (1980, p. 324). When we see a friend frown we can infer that he is angry. But we cannot do the same on the basis of our own facial expression when angry because we usually don't see it. An appeal to mirrors is fruitless, because we usually do not look into the mirror when angry and mirrors did not always exist. It seems that the proponent of the idea of analogy must assume that facial expressions do not play an important role independently from the behavior and situation. It should be pointed out, however, that we do have kinesthetic sensations which give us information about our face, because they are connected with other perceptions we have of our own face, for instance perceptions via our hands. But this observation does not help much.

The solution of the problem is that a facial expression is usually not more than a part of the behavior and circumstances. It is true that we do not observe our own facial expression when we are angry. We do notice the aspect of our environment that makes us angry as well as the rest of our behavior, which usually includes a variety of other items. When someone else displays the same kind of behavior when stimulated by the same environmental factor, we do not need to rely on his facial expression to determine that he is angry. We do see on such an occasion what kind of face a person makes when angry. This information we then use later for our interpretation of the behavior of others. So in this way facial expressions do play a role. The idea of analogy only implies that an isolated facial expression is not a starting-point for interpretation. But this is no problem, since our mental states are usually expressed by more than just our faces. Many people are used to ascribing what we read off from a person's behavior to his face and especially to the eyes. But in particular in the case of spontaneous behavior our mental states are expressed by our entire behavior, and our facial expressions merely accompany them.

The Acquisition and Justification of Knowledge

Broad rejected the view that knowledge of the mental states of others is *acquired* via analogy, but he distinguished between the acquisition and the justification of such knowledge (1980, p. 324). It is possible that we justify this knowledge by analogy but acquire it in some other way. The question is then how do we acquire it? Broad's most relevant suggestion is that such knowledge is not acquired, but that we have an innate instinct for ascribing mental states to beings with a certain kind of body and behavior (1980, p. 327, 330).

This view has been developed recently along Darwinian lines. The adult's belief in the mind of others is the result of natural selection. Beings who have this belief and who are able to discover the thoughts and feelings of others have an advantage in the evolutionary process over beings who are unable to do so; the latter are selected out. When I perceive that another person screams and writhes I do not *infer* that he is in pain. His screaming, in combination with mechanisms in my brain, *causes* me to believe that he is in pain (Levin, 1984, pp. 347ff.). This hypothesis is supposed to explain in particular the reactions of animals and infants to the behavior of others. These reactions, for instance smiling or becoming frightened, are supposed to be innate. I do not wish to quarrel with the idea that certain reactions and the tendency to develop certain capacities are innate. But I don't know whether an infant or animal believes in the mental states of others, and shall not speculate. Those who think they do know, regard the result of their interpretation as a fact, but other interpretations are possible. An infant's smile can be explained as well by an innate tendency to imitate as by an innate tendency to believe that the other person is friendly. In fact the first explanation strikes me as the most plausible one.

However we acquire the belief that others have mental states, this belief does stand in need of rational justification. An instinctive belief can be wrong, even if it has advantages. I think that our knowledge of the mental states of others is acquired by analogy. But if my arguments are found not convincing enough, my view can be taken as concerning the justification of our belief.

My view does allow that our knowledge of the mental states of others is sometimes intuitive, in the popular sense according to which we intuitively know the solution to a problem when this solution occurs to us suddenly. It does not follow that this knowledge is instinctive, however. The intuition can be explained, and turns out to rely on implicit reasoning which may or may not be correct.

OBJECTIONS TO THE IDEA OF ANALOGY

I will now examine certain objections to the analogy view. Doing so will allow further explanation and elaboration of this. The main objection is that the inference from only one case, our own, to many other cases is weak (Ryle, 1949, pp. 51-53; Wittgenstein, 1953, § 293).

I have already indicated that according to the analogy view it is not necessary to assume that we always start with our own circumstances and behavior. If we did, we would often be mistaken. Sometimes we would have nothing to go on, never having been in the relevant kind of situation or never having displayed the behavior in question. Only the foundation, the coming about of the common meaning of the terms for the mental relies on analogy. Suppose a child acts shy after doing something clumsy. Adults can then teach this child the term on the basis of analogy with their own case. Afterwards others can tell the child that they are in this state without there being any cause or behavior perceptible by the child. The child can apply the knowledge acquired in this way to others. In what follows I discuss analogy as a necessary foundation without claiming that we always infer from our own case. The question is whether we *may* in certain clear-cut situations infer from our own case, thus laying a foundation.

When a small child injures himself and cries, an adult assumes that he is in pain. This assumption can be justified by two principles, which I will discuss successively although they in fact operate together. The first principle is that a cause always has the same effect. The complete cause of the occurrence of pain—that is, the condition that is sufficient to produce the effect—comprises not only the injury but also the constitution of the body. So the adult assumes that the body of the child is roughly the same as his own. The fact that the child gives no sign of pain when he hurts himself only slightly is not surprising even if the adult himself has felt pain on similar occasions. There can be some difference. The child may be distracted, and the adult knows from his own experience that this is not unusual. But if a child displays no pain behavior when he injures himself badly the adult will find this curious. He rightly assumes that the child is roughly similar in constitution and that what causes pain in himself causes pain in others as well.

He may assume so pending proof to the contrary. It is possible that some—or perhaps all—other people differ from a particular person in one or more relevant respects. Their behavior may indicate this to that person. In some cases the person can try to produce the factor in question for himself in order to see what the consequences are for his mental experience. In this way he may discover, for instance, that whereas usually pain occurs under certain circumstances, if some substance is injected there does not have to be any pain under those circumstances (Ayer, 1972, pp. 212-214).

Then there is behavior. In our own case we can perceive that pain leads or even impels us to behave in a certain way. It is natural to assume that the same kind of behavior can and will have the same cause in others, unless something indicates that some other cause is probable.

This is an application of the second principle, according to which like events have like causes. Taken generally this principle is controversial. Some think that like events may have different causes, which is certainly true if the effect is described in general terms. When a house burns down this may have several causes. An expert may discover that there was a short or that the house was lit with gasoline. If all the details of an effect are taken into consideration, however, the same effect will have the same cause. So taken this way the principle is probably right.

In the present case the applicability of the principle in this form does not seem to be enough, however. For pain behavior can have a cause other than pain, since pain can be simulated. We do usually take this possibility into account, except when very small children are concerned. Behavior alone is not enough to be certain about another person's pain. But when there is no reason to suspect simulation it does strongly indicate pain as a cause. Also we cannot imagine a different sensation resulting in the same kind of behavior as pain does, since we don't know any such sensation. So assuming that others have the same constitution, there must be pain unless there is a reason for simulation.

The two forementioned principles are *jointly* sufficient to justify the belief that others have pain. We assume this without thinking about it. If a child displays no pain-behavior when there is a serious cause for such behavior, we wonder whether the child is normal. In the case of an adult we can assume self-control. When older children display behavior that is appropriate for serious pain when they seem to have sustained only a minor injury, then we suspect that they exaggerate.

In the case of pets we think there is pain when they display pain-behavior when hit accidentally. But when an animal's appearance differs too greatly from ours, as in the case of crabs and lobsters, we don't know what to think. We don't easily assume that such animals feel pain. If we are interested in the protection of the rights of animals we consult a physiologist about the animal's nervous system. In such cases there are not enough clues for the argument from analogy. These doubtful cases can make us realize that we base our belief that others have pain on their constitution and behavior, and on physical causes.

These reasons are sufficient to think that others do sometimes feel pain as we do and to fend off skepticism about the mental states of others. In an extreme situation, when someone is seriously injured and behaves as when in great pain, it is absurd to doubt, even if our knowledge of his pain is not direct.

VERIFICATION AND UNCERTAINTY

It may be objected that the argument from analogy cannot be definitely confirmed. For issues other than the mental states of others the correctness of this kind of argument can at least sometimes be verified (Ryle, 1949, p. 51). When certain symptoms suggest a particular disease, because on other occasions this disease has accompanied these symptoms, this suggestion can be checked by examining the body. But according to the analogy view we have no access to the consciousness of others. We cannot detect pain in others as we do in our own case. Consequently, this objection goes, on this view we can never be certain, whereas in reality we are sometimes certain. So there must be a different kind of justification.

Some mentalists reply that we are not in fact ever certain about the mental states of others, and so there is no problem with the analogy view.

It goes too far, however, to say that on the view that we know the minds of others by analogy we can never have certainty about their mental states. Sometimes the circumstances are such that we can be certain that another person is in pain even without perceiving the pain. We can be certain that there is pain when we clearly perceive a serious injury and striking pain-behavior, provided there is no reason to suspect simulation. These factors may occur together in an accident at home, for instance. This is true, as I have pointed out, because people are roughly the same in this respect.

Suppose that we see an accident, and are sure that a person is in pain, but later discover that the accident was staged for hidden cameras, and that the pain-behavior was acted. This kind of thing has happened. It does not indicate, however, that we can never be certain. We can check whether a staged event is at issue, although usually it would be rather strange to do so since such events are quite rare. But are we even then certain, isn't it always possible that there is something like this going on? This question can be answered by another question: why doubt if there is no concrete reason to doubt? If someone says that we cannot be certain that there is pain because of the possibility of unusual circumstances, whereas no one can think of a different concrete possibility, then this statement is empty when it concerns familiar situations like the one at issue.

It should be noticed that in the kind of case discussed above there is uncertainty about the publicly observable circumstances, not about the connection between the circumstances and a person's mental states. When we are certain about the external circumstances, we are also certain about the mental states of the person involved.

We cannot be certain, however, when we only perceive pain-behavior and no cause or vice versa while there might be reason for simulation. In such a case verification of another person's pain by direct perception is desirable but not possible. This is unfortunate but we have to accept it. Because such verification is not possible we are often uncertain even when we are very careful in our assessment of another person's mental states.

Ayer draws a useful comparison with statements about the past. I cannot experience another person's mental states, but neither can I observe my own past experiences now. To justify my statements about the past I can only rely on reports and other indirect evidence. Our knowledge of the past is indirect and based on induction. No report is infallible and any sign can be deceptive, but under certain conditions we can rely on them. In principle any story can be false, and it is impossible to test it by returning to the past in order to witness what took place then. So the claim that we know something only if we have certainty, and that we have certainty about something only if we can witness it leads to the impossibility of knowledge about the past. But our inductive evidence about the past does have value. In some cases it is so reliable that we can say that we know something that happened in the past (Ayer, 1972, pp. 200-201, 206-207). Knowledge about the past is sometimes even better justified by inductive evidence than by the possibility of our being a witness. This point is clear from the fact that sometimes we are present at an event but unable to distinguish some of its features. Nevertheless being a witness of something remains the basis for our knowledge.

Similarly in the case of other minds we sometimes have indications that are strong enough for us to say that we know that another person is in pain. Knowing something means that it is true. So strictly speaking we could use the word only when we have absolute certainty. But at least in empirical cases such certainty is impossible. We can say that we have knowledge if there is no indication that we've overlooked anything. Even in the case of our own pain we can make mistakes, as I have argued. For statements about his pain another person has one ground for justification that I don't have. But this does not mean that I cannot know that he is in pain (Wisdom, 1965, pp. 242ff.). When there are enough indications it is not necessary to perceive another person's pain in order to be certain of it.

As we saw, some mentalists think that a sincere statement that one is in pain cannot be false. On the other hand, statements about the pain of others could reach no greater degree of certainty than high probability, because they rely on mere indications and reasoning. I think that there are no absolutely certain statements about reality, neither about the physical nor about the mental. But suppose noticing one's own pain would constitute a stronger guarantee that there is pain than noticing the indications of another person's pain. Still sometimes the belief that another person is in pain relies on very strong evidence and quite simple reasoning which are sufficient for certainty.

Suppose it is False

I have described the reasons for thinking that, for instance, a crying child who has just had his finger caught in a door is in pain. But suppose that these reasons are insufficient, as some philosophers claim. The child's parents are only two people. They cannot assume that the child is in pain on the basis of their own case, and they cannot verify that the child is in pain. So we could suppose that the child feels an itch as the result of its mishap, and that when the same thing happens to other children some of them feel dizzy, others have sensations completely unknown to us, and yet others feel nothing.

In the first place I want to point out that if this were a true description of children, the philosophical problem could not even be formulated. Each speaker would mean something different by pain and no one would know what others meant by the word. For in that case children would learn to apply the word 'pain' to a wide variety of sensations. In fact a word like 'pain' would not be a name for a sensation, since 'pain' would be used for every sensation and it would be used also when there is none. Sentences about a person's pain in the first or third person would then also not be descriptions of his mental state. Sensations would play no role in communication, and Wittgenstein would be right: this wheel, which can be turned without anything else moving with it is not part of the mechanism (1953, § 271). Everyone would still speak of 'pain' on the occasion of behavior, but we would then not speak about pain but at best about 'a sensation.' It would be senseless to have names for different kinds of sensations. For we might speak of an itch when someone scratches and of pain when someone screams, but if people feel all kinds of things when scratching or screaming, the different names for sensations have no function. Sensations would be like the beetles in Wittgenstein's example (ibid., § 293): irrelevant to the use of language. But Wittgenstein cannot explain why we do have different words for different sensations, if they are not names for them and if they also don't refer to behavior, as he thinks. (Wittgenstein's view that statements about the mental states of others are expressions of the speaker's attitude will be discussed later on.)

Two of the four cases imagined strike us as absurd, because we experience ourselves that a bruise does not cause itching or dizziness and that those sensations do not lead to screaming whereas pain does. The idea that a child screams when he has a sensation that we don't know is not absurd, but this is of course very implausible in the case of a bruise. Such a case would require a special explanation. If someone suggested that the child feels nothing, we would ask why he thinks that the bruise does not cause pain in this case and why the child does scream. If we get no satisfactory explanation we can reject the suggestion as wildly implausible. We would be right to disregard the philosophically inspired answer: 'Why could one not suppose this? The normal assumption that the child is in pain is after all insufficiently justified by cause and behavior.' A special justification is required for the supposition of this kind of extraordinary case.

The experience of pain is roughly similar in different people and has a natural mode of expression, although such expression can be controlled or repressed. Differences between individual people and between cultures create problems for inference from one's own case to other people's mental states. A smile can express kindness but also contempt. Or it can be a habit, a mask that means almost nothing. Children adopt the stylization and way of using originally natural expressions from the people who raise them. Consequently as adults they can interpret the mental states of other members of their own culture.

Defense against Scepticism

So Wittgenstein is right in claiming that we are sometimes certain about another person's pain (1953, §§ 224, 303). But he is wrong in thinking that mentalism cannot account for this fact. His view allows for certainty only in the sense that we can sometimes *say* with certainty that another person feels pain, because the current norms for saying so are satisfied. But this is not enough. For it needs to be determined also whether and how these norms are justified.

According to Ryle if dualism were right, then we could have no knowledge of the hidden minds of other people. He explains this point on numerous occasions (1949, pp. 22, 51, 64, 87). If dualism were true a robot could have an intelligent soul which does not manifest itself, or someone could seem to act intelligently while being a robot. But, Ryle claims, in ordinary life we do have decisive criteria for distinguishing mechanical movements from intelligent behavior (ibid., p. 22). He speaks about Cartesian dualism, but uses this argument to reject any kind of dualism or mentalism. For he claims that his behaviorism is the only way out. Only behaviorism would not lead to scepticism about other minds and then to solipsism—the view that a subject can know of the existence of his own mind only—because the argument from analogy does not work. I have now shown that his argument does not undermine the argument from analogy and so also does not affect mentalism.

Ryle's argument applies only to two kinds of dualism. The first is the view that souls have no connection to the body, so that no one could know whether other bodies are ensouled. His objection also has some force against the view that there is interaction between body and mind, but that the mind is so independent of the body that different souls could be lodged in physiologically indistinguishable bodies that display the same behavior. On that view someone could know that other bodies are also ensouled, but not what those souls are like exactly.

Other forms of dualism and mentalism do allow for the possibility of knowing the minds of others. This is true of views on which physical and mental processes run parallel, or the mind interacts with the body without interrupting the causal chain of the physical world (Addis, 1965, pp. 47-48). I will defend a view that allows only this kind of interaction. Moreover on my view each mental process is accompanied by a physical one in such a way that there is no difference in the mental process without a difference in the corresponding physical process and vice versa. I have in fact already assumed this view.

OTHER OBJECTIONS

I will now turn to objections that arise from behavioristic and related views, whose positive claims I will discuss at the end of this chapter. According to these objections the idea of analogy is conceptually untenable.

The idea of analogy presupposes that the meanings of words like 'pain' are essentially determined by one's own experience. I have defended this presupposition in the preceding chapter. It has been objected that on this assumption it is hard to see what the word would mean when applied to another person's sensation. The following reply is not supposed to work: the supposition that another person is in pain is the supposition that he has the same as I have often had. For we cannot simply apply the meaning of 'the same' to another person (Wittgenstein, 1953, §§ 350-351). Malcolm (1975, pp. 132, 137) claims in addition that on the analogy view we cannot, after noticing pain in ourselves, notice *the same in others*. For on this view behavior and circumstances do not function as criteria for the same. Without behavior as a criterion that gives certainty we could not determine that the same occurs in another person. And if we cannot do this, then 'the same,' when applied to others, has no meaning.

A criterion in the Wittgensteinian sense is not necessary, however. For behavior and circumstances are *symptoms* which are sufficient indications that others have the same sensations I have had if they resemble my behavior and circumstances.[2] In this way we can determine that another person is in pain, and, as we saw, the common meaning of terms for the mental can be generated. It is not necessary that we can always determine whether the application of these terms to others is correct.

When we say that another person is in pain, we judge that this person is in a state which we would call pain if we were in that state ourselves. So we judge that the person is in the same state as when we are in pain (cf. McGinn, 1984, p. 121). The belief that the other person is in pain does not have to be 'explained' by the belief that his experience is the same as mine. If another person is in pain it follows automatically that his experience is the same. Wittgenstein does admit this last point (§ 350).

If 'pain' were synonymous with 'pain experienced by me' the term would not apply to others. But if the word receives its meaning for me via my pain, it does not follow that the term thereby becomes synonymous with 'pain experienced by me.' It comes to mean 'pain,' which is independent of 'I' who experienced it. That is, 'I' is thinkable and imaginable without 'pain' and vice versa. So there is no problem for applying the word to others and for saying that they have the same sensation (Levin, 1984, p. 353). We can see pain as a state we sometimes have, and which we can distinguish from the thinking I that detects this state. Also, we can imagine that another person has this state. We know what 'pain' means even when we feel none, because we remember it. When we say that we were in pain yesterday the word has the same meaning as when we say we are in pain now. Similarly we know what it means when we apply it to others, even though we do not have the others' experiences.

In *Individuals* Strawson raised an objection which relies on his conception of the person. He thinks that a necessary condition for ascription of mental states to ourselves is that we ascribe them to others, or, if the opportunity for doing so does not occur, that we are willing to do so. He relies on a logical point: the idea of a predicate is correlative with that of a *range* of distinguishable individuals to whom the predicate can be ascribed meaningfully if not necessarily truly (1971, p. 99, fn. 1).

It is true that a predicate must in principle be applicable to more than one case. But it is not necessary that it be applicable to a range of cases of which it is *true*. Maybe there is no such range, or maybe we don't know whether it may be applied to the cases of the range. Strawson admits this, but that really undermines his point about predicates. For then we don't know without an argument from analogy whether we can ascribe the predicate to others or not.

If the application of mental predicates to myself presupposed that I affirm them truly of others, then the existence of my mind would imply the existence of other minds. But Strawson only says that I must be ready to affirm mental predicates of others. This claim leaves open the possibility that I do so incorrectly. So on his view the existence of my mind does not imply the existence of other minds and the argument from analogy is not superfluous, as Ayer argued in 'The Concept of a Person' (1973, p. 105).

Secondly, the range to which a mental predicate is applied could belong to one person. This person can be affirmed over time to have pain in his hand, his leg, and his head, and many other places. In that case the requirement is satisfied. It is not necessary that the predicate be applied to more people.

Strawson has another arrow in his quiver. He suggests that a Cartesian could take the following view. We can identify bodies, and this gives us an indirect way of identifying subjects of experience. Another subject is then 'the subject of those experiences that have the same unique causal relation to the body N that my experiences have to body M.' Strawson thinks this is a useless answer. He thinks it requires that I have noticed that *my* experiences have a special relation to body M, whereas the right to talk about *my* experiences is at issue. As long as I continue to speak in the Cartesian fashion about experiences on the one hand, and bodies on the other, I have noticed at most that experiences, *all* experiences, have a special relation to body M. The Cartesian needs the word 'mine,' but Strawson claims that he cannot justify its use. For suppose that private experiences are all we have to go on for the identification of subjects of mental states. Then we cannot say that a private experience is another person's for the same reason that, from my own point of view, I cannot say that an experience is mine. All private experiences would be mine, that is, no one's. Strawson concludes that we can only ascribe mental states to ourselves if we can ascribe them to others (ibid., pp. 100-101).

I think, however, that there is nothing wrong with the Cartesian answer that Strawson rejects. It is true that we need to explain how we get 'I' and 'mine.' It makes sense to speak of 'I' because there are others. First a person notices that a body and private experiences stand in a special relation. He also notices that there are other bodies. As soon as he realizes that those bodies are coupled with subjects of experience, in the way he now knows, it begins to make sense for him to speak of 'I' and about another person as 'he.' A Cartesian or mentalist can say: another subject is 'the subject of those experiences that stand in the same unique causal relation to body N as the familiar experiences to body M.' The familiar experiences are his own. Those of the other person he merely supposes to be there. But he does not have to say 'mine' because only his own are known to him. As soon as he acknowledges another subject he can say it, however, for then there is a contrast between 'I' and 'he.'

Strawson claims that if all private experiences were mine, they would belong to no one. But he should have said the following: if all private experiences were mine, they would belong to a person who would probably not speak of 'my private experiences,' since 'my' would be superfluous. The pain that I feel is my pain. But if I recognized no other subjects with pains I would not have to speak of 'my' pain. If there were no other organism besides me, I could still ascribe pains to myself, but the word 'myself' would be superfluous for lack of contrast.

Scheler has objected that the idea of analogy does not logically lead to the view that there is another, different 'I,' but only to the postulation of *my* I, which exists again (1922, pp. 234, 236). The projection of the 'I' is probably also what bothers Wittgenstein when he emphasizes that we should imagine that another person is in pain, not that we ourselves feel pain in some part of another person's body (1954, § 302; cf. also Kripke, 1982, pp. 114ff.).

But for us another person is another body that has roughly the same kinds of mental states as we do, and that has the same kind of 'I,' whatever that is. Of course we find the differences between ourselves and others very important. But these differences presuppose a high degree of similarity, which includes sensations, feelings and thoughts. Some of this supposed similarity may be lacking—which can already lead to isolation— but if too much is missing we do not recognize the other (fully) as another human being. Scheler thinks that we know that there are others because they differ from us, and are inscrutable in their individual differences. I think this is not right. Another person can be understood as a separate human being, as a distinct individual, only on the basis of a common humanity. He is another human being for us because of similarities between him and us, although he also differs from us. He is another human being because he speaks the same 'language,' be it a genuine language or the 'language' of to us intelligible labor, habits and the like. If he speaks a different language it must be roughly translatable into our own. In the past serious consideration has been given to the possibility that people who belonged to recently discovered tribes and whose customs differed dramatically from Western customs did not have souls, that is, were not human. The need for a common ground is clear within a culture. When someone makes something that fits insufficiently into existing artistic categories then it is not regarded as music or painting. Such assessments may be completely wrong, but the fact that they are made indicates our reliance on common categories.

Scheler contends also that the ascription of mental states to another person on the basis of his behavior requires that we know already that he is another human being (1922, p. 234). When a rope writhes we do not ascribe pain to it. So knowledge by analogy could be at most secondary. It has been argued as well that the argument from analogy requires background knowledge about the beings to which it is applied, and that this knowledge is absent if the mental is a non-physical property, thus differing radically from everything else (Carruthers, 1986, pp. 20, 22).

We have background knowledge about the mental as something non-physical, however, because we know mental properties of ourselves. And we have enough background knowledge about human beings so that the idea of analogy can account for the fact that we see something else as a human being. Before we ascribe a sensation or intention to something other than ourselves we have to know more than just a limited bit of behavior. For instance, we don't ascribe pain to something merely on the basis of certain movements but we require that it also has the form of a familiar organism, and that it walks, breathes, eats, etc. In short we require a variety of data indicating that it is a human being and that it has the kinds of sensations humans have. This point is no problem for the analogy view. It merely means that we don't rely solely on the piece of current behavior on which we focus when making a judgment about another person's mental state. Our view that something is a human being relies on other data which at the same time give us reason for seeing an analogy. We ascribe to him not just pain, but also other sensations, which together amount to his being a human being for us. Another human being is something to which we ascribe on the basis of his behavior fundamental mental capacities which we ourselves also have. So we don't have to know beforehand that he is another person. The analogy view can explain how we come to see other beings as human.

BEHAVIORISM AND SIMILAR VIEWS

The analogy view enjoys less popularity nowadays than the behavioristic account of knowledge of other minds. According to behaviorism we know another person's mental states directly in his behavior. If agitations, moods and inclinations are nothing other than behavior—or dispositions to behave—then we simply perceive those mental events. We perceive a person's sadness in his tears, his anger in his yelling. We are supposed to be able to observe that another person is thinking. This observation would in principle be no different from the way in which the thinking person perceives his own thought introspectively.

Knowledge of other minds is no problem on this view, but my discussion of behaviorism should make it clear that this view of the matter is not right. An observer can only perceive another person's bodily attitude and conclude from it that that person is thinking. But he cannot observe the thinking itself, let alone the content of the thoughts. If we stick with the example of pain it is immediately clear that we do not observe the pain of others, but only his behavior.

In some cases, however, behaviorism seems to be supported by our experience. For we often say that we see or hear that someone is sad or aggressive, and we do not have the experience that in these cases we derive statements about a person's mental states from his behavior.

Often we can make these kinds of statements on the basis of a fixed connection between behavior and feeling. When in our society a person bursts out in tears in company we know that he is sad. In that case we so to speak 'see' the sadness, though not literally. During a funeral we may assume sadness in the case of this kind of behavior except in the case of a known pretender. But in a culture where it is part of a ritual that all the women present wail on certain occasions, we will have to rely on reasoning to determine whether the wailing of a particular woman indicates sadness. In short, we sometimes don't have the experience of drawing conclusions about the mental from behavior, because the connection is so obvious. Nevertheless even in those cases we do interpret the mental on the basis of behavior. These interpretations can be radically wrong, even if we observe the behavior correctly. The more natural the connections between behavior and the mental, and the less they are determined and modified by the dominant culture or subculture, the less likely we are to make mistakes.

Nevertheless, even if certain reactions always accompany certain sensations and feelings so that we are always in a position to make the right inference about the mental, we still do not perceive the sensations and feelings of others, but only their external reactions. On the basis of these reactions we seem to be able to conclude *that* a person is in a certain mental state, but we cannot perceive the state itself (Aune, 1963, p. 198). Our perception that someone is in a certain mental state contains an inference which is so obvious that we usually don't notice it. It becomes explicit, however, when we realize that we have made a mistake.

There are other contexts where there is in fact an inference but in which perceptual terms like 'see' are often used. We say, for instance, 'now I see that you were right,' or 'I see what you intend to do.' In such cases we mostly do see something in the literal sense, but what we claim to see is in fact known on the basis of insight or inference (Vendler, 1984, p. 10). We do not literally see that someone is sad; it is an insight, that we acquire on the basis of perception.

When another person's feeling is directed at us, for instance in friendliness or aggression, another factor strengthens the impression that we perceive the mental states of others. Behavior is aggressive only if its subject has the *intention* to attack. We cannot perceive this intention and so we have to infer it from behavior. But we can see or understand that the behavior poses a danger for us, as is the agent's intention. We see this just as we see that an inanimate object is going to harm us, as when the sea destroys a dike.

When an arm lashes out dangerously in our direction, we see the movement of the arm. In the case of such danger we can limit ourselves to a claim about—or a reaction to—what the other person's movements (will) mean to us: danger to our body. This does not require knowledge of the other person's state of mind. We have a tendency to identify what the behavior of another person means to us with what it is. This tendency often leads us to think that we perceive another person's mental states directly. When another person's behavior is harmful to us we think that we know his malevolent state of mind. But he may not be in such a state.

In the case of symbolic behavior, such as the shaking of a fist from a distance, we can limit ourselves to an assessment of what is coming, as we do in the case of a defective dike. In that case we do make a projection on the basis of the data—about what is coming on the basis of what is happening now—, but not necessarily about mental states. In fact a projection about the future on the basis of symbolic behavior often contains a claim about the mental state of the other person, but we can draw the distinction. This distinction allows us to realize that an appropriate reaction to behavior does not necessarily indicate any understanding of the mental state of the other person, not even the realization that the source of the threat is animate. But in fact we often ascribe aggression to another person on the basis of the threat he poses to us. We don't know the other party's state of mind, but we think we do. We used to ascribe aggression and other inclinations even to inanimate objects.

Animals and very young children can react appropriately to a threat or an expression of friendliness. Scheler has adduced this point against the idea of analogy on the ground that a baby certainly is unable to carry out the argument from analogy (1922, p. 233). But a baby is also unable to say and no doubt unable to think that a smile indicates good will. Probably he makes little or no distinction between himself and others, and he is not even able to see this. The whole problem does not arise yet.

This point is clear from the fact that people sometimes ascribe mental states to the inanimate world, as Scheler reports about 'primitives.' The issue is only what something means 'for me' or in this case 'for us members of the tribe.' For instance, nature is 'angry' at the tribe. In itself nature does not have any such states; the anger exists only in the mind of the members of the tribe. Their reaction to natural phenomena is certainly not a reaction to 'anger,' because there is none. They ascribe mental states to nature, because they interpret it on the basis of its effects on their lives.

When there is a mental life, an organism can also react on the basis of consequences for itself only, without knowing the mental state of the other organism. Suppose that a gazelle has no aggression, then she cannot know the mental states of a pursuing lion. Yet her flight is an appropriate reaction.

Philosophers sometimes appeal in this context to the spontaneous reaction of animals and small children. But this move is rather dubious. For such reactions are susceptible to various interpretations. Levin (1984, p. 344) claims that at the age of sixteen months his child believed that his mother was angry when she scolded him. But how can he be so sure? Many children at that age are frightened not only by a loud voice but by all sounds that are loud or suddenly increase in volume (Bowlby, 1981, p. 134). Reactions like fear, shrinking, running away do not require a belief about another person's mental state. The recognition of the external facts is enough.

Plessner (1953, pp. 172ff.) claims that the intentional attitude and mode of expression of organisms with respect to their environment is psychophysically indifferent. If someone understands the meaning of an organism's attitude, he understands nothing psychological. The intentionality of the living body with respect to its environment is neither subjective, nor objective, but something in between. When we say 'I see that he is angry,' this means according to Plessner not that I know the existence and the nature of the anger, but only his attitude with respect to his environment (ibid., p. 174).

We can give the following reply to this view. The intentional attitude with respect to the environment is not psycho-physically indifferent but mental. This is because it is intentional. It is possible, however, that an organism perceives that another organism is about to attack its environment without knowledge of the mental states of that organism. But in that case it sees, or rather infers, only what the other organism will probably do to its environment, in the way in which we can see that a dike is in bad shape and about to break. On the other hand it will usually see the other organism as a whole as animate on the model of its own intentionality. But if it does not at all ascribe its own kind of intentional states to the other being, it will regard it as a mechanism. It can know the other being's intentional states and anger only on the basis of its own experience of these states. When someone says that he sees that another person is angry, this normally implies that he claims to know the mental state of the other person.

Along the same lines it has been adduced that people immediately see faces as angry or friendly. This aspect is supposed to be a primary mode of existence of faces, which precedes the division into mind and body. This point does not establish the psycho-physical indifference of the attitudes in question, however. For saying that someone is angry or friendly, and is not simulating, requires a decision, based on observation, about the person's mental state and intentions. We assume that the person is ensouled, and do not see his face as psycho-physically indifferent. We do not see it as a mask, but as something ensouled. The fact that we seem immediately to determine its expression does not count against the idea that we make a decision: we can do so immediately because we are used to giving such interpretations. Furthermore we make mistakes while doing so. We see the heads of certain kinds of dogs immediately as 'sad, depressed,' but we do not thereby know the mental states of these dogs. In a general sense, if the primary mode of existence consists in being in and displaying a certain mood then the primary mode of existence is psychological.

Seeing a face as angry or friendly does precede the distinction between the physical and the mental, but this does not count against this distinction. Life precedes all distinctions; when we were still in the crib we did not make these distinctions either. The question is whether the distinction between the physical and the mental can be maintained in this case, and it can. The physical state of a face that is seen as friendly can be imitated by a person devoid of friendliness, or by a cast of a friendly face, which is of course not even animate.

Finally, if we include certain kinds of behavior in the definition of friendliness and anger, then these moods are by definition at least in part perceptible by others. I do not wish to claim that no supposedly mental concept could be defined in this way. In the case of a concept like 'pain' this approach would be wrong. But for some emotions this kind of definition has a certain plausibility. If MacIntyre's claim that feelings have no link to any particular behavior is right, then this kind of definition won't apply in the case of emotions either (cf. ch. 2). Nevertheless if this kind of definition is adopted, then the physical component is perceptible by others, but the mental component is not.

Linguistic Behaviorism

Wittgenstein originated the view that the mental is not identical with behavior, but that in the case of certain behavior we are conceptually justified to say that someone is in what is called a mental state. Such behavior is a criterion for ascribing mental states (cf. 1953, §§ 56, 146, 253, 258, 354). It is not very clear what criteria in the Wittgensteinian sense are. A plausible characterization is that a criterion for ascribing a property is something that, by definition, justifies the ascription of the property (Albritton, 1968, p. 244). So this kind of ground relies on a convention and differs from a symptom, which can be used as inductive evidence gathered by experience.

We teach children the word 'pain' on the basis of a certain kind of behavior that they or others display under certain circumstances. When afterwards they apply the word to others on the occasion of that kind of behavior under the same kind of circumstances they play the language game correctly. They say correctly that the other person 'feels pain.' According to linguistic behaviorism the actual state of that person is irrelevant. The nature of that state does not matter for linguistic communication, because private objects can play no role in language (Wittgenstein, ibid., § 304). Words like 'pain' are not supposed to be names for certain 'inner' states. The statement 'he is in pain' is thus not really a judgment about his 'inner' state. Language is public and must be used according to public criteria, which are provided by behavior. The meaning of a word is its use, even if it concerns our mental states.

According to the later Wittgenstein there must be an outward criterion for speaking about 'inner processes' in others (ibid., § 580). Even when a symptom is recognized as such it must ultimately be connected to a criterion. A general reason for this view is that without a public criterion there could be no certainty, which relies on conventions (Wittgenstein, 1958, pp 24-25; cf. Chihara and Fodor, 1968, pp. 400-401). A particular reason is that 'I am in pain' is not, according to Wittgenstein, an observation of a mental state, but something that replaces pain behavior. If it is not an observation of a mental state then the 'I' can also not correlate his mental state with his behavior. The possibility of such correlations is the basis for the argument from analogy. Without it the argument cannot get off the ground. For Wittgenstein the perception of others comes first. We observe their pain-behavior. This behavior is supposed to be a criterion and not a symptom. It could not be a symptom of anything, since we cannot connect it with pain via our own case.

This view may be coherent, but its premisses are false. Statements like 'I am in pain' are observations of mental states, as we saw in chapter 3. So it is possible to see a correlation with one's own behavior, which then can serve as a basis for the argument from analogy. Something physical like behavior is necessary only to learn the language about private states, but not to speak about them once this language is learned. Words like 'pain' are names for mental states in our own case, and there is no good reason to say they are not when applied to others. When we say that someone is in pain, we make judgments about his mental states. These states are relevant for the correctness of our judgments. Sometimes another person's behavior justifies our statement that he is in pain, in the sense that there is sufficient reason for making this statement, but we are in fact taken in by an effective simulation. In such a case we play the 'language game' correctly, but make a mistake anyway because of his real mental states. The question whether we are right in ascribing the empirical state 'pain' to another person is not the same as the question whether we play the language game correctly. Behavior that often accompanies pain is not part of the concept of pain, since pain can occur without that behavior. For this reason a conceptual justification is never enough to determine whether someone is in pain. I have already argued that even if behavior is not a criterion but a symptom, sufficient certainty about the mental states of others can be achieved.

As Malcolm argues, it follows from Wittgenstein's view that someone who has never been in pain nevertheless understands what he says when he ascribes pain to others. For on his view the meaning of the term 'pain' is not derived from our own case. For Malcolm, understanding a concept consists in using it adequately, and someone who has never felt pain could still learn to use the word appropriately. It follows that he would understand it. A person who never felt pain could learn to determine when other people are in pain on the basis of their behavior. Malcolm believes that he could show as much concern for the suffering of others as normal people (1972, pp. 46-48).

It must be objected, however, that there would be a difference between the use of 'pain' by a normal person and by a person without pain, if the two underwent the same learning process. Even if the man without pain got extra training there would still be a difference in the use of the word. Once he has the concept 'pain,' a normal child can discover other sources of pain and other forms of pain-behavior from his own case. He can then apply this knowledge to others. The man without pain could not learn these things on his own. He would have to learn them from others. In order to use the word 'pain' correctly he would have to memorize, and occasionally consult, a list of forms of pain-behavior and causes of pain. No such list could be complete. Consequently he would occasionally falter, and be exposed as the well-trained parrot he was. He would also not be able to empathize with those in pain, although he could pretend. If he could feel other very unpleasant sensations, and if he were told that pain is also bad, he could empathize as with someone who feels something very unpleasant. In that case his empathy would again be based on knowledge of his own feelings.

On my view this Wittgensteinian view is incorrect because the meanings of words for sensations are based on having those sensations. I have indicated why we may suppose that others have the same experience that we have when we say that we are in pain, so that the word 'pain' stands for a definite state that we can ascribe to others.

Having an Attitude

Just what, on the Wittgensteinian view, is this use of 'he is in pain' which is supposed to be its meaning? In the first place Wittgenstein thinks it would not just be wrong to ascribe pain to inanimate objects such as ovens, pots and pans. It would be unintelligible, because they display no pain-behavior. We can ascribe pain only to people and to other living beings that display behavior that resembles human behavior (1953, §§ 281-284). The pain-behavior is supposed to be an essential component of the concept 'pain' (Pitcher, 1964, p. 306), that is, it is a criterion for the application of the concept.

But in reality this behavior is necessary only to *learn* to talk about pain. One could say, losely speaking, that it makes no sense to claim seriously that an oven is in pain. The reason is, however, that it is such a strange mistake. It does make sense, and sometimes it is correct to ascribe pain to organisms that display behavior very different from ours, and from that of animals familiar to us. We don't do so very easily, because without familiar behavior we have no clue, but sometimes that is a shortcoming in us. Furthermore it makes sense, and it is no doubt right, to ascribe pain to someone who undergoes surgery unanesthesized and whose vocal cords and muscles are paralyzed.

Wittgenstein seems to think that believing that another person is in pain amounts to taking a certain attitude toward that person, such as compassion. So it isn't *because* we ascribe the pain to the other person that we have the attitude. Rather, having the attitude is identical with the ascription.Generally speaking, ascribing 'souls' to other people is taking a certain attitude with respect to them (ibid., §§ 287, 310, 420, p. 178).

It is not really possible to discuss this general claim briefly, but insofar as it bears on the ascription of sensations and other mental phenomena, it is blatantly false. For while believing that another person is a living human being like us, and that he is in pain, we can take any attitude with respect to him: compassion, sadistic pleasure, the businesslike attitude of a mechanic whose job it is to do something about it, or complete indifference. The state we ascribe to a person does not determine our attitude toward him. So the belief about his state and our attitude are not the same thing, and the attitude cannot replace our belief (cf. Locke, 1971, pp. 84-85). It would be nice if compassion and helpfulness always accompanied the conviction that someone is in pain. In that case I would still argue that they are not the same as the conviction. Since there is no stable connection between the two, the view that they are identical is obviously untenable.

Moreover this view breaks down completely for the ascription of different kinds of sensations to others. What particular attitude of the speaker is represented by 'he is dizzy' or 'he has an itch,' and how would these attitudes differ from each other? This question would have to be answered in order to defend the view in question. In these cases it is even clearer than in the case of pain that the speaker can take just about any attitude toward the person he is talking about.

We can conclude that behavioristic approaches offer no viable alternative to the idea of analogy which I defended in this chapter.

Notes

1. 'Nun kann ich von einem denkenden Wesen durch keine aüssere Erfahrung, sondern bloss durch das Selbstbewusstsein die mindeste Vorstellung haben. Also sind dergleichen Gegenstände nichts weiter als die Uebertragung dieses meines Bewusstseins auf andere Dinge, welche nur dadurch als denkende Wesen vorgestellt werden' (Kant, 1781, p. 342).

2. Ordinarily, behavior that is a manifestation of a mental state is not called a symptom. In ordinary language a symptom is, for instance, a half-suppressed gesture that betrays a mental state (Austin, 1979, pp. 107-108). In what follows the term is used in a somewhat broader, philosophical sense, as the opposite of 'criterion'.

7. THE MIND-BRAIN IDENTITY THEORY

The next two chapters will be concerned with materialism and functionalism. Many materialists regard behaviorism as inadequate, and thus
think that mentalism is in part acceptable. But they want to identify the
mental with the physical, and this goes against mentalism as I have
defined it. The same applies to some extent to functionalism, which is
related to materialism.

Materialism has a long history and comes in many varieties. As a result
there are different interpretations of the term 'materialism.' Some views
that were regarded as materialistic at one time are no longer so regarded.
During the nineteenth century the denial of dualism—the denial of the
view that there is a soul that can exist apart from the body—was often
thought to amount to materialism. Now the view that there are separate
mental states, even if they depend on the body, is usually regarded as
dualistic or mentalistic. I will here only discuss the modern form of
materialism.

The modern form of materialism, the identity theory, must be distinguished from behaviorism. According to the identity theory there is
something that does not amount to behavior and that may be called
mental. But the mental is nothing other than electro-chemical processes in
the nervous system, in particular in the brain. Thus Place (1964) attacks
Ryle's behaviorism, and defends the view that consciousness is something
other than behavior; but then he claims that consciousness is nothing
other than certain processes in the brain.

Materialists adopt the scientific idea that mental processes are correlated with certain operations of the nervous system and the brain. A
mentalist can admit this idea too. But materialists add the philosophical
idea that these mental processes are identical with the corresponding
physical processes. The existence of a correlation is necessary but not
sufficient for materialism; it is compatible with various other theories.

An essential difference between behaviorism and materialism is that on
the former view terms for the mental have the same *meaning*, on the latter
view they have the same *reference* as other terms. Behaviorists hold that
terms for the mental mean the same as expressions for behavior and
dispositions to behavior. Materialists don't think that a term for the
mental, for instance 'afterimage,' *means* the same as the term for the

brain process that the mental term refers to as well. The position that terms for the mental mean the same as physiological terms would be indefensible. The materialist admits this, but claims that they refer to the same things as physiological terms, namely to processes in the brain.

Despite these important differences there are similarities between materialism and behaviorism. Behaviorism can be called a form of materialism, because it allows only movements of organisms. Furthermore for behaviorism the notion of a disposition is central, and besides it is probable that the body has a certain physiological structure on which those dispositions depend. If the behaviorist incorporates this view into his theory he has an explanation for the existence of these dispositions.

MEANING AND REFERENCE

So the difference between meaning and reference is important to the materialistic identity theory. This difference can be easily illustrated by means of the example of the terms 'morning star' and 'evening star,' which differ in meaning but have the same referent: the planet Venus. According to the materialist, science discovers the reference of the terms for the mental. This reference consists in the electro-chemical processes in the brain, which are also called central state processes.

There are, however, two reasons why the example of the morning star and the evening star is not very suitable for explaining the identity theory (henceforward the IT). The first reason is that one can say that 'the morning star' and 'the evening star' don't refer to the same thing because they refer to Venus at different moments in the course of this planet (Polten, 1973, pp. 27ff). Secondly this example rather provides a reason, although not a good one, for adopting a double aspect theory. On this interpretation the terms 'morning star' and 'evening star' refer to two aspects of the same thing, the planet. Similarly the terms for the mental and for the physical could be said to refer to two aspects of the same thing. Although materialism sometimes comes close to double aspect theory, it is different from this view, which I will discuss later (cf. Feigl, 1967, pp. 80, 82; Popper-Eccles 1977, pp. 82-83).

Some materialists appeal to the following examples of what they regard as identity. They think that physics has discovered, for instance, that heat—the sensation of heat—is the same as the average molecular motion energy of the air, and that sound is the vibration of the air at a certain frequency. Similarly physiology could discover that sensations such as pain are certain processes in the nervous system (Churchland, 1985, pp. 15, 33 and passim).

If such identities were acceptable, materialism would have a solid basis, but they are not. Physics textbooks may claim that heat is the energy of molecular motion, but we must distinguish between this so-called heat on one hand, and heat qua sensation on the other hand. The sensation of heat is not the same as molecular motion. A physicist can define the heat he studies as molecular motion because he is not concerned with the sensation.

So there is a source of confusion here in that 'heat' refers to two sorts of phenomena. Originally the word only referred to the sensation, later it also started to be used to refer to the motion of molecules. It should be pointed out, moreover, that the physicist can do without the term 'heat.' The sensation is the starting-point for discovering the energy of molecular motion, but the term 'heat' is now no longer necessary in physics. The same counts for other anthropomorphic terms like 'force.'

The question of the relationship between the sensation of heat and the motion of molecules is a philosophical one. It is easy to see that the sensation of heat and the molecular motion in question are not identical. For the motion can exist without the sensation when there are no organisms around with the necessary sense for heat. Secondly, the same person sometimes feels warm, sometimes cold in the presence of the same average energy of molecular motion. If both his sensation of heat and his sensation of cold were identical with the energy, then the two sensations would be identical, which is absurd. So the sensations are not identical with the energy. Thirdly, simultaneity is a strict condition for identity, and this condition is not satisfied. The sensation of heat occurs after the motion of molecules in the air. This motion acts on the skin and causes a physiological process and the sensation. In the fourth place, materialists want to show that sensations like pain are identical with processes in the nervous system. But if a sensation is identical with such a process it cannot at the same time be identical with the motion of molecules, for that would imply that the latter is identical with a process in the nervous system.

In another example of the same kind the error is less obvious. P.S. Churchland (1986, p. 326) thinks the fact that an object is blue can be identified with its disposition to reflect electromagnetic radiation of a certain wave-length. Because she calls blue a property of the object this idea does not seem susceptible to the above objections. But is blue such a property? It seems that way to people who are not color-blind. But scientifically speaking blue is not a property of the object at all. The object only has the disposition to reflect a certain kind of radiation which gives some organisms an impression of blue. Blue is an impression, a sensation. The reasons mentioned in the case of heat, except maybe the second one, also explain why color cannot be identified with radiation.

A claim that is acceptable is that the molecular motion or radiation causes the sensation. This idea is sometimes mentioned in physics textbooks.

If a materialist assumes that the identity of the sensation of heat and the motion of molecules has already been discovered he begs the question. Furthermore *this* identity is in any case impossible. He will say, for instance, that the sensation of heat is (no more than) a different way or medium of representing or knowing the molecular motion (P.M. Churchland, 1985, p. 34). But this enigmatic formulation contains the problem that needs to be addressed. For it does not seem to be true that the sensation of heat gives us any knowledge about molecules and their motion.

Other often cited examples are the fact that water is H_2O and the example of lightning. These cases do not immediately give the question a materialistic turn on a pseudo-scientific basis. Science has discovered that the term 'lightning' refers to a kind of electrical discharge. The terms do have different meanings, but the same referent: the electrical discharge. When someone who knows nothing about electricity speaks about lightning, he speaks about a kind of electrical discharge without knowing it. Similarly when we speak about mental processes we supposedly speak about brain processes without necessarily knowing it.

At this point an important problem arises for the IT. Properties of lightning are also properties of the kind of electrical discharge that is identical with it. If it is true that lightning sometimes strikes people it is also true that electrical discharges between clouds and the earth sometimes strike people. If it is true that electrical discharges between the clouds and the earth sometimes strike people, then lightning sometimes strike people. In general if a and b are identical they have the same properties. But it is not in general true that mental states and their physical correlates have the same properties. Pain can be sharp or dull; it makes no sense to say the same of brain processes. It makes sense to say about molecular motion in the brain that it is slow or fast, straight or circular, but it makes no sense to say these things about the sensation of pain.

This is a fundamental problem for the IT. How can one maintain that a red afterimage is identical with a certain electro-chemical process in the brain, while the afterimage has a property, red, which the process in the brain lacks?

Topic Neutralism

Smart tries to deal with this problem in his important article 'Sensations and Brain Processes' (1970). He proposes the following formulation of having a red afterimage: 'There is something going on in me which is like what is going on when I really see something red (p. 60).' So he uses neutral expressions like 'something is going on.' Supposedly one can substitute the brain process for what is going on. This view is called 'topic neutralism'. 'I am in pain' can be transformed in this way into 'there is something going on which is like what is going on when I hurt myself, cut myself etc.'

How does Smart arrive at this 'translation,' which strikes one immediately as inadequate? He relies on an article by Place (1970), who argues that we learn to describe our conscious experiences by means of terms for properties of generally accessible things. We learn to use the term 'green' on the basis of observation of objects that are visibly green for everybody. In this way we acquire the ability to say about a private afterimage that it is green. This is an acceptable view which I have discussed in relation to Wittgenstein. But Place thinks wrongly that it follows that when we describe an afterimage as green, we do not thereby claim that something exists, the afterimage, that is green (1970, p. 50). This view underlies Smart's (1970a, pp. 161ff.). But the fact that we have learned the word 'green' from applications to public objects does not mean that we don't apply 'green' in the case of a green afterimage literally and correctly to something green, whatever this 'something' may be.

Let us consider another example. When I say that I feel a 'burning' pain—while there is no fire in the literal sense—I use 'burning' figuratively. I express the fact that I feel a pain that is like the pain one feels when touching a burning stove. The difference with the first example is that 'burning' is not used literally here. But this does not affect the reality of this property of my pain. The term has become, in a sense, also a literal term, as happens with many terms, including physical ones. In any case my experience has a certain quality which is no less real if it is described by means of a term that does not apply to it literally.

Topic-neutralism is unsatisfactory for the further reason that in fact I can and do say more than that 'something' occurs: that a red or green impression presents itself to me. We can certainly assume that a neural process takes place. It does not present itself to me, however, but only to the physiologist who studies me. It is equally clear that I say more than that something is going on in me when I say that I have a red or green impression or pain, namely that a particular familiar phenomenon presents itself to me.

Moreover someone who is conscious of a red afterimage does not have to be conscious of any brain process. He need not notice a brain process at all or know about any. Yet he is conscious of something, he has noticed something. This must be something non-physical, namely the properties of the afterimage, and those are properties that the brain process does not have. So the afterimage is not identical with a brain process (Shaffer, 1970, p. 119; 1970a, p. 137).

The materialist reply is that when someone is conscious of a red afterimage he is conscious of a brain process, because the afterimage is identical with the brain process, but he does not notice that it is a brain process (Smart, 1970a, p. 164, n. 8; Levin, 1979, p. 138). This would mean that we can be conscious of something without knowing that it exists and without knowing anything about it.

THE DIFFERENCE WITH OTHER IDENTIFICATIONS

The idea of being conscious of something has specific consequences that cause problems for the view that mental processes are brain processes. Suppose that a person P is conscious of water and does not know that water is H_2O in liquid form. We may now say that P is conscious of H_2O, because he is conscious of something that is called H_2O in chemistry, even though he does not know that it is called H_2O. And P knows something about H_2O -, namely what he knows about water, even though he does not know that he knows something about H_2O. P does not know that water is also called H_2O. If he is told that water is H_2O in liquid form he can truly say that he was already conscious of H_2O and knew certain things about it. He now knows that H_2O is drinkable because he already knew that water is drinkable. This account applies also to the identity of lightning and electrical discharge. We learn something about electrical discharge by being informed of the identity.

But we cannot say about someone who is conscious of an afterimage that he knows of the existence of a brain process via the afterimage, let alone that he would know any properties of the brain process in this way. He may or may not know about the brain process from his study of physiology. But he cannot acquire knowledge about a brain process from learning that the afterimage and the brain process are identical. Nor can one acquire knowledge of afterimages from learning about such an identity. When someone is told that an afterimage is identical with a brain process he learns nothing about the brain process, however much he knows about the afterimage, and vice versa.

But can't we say that he is at least conscious of the brain process by being conscious of the afterimage although he does not acquire any knowledge about the brain process in this way? No, for 'consciousness of a brain process' refers to what the brain-physiologist is conscious of when he watches a projection of a brain process on a screen. Someone who has an afterimage is certainly not conscious of a brain process in that way. But in what way is he conscious of it? There is no answer to this question. The statement has no content. So there is no parallel with the case of the identity of water and H_2O or lightning and electrical discharge. The claim that consciousness of an afterimage is consciousness of a brain process cannot be defended by an appeal to such scientific discoveries.

This is the fundamental reason why the IT does not work. Smart, who thinks that mental terms refer to brain processes, appeals to the distinction between the meaning and reference of a term. This distinction is supposed to explain why what applies to brain processes does not apply to sensations (1970, p. 62). I have shown that the identity of brain processes and mental processes is in any case not of the kind we know from science. That is the kind Smart has in mind. If it does not follow from the identity that what applies to brain processes applies to mental processes, the claim of identity is empty and hardly susceptible of refutation.

One can know everything about a person's physical constitution without knowing his mental states. The description in physicalistic terms in particular provides no information about mental states known as qualia, which include sensations (Jackson, 1982, pp. 128-130). If a person who is color-blind knows everything about brain-states and their properties he does not thereby know everything about the sensation of red. If everything were physical including red, it should be describable in physical terms, but this is not the case (Madell, 1986, p. 155). It has been argued that knowledge of the mental is not knowledge of facts but only a practical ability for recognition, and that complete knowledge of brain-states does not have to result in this skill (Carruthers, 1986, p. 144). This argument does not work, because recognition implies knowledge. Recognition of mental states relies on knowledge of empirically given states of consciousness, as I argued in chapters 3 and 5. It is clear that these are genuine states also because knowledge of them can lead to statements that something is the case.

If the materialist still maintains that he knows another person's mental states because they are identical with that person's physical states which he knows, this claim has no content.

So what is said about a brain process does not apply to sensations and vice versa, despite their supposed identity. But then brain processes and sensations share no properties, at least insofar as we know. And if we assume that phenomena can be completely reduced to properties and that there is no bearer of those properties, then phenomena that share no properties are not identical.

If one assumes that there is a bearer of properties x, then x has both physical and mental properties. But since according to the materialist the mental is indeterminate, x really has only physical properties, and according to the IT x itself is physical. Terms for the mental cannot refer to physical properties, as we saw, because brain processes and sensations share no properties. They could refer to the physical bearer x. But since nothing can be said about x apart from its properties, this is a metaphysical claim which can be neither supported nor refuted.

There is here a remarkable resemblance with the way in which philosophers used to defend the catholic dogma of transsubstantiation, the transformation of bread into the body of Christ. The properties of the bread remain the same, they argued, but the substance of the bread, the x which is the bearer of these properties, is changed into the substance of the body of Christ. We don't see the change because the properties don't change. When converted into the linguistic terminology of meaning and reference the argument runs as follows. If a doubting Thomas uses the term 'bread' and the terms for the properties of bread such as 'nutritious' for the 'sacred host' (the changed bread) this is correct insofar as the meaning of these terms is concerned. But this person does, without knowing it, refer to the substance, the bearer of the properties, the body of Christ. Fortunately the believer does know this. Similarly non-materialists are supposed to refer to something physical by means of terms for the mental without knowing it. But fortunately the materialist does know this, assuming that he regards such a medieval argument as useful.

Some formulations of this metaphysical claim are reminiscent of the double aspect theory, according to which there is a bearer x which has both physical and mental properties, while nothing more can be said about this x. The IT claims that x is physical, but otherwise this x is equally undetermined, because the physical nature of x cannot be identified with its physical properties. The difference between the IT and double aspect theory is, however, that the latter does not conflict with empirical facts.

P.S. Churchland argues (1986, pp. 328-330) that the above arguments do not show that introspective consciousness of sensations *could* not be introspective consciousness of brain-states. She thinks that one cannot conclude that the qualia of my sensations are not properties of my brain-states on the basis of (1) the qualia (qualitative properties) of my sensations can be known by me in introspection and (2) the properties of my brain-states cannot be known by me in introspection. For being recognized as something or believed to be something is not a real property of the object itself, but it is a property of the object "as apprehended under some description" or "as thought about in some manner." If Oedipus marries Jocaste and does not think that he marries his mother, Jocaste can nevertheless be his mother.

This last point is correct, but it is of little use since all properties are attributed by us in this way. We can only speak about properties of things because we ascribe those properties to them. One may make a mistake doing this, but it will have to be shown that a mistake has been made. This requirement is the more urgent if a whole category of statements is at issue as is the case here, namely statements ascribing or withholding properties.

The property at issue here is a relational one: '(not) knowable by a certain cognitive faculty.' This property is a relation between the knower and the object of knowledge. But our conception of this property cannot be undermined simply by pointing out that the property depends on our thought. If Churchland thinks that properties of my brain-states can be known in introspection she must provide a solid argument. It is not enough to say that this is true because my qualia are my brainstates. If someone claimed that he knew his brain-states by introspection and sent the information acquired in this way to a journal, he would be regarded as a fool by brain-physiologists, and I think they would be right.

I know of no argument that makes it plausible that qualia are identical with brain-states. It is true, however, that there is no decisive argument against the *possibility* of this identity. Such an argument would require knowledge of all future scientific discoveries and theories that could radically alter our picture of reality. This is impossible.

The Monadic Thesis

It has been argued that the objection that properties of sensations do not apply to brain-states is met by the monadic thesis. According to this thesis someone's having a sensation does not amount to a relation between that person and something else, the sensation. Rather it means that the person is in the *state* of having the sensation. The main argument in favor of this claim is that sensations depend on the person's consciousness. Pain that is not experienced by a person does not exist. This thesis is not uncontroversial (chapter one), but certainly defensible. Next it is claimed that because the sensation does not exist independently, the properties of the sensation need not apply to the brain process. We ordinarily say that the afterimage of a color can become fainter. This property does not belong to the corresponding brain state. But this fact cannot be used against the IT according to Levin because the materialist does not say that an afterimage is identical with the brain process but that the state of having the image is identical with it. About this state it cannot be said either that it becomes fainter (Levin 1979, pp. 97-100).

There is already a problem, however, with this particular example. If it is better not to say that the afterimage becomes fainter, we will have to say this about the *state* of having the afterimage. Different states of having a sensation can be distinguished introspectively. Any theory has to take this fact into account. This distinction can be drawn only on the basis of the properties of those states. Whether we speak of an inner object of a sensation or of a property of a sensation does not make any difference in the present context (Robinson, 1982, p. 7). If a property were at issue it would have to be possible that it also apply to a brain state, which is not the case. This would have to be possible because according to the IT a particular state of consciousness is identical with a particular brain process. The monadic thesis merely moves the problem around, as Fodor has shown (1968, pp. 105-106).

Lycan (1987, pp. 16-17) argues, along the same lines as Levin, that pains are not objects, not phenomenal individuals. The having of a pain is an event, and according to Lycan events do not have individual essences. So feeling the painfulness of pain is not essential to having a pain, and we may identify the having of a pain with something else, namely a brain event.

But events, like objects, do have individual essences. Lycan describes a certain action as a succession of events without giving it a characterizing name. This makes it impossible to decide what is essential to it. Different people would regard different parts of the action as essential. But the same holds for the description of a collection of objects in a room. One cannot decide which object is essential unless the collection has got a defining or characterizing name. Named collections or objects, however, have essences, as do named events such as 'driving a car' and 'stopping'. The essential properties of these events can be described. If a particular event does not have these properties, it is not 'driving a car' or 'stopping'. Likewise the phenomenal character of a pain-event is essential to it. Without this character, the feeling of painfulness, it would not be 'having a pain'. Therefore having a pain cannot be identified with something else.

Topic neutralism, which also underlies D. Lewis's more recent functional materialism, was initially regarded by Smart and others as claiming synonymy. But it is intuitively clear that 'pain' does not mean the same as 'what happens when I cut my finger' or any other definition of this kind. If 'pain' meant the same as some such definition it would be true by definition that cutting one's finger hurts. This is clearly not a matter of definition, however, but an empirical fact (Levin, 1979, p. 113). An analytic topic neutralist could try to deny that he must draw this conclusion. He could reply that the causal relation between being injured and feeling pain is contingent end empirical, but that pain is by definition identical to whatever is contingently caused by an injury.

Levin argues convincingly on the basis of an argument he borrows from Kripke (1981, pp. 144ff.) that this reply also leads to counter-intuitive results. If 'pain' means 'what happens when I cut my hand' it is a necessary truth that whatever happens when I cut my hand is pain. But this is certainly not right. If my nerves would be of a different nature then a cut could lead to an itch rather than to pain. Logically speaking it is possible that a cut causes an itch even given the kind of nerves I have. It is merely a contingent truth that pains and not itches play the causal role they do. But according to analytical topic neutralism the result of cutting one's hand, whatever it is, is pain, even if this result is a sensation of an itch. This is clearly incorrect. We could, of course, start to call itches 'pains,' but they are something different (Levin, 1979, p. 114).

Levin argues furthermore that formulas like 'what happens when [public event]' determine what mental terms like 'pain' refer to. A mentalist can agree with this. But it is not clear how the resulting position has any materialistic implications. Private states like sensations must get public names on the basis of something public. But it does not follow that the private sensation itself is also something public and material. Levin's criticism of the analytical interpretation of topic neutralism makes it useless as a materialistic argument, although he does not seem to realize this.

It is instructive to compare the materialist position with Wittgenstein's. Although he was not a materialist, his views are useful for materialists. For him behavior and circumstances are criteria for statements which contain mental terms, but the mental itself is not described by those statements. The mental is ineffable. The materialist gives less emphasis to behavior than to the circumstances, in particular the causes of mental states. Also he does not conclude that the mental is ineffable. Rather he assumes that if the mental cannot be described it does not exist, in any case not qua mental. If mental properties of the mental cannot be described, it follows that the mental does not have such properties, and is thus indeterminate. On the other hand, physical properties can be described. So, on this erroneous view, if the mental has properties they must be physical. Wittgenstein is also useful for eliminative materialism, which I will discuss later.

Reduction via the Response

Armstrong has tried a different strategy to 'neutralize' the mental, that is to strip it of its special status. He focuses on the response as opposed to the stimulus, but does so in a different way from logical behaviorism. For Ryle a disposition is nothing other than the probability that a certain kind of behavior will occur. For Armstrong, on the other hand, this disposition is a part of the subject's physical constitution which is the cause of the behavior. This is a natural materialist modification of Ryle's view. Armstrong thinks that the concept of a mental state is the concept of a state that is apt to produce a certain kind of behavior (1971, p. 82). This concept does not determine the nature of this state. Scientifically speaking it is something physical. Perception is supposed to be nothing other than the acquisition of beliefs or information about the environment. Beliefs furthermore are the capacity to display selective (physical) behavior (ibid., pp. 209-210, 248-250, 300). These mental states are then identified with states of the central nervous system along Smart's lines (ibid., pp. 355ff.). Armstrong regards sensations as perceptions and defines mental images in terms of their relationship to perceptions (ibid., p. 301). Consequently the import of his analysis depends on his view about perceptions.

He eliminates the mental by taking the perspective of an external observer rather than the subject of mental states. He defines a person's mental states in terms of the results of those mental states that are observable by others, that is, in terms of behavior. A person's perceptions and sensations result for an observer in that person's ability to display selective behavior. For instance, when we have an itch somewhere, we may scratch there. Armstrong's definition reduces the content of a perception or sensation (the itch) to the ability to display certain behavior (the scratching). In reality itches, as well as other sensations and mental phenomena, are more than that. They are something in themselves. They certainly provide the possibility for selective behavior, but for the subject himself they amount to more than this. It is incorrect to define the mental in terms of the perceptions of an external observer, who lacks the mental states in question and cannot perceive them.

From his perspective Armstrong cannot acknowledge the reality of the special nature of a person's mental impressions. Thus he considers it an illusion to think that someone who is in pain or sees something red acquires knowledge about the nature of these properties. The senses are not supposed to provide knowledge of the property that red objects share nor of the property common to people who are in pain (ibid., pp. 276,

314). According to Armstrong they do not give us knowledge of red and pain.

However, as Swinburne (1987, p. 39) has argued, our perceptual beliefs about the possession by objects of secondary qualities such as 'red' or 'loud' would have no content if we did not have knowledge of our sensations. A person would not understand a belief that an object is red, and so could not acquire such a belief through perception, unless red objects normally caused in him sensations of red. Armstrong's denial of our knowledge of our sensations expresses the anti-empirical and meta-physical orientation of these philosophers who, on the other hand, appeal to science for support of their position. If we did not see and identify the property 'red,' we could not pick out red objects. Also we may know this property even if circumstances make it impossible to pick out any red objects.

COEXISTENCE IN SPACE AND TIME

Another important problem for the IT is the fact that identity requires coexistence in space and time. Coexistence in time causes no problems as long as the materialist does not identify the mental with causes in the external world. In chapter 1 we saw, however, that it is difficult, if not impossible to determine where mental states occur. There is no reason for thinking that an afterimage occurs in a particular place in the brain. And what is the location of a thought? It cannot be found. The most plausible solution is to say that a mental state is where its subject is. But the physiological counterpart of a thought is only in a part of the brain that needs to be specified by science. We often feel pain in a particular place, for instance in an arm or a leg. But there is a physiological counterpart for a pain not only where we feel it but also in the spinal cord and in the brain.

One might suggest that the issue does not concern the counterpart of pain but the counterpart of 'the experience of pain,' and that the latter can be found where the subject is. In this way there can be said to be coexistence in space to some extent (Th. Nagel, 1970, p. 218). But as soon as one tries to find a more specific place for the experience of pain the effort becomes pointless. For mental phenomena are not extended, whereas a physiologist can determine quite precisely what nervous process is correlated with a particular pain. Consequently the requirement of coexistence in space is not met, at least not with sufficient precision.

Malcolm (1972) points out the following problem for the IT. According to the IT the identity of the mental and the physical is not logical but contingent and empirical. Consequently the method for determining whether a thought or the experience of pain takes place in the brain should be independent from the method for determining the location of the correlated brain process. Since the IT is supposed to rely on past and future scientific discoveries, the location of a thought or experience will have to be determined empirically, probably with the help of scientific instruments. But such an undertaking is unintelligible. No observation or research with instruments could detect the presence of a thought in the brain, unless the research is conceived as determining a brain process whose occurrence is then used as a criterion for the occurrence of a thought. But if the research is conceived of in this way, the identity is not contingent or empirical (Malcolm, 1972, pp. 67-70).

At most one could agree, once the IT has been made plausible in other ways, to assign the same location to mental phenomena as to physical phenomena with which they are supposed to be identical (Shaffer, 1970, p. 116). But in the first place I think that spatial coexistence is such an important criterion for identity that such coexistence must be established before identity can be accepted. It would be acceptible to say only about less important points that they can be derived from other, more important grounds for accepting the IT. Secondly if this maneuver is regarded as legitimate, it is hard to see what it means. For it makes no sense to ascribe extension to mental phenomena like pains or thoughts, unless one is speaking metaphorically. But precise location requires extension.

PUBLIC VERSUS PRIVATE

Another problem for the IT is the fact that physical processes are public and mental ones private. The fact that mental states are not absolutely private makes little or no difference. Some mental processes, like dreams, are highly private whereas the corresponding physical processes are accessible to any physiologist.

I know best what dreams I have and whether I am in pain. That is, I have epistemic authority over these mental phenomena (cf. ch. 3). Others can in principle know everything about my brain processes but not about my pain. When a statement is about something private it cannot be about something public. 'I am in pain' is about something private and thus cannot be about something physical, which is public (Baier, 1970, pp. 97-98).

It has been replied that being private and public are not real properties of the mental and the physical, but that they are merely assigned by us. For this reason the above argument is supposed to have no force (Carruthers, 1986, p. 140). But this is too fast. If these properties, which are relations to knowers, are assigned by us, this merely implies that the objects do not necessarily have these properties and that the argument does not necessarily work. It does not follow that the argument in fact does not work. Until proof to the contrary we can regard it as in fact sound.

THE ELIMINATION THEORY

A problem with the IT is that when the mental is identified with the physical, it seems to follow that some physical processes are mental. Consider the materialist claim that 'X is a mental process of type a' is equivalent to 'X is a brain process of type a'. This claim seems to imply not only that mental events have physical features, but also that some physical events have non-physical features (Feyerabend, 1970, p. 140; Rorty, 1970, pp. 190ff.). This is a result of the fact that the IT has a mentalistic starting-point from which it then arrives at a materialistic conclusion.

In fact the same starting-point could be used to make the opposite choice, as Feigl did (1967, pp. 80, 86). He claimed that terms for some physical processes in the brain refer to what he calls 'raw feels', that is, unconceptualized sensations and feelings, which are supposed to be what is real.

In order to avoid such unwanted implications it has been claimed that what is called the mental does not exist and that in the future it will be possible to say everything in physicalistic terms. This view is known as the materialistic elimination theory (Feyerabend, 1970, pp. 144ff). We know now that demons don't exist, and that they were products of invention and hallucination. We can express this insight by saying either that demons are products of the mind or that demons don't exist. The latter is the best way of putting it in this case. According to the eliminationist we will come to realize at one point that the mental does not exist. When science will have progressed enough we will be able to describe everything that exists in terms of physical science. Instead of mentalistic expressions we will be able to use physiological terms. Instead of 'I am in pain' we wil then be able to say 'my C-fibers are firing'. The expression 'I am in pain' will be useless. If this way of speaking did not develop quickly it would only be because it is impractical. Theoretically speaking it is quite possible and that is what the philosophical question is about (Rorty, 1970, p. 196ff).

There are obvious objections against this view. We can say about demons that they don't really exist. They only seem to exist for a hallucinating mind. But the existence of mental phenomena cannot be denied in this way. Even if demons do not exist, the belief in demons and the hallucinations do or did occur. Beliefs and visions are existing mental phenomena.

Suppose that in the future talk about C-fibers replaced all talk about pain. That would mean that one expression is used to refer to two different phenomena. It would be the same as when we decided to use the term 'man' to refer to both men and women. It would not mean that women no longer existed but that the word 'man' acquired the more general meaning of 'human being' which includes both sexes (cf. Levin, 1979, pp. 149ff). When a materialist says that the statement 'my C-fibers are firing' after replacing 'I am in pain' only applies to the physical phenomenon, then he must accept one of the following theses. a) Pain does not exist at all. It is a product of the imagination or superstition like demons and fairies. This view is nonsensical. b) Alternatively he could hold that when we say that we are in pain we really report on a state of the nervous system, even though we are not concious of such a state. The latter position is adopted by Rorty (ibid., p. 201). But this view presupposes that pain is identical with something material, which is the identity theory. So the elimination theory needs the identity theory which I have already criticized.

A materialist who wants to defend such a new linguistic convention must first provide a good reason for it by showing the identity of mental states and brain processes. This requires that what is true of the one is true of the other. The materialist puts the cart before the horse when he says that we must adapt language in such a way that what we say about the physical also applies to what is called the mental. He must argue first for what he wants to achieve in this way.

Rorty has in the meanwhile dropped eliminative materialism (1980, II, 6). He no longer wants to say that mental phenomena don't exist, because this approach leads to conceptual problems. He thinks now that the materialist should limit himself to the claim that when science will be sufficiently advanced no predictive, explanatory or descriptive power is lost if only physicalistic language is used for the mental. Suppose a cerebroscope which can provide information about everything in the brain gives all correct statements about the mental and can correct anything someone says about his pain. It is then pointless to wonder whether this shows that pain does not exist as a mental state. Talk about the mental would lose its meaning as reports about something real. (It can keep its meaning as a social exchange among people, as a language game.) If statements about the mental are not incorrigible, then the mental can no longer be distinguished as a separate category. When all research about the mental will be done by cerebroscopes and not at all by relying on statements from subjects about their own mental states, then the physical will have won, or so Rorty claims.

It is not surprising that a materialist with this ideal appeals to Wittgenstein (Rorty, ibid., p. 69 and passim). For according to Wittgenstein the realization of this ideal has already begun: statements which include mental terms are not statements about the mental. The materialist can add that once statements about the physical will be supplemented with descriptions of brain mechanisms, they will also describe what we now call the mental.

Rorty expresses faith in a future that his monistic view makes him regard as ideal. But this expectation is unrealistic. Physiology can already predict certain mental phenomena. In some cases it can do so better than their subject, as in the case of someone taking a mind altering drug for the first time. The use of the terminology for the mental has remained unaffected, however. A physiologist wil say that he knows what the effect of the drug is on the body and also how it influences the mind. He regards the effect on the mind as something different from the effect on the body.

I have already shown in my discussion of epistemic authority (ch. 3) that the physiologist's knowledge about the mental relies on statements of subjects about their own mental states. He must use those to arrive at his psycho-physiological correlations. Statements about one's own mental states may not be in principle incorrigible, but their private nature makes them sufficiently different from statements about the physical.

The proponents of the linguistic change argue that what they contemptuously call 'folkpsychology' is a theory. For that suggests that it can be replaced by a different theory. Thus P.S. Churchland regards 'folkpsychology' as a theory that uses mentalistic concepts like sensation, perception, desire, expectation, intention. According to many philosophers the concepts of 'belief' and 'desire' form the basis for explaining action in this theory. We think that often people act because they want something and have certain beliefs about what it takes to satisfy this desire (Churchland, 1986, pp. 299-300). This psychology is supposed to be a theory in so far as it provides explanations and predictions. Moreover the application of mental terms depends on learning generalizations. Thus a statement like 'I am in pain because I cut myself' is supposed to be a theoretical claim. According to Churchland this folkpsychology could be completely wrong. She contrasts it with psychology as it is practiced in universities, which she regards as a truly scientific form of psychology and which she thinks could eventually replace folkpsychology (ibid., pp. 303, 307, 384, 396).

It should be pointed out, however, that psychology as we know it uses mentalistic terms and thus, on Churchland's view, falls under folkpsychology. She does in fact include results of academic psychology in folkpsychology (p. 302). So it is better to use a neutral term for it: 'psychological psychology.'

If the term 'theory' is given the very broad interpretation that Churchland wants to give it, then folkpsychology is by definition a theory. A child who says that he does not want to eat something 'because he does not like it' is then already theorizing. But this is an artificial use of the term 'theory', which relies on very minimal criteria for the theoretical. It is not true that any generalization of our observations about the world amounts to a theoretical claim (Madell, 1986, p. 166). Churchland adopts her position because it allows her to claim that this so-called 'theory' can be replaced by a different, genuine theory, namely neuro-physiology.

We, the lay people, often do have views which are potential real theories. Some of these are shown to be wrong by psychological research. Folkpsychology is not a theory but it does contain a variety of more or less theoretical ideas.

The central question is whether basic concepts of psychological psychology such as belief, perception, sensation and desire can be replaced by neuro-physiological ones. Although these concepts do not constitute a theory in any strict sense, they have changed over time to some extent. Nevertheless it is unlikely that they will be discarded because incorrect. For although they are formed by thought they are very close to the phenomena. The concepts of sensations, beliefs, desires and feelings are much less theoretical than concepts from natural science or from the humanities like 'collective unconscious' (Campbell, 1986, pp. 145-146). For this reason the chance that they are inapplicable is much less great. Their meanings may change somewhat, but they continue to be mentalistic. The view that our actions result at least to some extent from our desires and beliefs is hardly a theory. The statement 'I am leaving because I want to have something to eat and I think that the baker is still open' does not rely on a theory, unless one is willing to call any simple thought a theory. Only careful analysis of human motivation requires theorizing. Churchland's view that folkpsychology may be completely wrong implies that *all* ordinary statements of the kind I have mentioned—such as 'I don't eat it because I don't like it'— as well as *all* statements of academic, psychological psychology could turn out to be wrong. A view that has these implications relies on a strong faith.

DETERMINISM AS A MOTIVE FOR MATERIALISM

We have seen that the desire for public verifiability as found in natural science is a motive for modern materialism. Another motive is the desire to acknowledge only what is covered by the laws that govern the physical (Smart, 1970, p. 54). But this motive is stronger than the theory it inspires.

This motive is clear in Davidson's materialism. He relies on three premises (1980, p. 208). 1) At least some mental events interact causally with physical events. 2) Where there is causality there is a law in the strict sense. 3) There are no strict deterministic laws that allow prediction and explanation of mental events (the anomalism of the mental). Davidson regards as mental what is described by certain concepts, such as belief and hope; the physical is what is described by physical concepts. These three principles result in a kind of contradiction, he argues. For it follows from 1 and 2 there must be at least some laws about the mental.

Davidson assumes the first two principles but tries to argue for the third. He claims that existing psycho-physical correlations or generalizations are not laws in the strict sense, but merely state probabilities. For when we give mental explanations we must consider the entire system of a person's beliefs and intentions. A description of this system cannot be translated into physical terms. Mental and physical predicates are not made for each other (ibid., p. 218). Our psycho-physical generalizations do have practical value. But they can be made precise only if we switch to the concepts of a comprehensive closed theory such as physics (p. 219). Precise laws can be formulated only within such a closed system.

Furthermore he assumes that when the mental is described as mental it is not subject to laws, but that it is when described as physical. He also assumes without argument that physicalistic terms can refer to mental events (p. 215).

He then argues as follows. Suppose that m (a mental event) causes p (a physical event). Then m and p fall under a strict law when described in a certain way. This law can only be physical, for the mental does not constitute a closed system as is required for strict laws. But if m falls under a physical law then it has a physical description, for this means that it is a physical event. This materialistic monism without psycho-physical laws reconciles the three principles, for if the mental is also physical it does fall under the laws of physics.

What is the force of this argument? The first principle states that interaction between the mental and the physical is possible. This is a plausible view. Furthermore it is possible that causality presupposes a strict law, but Davidson moves too fast when he lays this down as principle (2). In quantum theory strict determinism has been abandoned. Perhaps there are only statistical laws for the mental. So this premise is not very strong. On the other hand, if one accepts (2) one must also accept—and this is possible—that there are strict laws about the mental.

In this way the contradiction would be avoided. It may be that these laws have not yet been discovered for certain practical reasons such as the complicated nature of the causal relations at issue. Or it may be in principle impossible to discover these laws.

If such laws cannot be discovered for the mental, as Davidson argues, then how could they be found if the mental is included in the physical? That move does not solve any problems. The problem is merely claimed to be solved by a verbal maneuver.

On the one hand Davidson says that psycho-physical laws are impossible because, among other things, there are insurmountable problems in the translation of language about the mental into language about the physical. On the other hand he acts as if those problems do not exist when he states his conclusion. If the language about the mental cannot or can hardly be translated into language about the physical, then no (or hardly any) description of the mental in physical terms is possible. (Unless he thinks that the mentalistic description of the mental can be dropped completely and replaced by a physicalistic description. This would amount to eliminative materialism, which I have already criticized.)

An obvious solution to the problem Davidson brings up is that causality does imply a certain lawlikeness, but not strict lawlikeness. Regularities or tendencies as those found in psycho-physical correlations, are then sufficient for causal relations. Davidson himself also can detect psycho-physical causal interaction only on the basis of such tendencies, since he thinks that there are no strict psycho-physical laws, and he does not claim that we know any physical laws about the mental. So his dilemma depends on a view that he rejects as unsatisfactory (Ayer, 1984, p. 189).

Davidson's argumentation reveals his motivation. No strict deterministic laws about the mental have been found, but there must be such laws. That is why the mental is claimed to be physical, for this move allows us to say that there are such laws, although we have not found them.

The most fundamental reason for rejecting materialism is, I think, that it relies on a metaphysical reduction. Materialists think that everything that exists consists in one kind of phenomenon. Touch and kinesthetic sensations primarily give us our conception of the material. What is perceived by those senses is supposed to be all there is. What in fact presents itself to a variety of other senses, for instance pain and flavors, is thought to be identical with the objects of touch and kinesthetic sensation. What is provided by the senses, sensations, is supposed to be the same as their physiological operations.

Other materialists make statements like: my mental state is a (direct) experience of a correlated state of my nervous system, which is experienced in a different, indirect way by a physiologist (Wilson, 1979, pp. 81-82, 94). Such statements are reminiscent of double aspect theory, which will be discussed later. They are suggestive, but it is not clear how they should be understood.

In natural science discoveries are made that show that certain things are composed of other, until then unknown things. Scientific reduction consists in finding theories that explain various kinds of phenomena and this is quite useful. The danger of the kind of philosophical, terminological reduction that materialism relies on is that phenomena and problems associated with them are analyzed away. This can actually obstruct a scientific approach, as has been pointed out by Popper (1979, pp. 60-61).[1]

We don't know whether in the future a yet to be developed, utopian neuro-physiological theory as envisioned by P.S. Churchland (1986, p. 332 and passim) will make a reduction of the mental to the physical possible. Neuro-physiology continues to discover correlations between brain processes and mental processes. The increase in such discoveries is not a reason for adopting reductionism. But it is possible that revolutionary discoveries will be made that lead to a completely different neuro-physiological theory which does make a reduction plausible. It would be foolish to exclude such a possibility. But we have no knowledge of such a scientific revolution and we have to make do with what we know now. On the basis of our present knowledge we can only conclude that there are no good reasons for identifying the mental with the physical.[2]

Notes

1. For a further analysis of materialism, especially of those forms of it that purport not to be reductionistic, see Robinson (1982).
2. I will discuss the so-called token identity theory in the chapter about functionalism.

due to fatigue, an effort is required. So the suggestion that mental states are theoretical entities runs contrary to the facts.

The second objection also depends on the contrived nature of the view. This objection applies if theoretical entities are interpreted realistically. This is no longer common in modern science, but where mental states are concerned it is not unusual. According to such an interpretation it is logically possible to observe a theoretical entity. If this possibility is realized, which may happen in the future, the entity loses its theoretical status. On this view it must make sense to speak of observation of such an entity, although it has not yet happened. But it seems impossible that we would ever observe the sensations of others. As I have pointed out, we do know our own sensations, but by calling sensations theoretical entities one ignores this knowledge for some reason.

It follows that the proponent of this view commits himself to materialism about these entities. For he will be able to observe them eventually only if the mental is physiological in nature (Fodor, ibid., p. 99). This consequence as well makes the view unacceptable (see chapter 7).

The view that mental states are theoretical entities has strange consequences for the additional reason that on this view the ordinary mental states of others, such as their sensations and feelings, are theoretical entities. If this view implies materialism it follows that the existence of these mental entities in others is not only compatible with materialism, but that it would logically imply it. This is inconsistent. For the proponents of materialism think that the truth of their view depends at least in part on the discovery of empirical facts. Even more strangely, if materialism turned out to be false, which would happen if discoveries incompatible with it were made, it would follow that the mental states of others don't exist (Sussman, p. 285).

I think this shows that the view that mental states are theoretical entities is set up so that materialism follows. For the proponent of the identity theory is not inclined to deny the existence of sensations and feelings in others. And if those entities exist, then the view that they are theoretical entities implies that materialism is true.

Sometimes it does make sense to *suppose* that others are in some mental state or other which explains their behavior. This is so when we are not sure whether some mental state caused the behavior or, if we are sure about that, what mental state was the cause. But when we do know that some particular kind of mental state was the cause it is misleading to speak of 'supposing.' And it is clear that we can do more than merely make suppositions about the mental states of others (cf. ch. 6).

One may insist that we cannot get beyond suppositions, and that the mental is a theoretical construct, on the ground that we cannot perceive the sensations of others. But then one must keep in mind that sensations are not theoretical entities of the kind of which molecules used to be an example. For when the existence of molecules was merely supposed they had never yet been observed. On the other hand, we do know sensations like pain in our own case by reflection.

Under certain circumstances, as in nineteenth century physics, it makes sense to think that theoretical entities are in principle observable. Physiologists can of course also posit *physical* theoretical entities to explain behavior. But the postulation of mental states as theoretical entities is not a scientific, methodological move, but a philosophical one motivated by the desire to regard the mental as physical. For the idea that they are theoretical entities is followed by the claim that they must be material, because otherwise they cannot be observed, but it is clear from the start that they cannot be observed in others. It is characteristic of the mental that it cannot be observed directly in others. The demand that such observation is possible, because it is possible for material things, amounts to the demand that the mental has a material feature. This is not a methodological move, but philosophical extortion. If one really wants to apply the notion of a theoretical entity to the mental, part of the content of that notion—that it be in principle observable in all cases—must be given up.

THE MENTAL IS NOT ALWAYS AN HYPOTHESIS

A good example of the conception of the mental as a theoretical entity found in articles by Dennett, for instance his article about mental image in *Brainstorms* (1981, ch. 10). He does not use the term 'theoretical enti there, but he expresses roughly the same idea with the term 'hypothes Dennett discusses two approaches to mental images. One of these he the scientific approach. According to it mental images are defined a causes of beliefs about mental images as manifested in statements a them. On this view all our statements about mental images are theses. 'Science' must determine whether these hypotheses are right p. 179).

According to Dennett it is plausible to think of mental i structures in the brain that carry information. It is appropri them images because they have certain structural and functi ties. Science may show that the normal causes of our belief images are such brainstructures. In that case the mental i *identified* with the brain-structure. On the other hand if s ut these images turn out to be caused by things in the br the specific features of images, then we must say, according to Dennett, that our beliefs are (largely) false (ibid., pp. 186-187).

It is a mystery, however, how science could discover that beliefs about mental images are caused by structures in the brain which do or do not have the features of mental images. For in its search for causes modern science does not consider the question whether they resemble their effects. A can be the cause of B without in the least resembling B. Of course once the cause has been found one may form a view about the resemblance of A and B, but that is not a scientific issue, but a philosopical one.

Dennett makes the refutation or confirmation of identity depend on the question of resemblance between cause and effect, but that question is irrelevant. Suppose that someone's belief that he has a mental image of his parental home is caused by a brain-structure that 'resembles' that image. This resemblance does not confirm that the person has the mental image, and it is not a reason for identification. Nor does the absence of a resemblance between the brain-structure and the mental image show that the person does not have the mental image.

The following two aspects of Dennett's approach are rather striking. The first one is his application of the notion of an hypothesis to *all* beliefs of *all* people about mental images. In his article he uses 'beliefs' not only for theoretical opinions about the nature of mental images, but also for simple claims like 'I had a mental image of my parents' home.' He is talking not just about simple claims by people whose reports we have learned to distrust, but about claims by all people (ibid., pp. 177, 179). Mental images are defined as the causes of our beliefs about them, but otherwise we are not supposed to know anything about them yet. This is how he makes mental images theoretical entities.

A refusal to believe all claims people make about their mental states shows scientific caution. But to regard all reports about mental states as hypotheses, even when there is no reason to doubt that the subjects are sincere and capable, is a philosophical doubt for which there is no rational, empirical ground. It is the kind of methodical doubt that Descartes recommended for the existence of the external world, but applied to the existence of the mental. It is certain that at least some people sometimes have mental images. So the doubt which is presupposed by Dennett's position is as unfounded as the Cartesian doubt about the existence of the external world.

Some philosophers, for instance the materialist Armstrong (1971, p. 343), regard belief itself as a hypothetical, theoretical notion, not only in the case of others, but also in our own case. It follows that it is logically possible that further research results in the conclusion that no one ever had a belief. But that is a self-refuting position, because it is itself a belief (Lurie, 1979, p. 253).

My second objection to Dennett is that he assumes that any research about the mental will fall within the scope of natural science. It follows that the result can only be that mental images are something like brain-structures, which can be identified by physiologists. But this assumption is unjustified. It is possible to do psychological research according to a methodology that is rationally and empirically sound but without considering physiological entities such as brain-structures. Such research can be done, for instance, by means of introspection, as I argued in ch. 3. There I discussed Dennett's view that introspection is not a source of knowledge about our own mental states and concluded that it is implausible.

Mental images are pictorial

In an earlier book Dennett has argued that mental images are not pictorial, but descriptional and therefore do not deserve to be called images. We can imagine things without going into great detail. If I imagine a man I need not also have imagined him as having a certain hair colour or a hat. This is like describing, that can be as undetailed as I like, but according to Dennett quite unlike drawing a picture. In a picture a man must either have a hat on or not. Dennett gives another illustration. If seeing or imaging is having a mental image, then the image of a striped tiger *must* - obeying the rules of images in general - reveal a definite number of stripes showing, and one should be able to pin this down with such questions as 'more than ten?', 'less than twenty?', but often one cannot do this (1969, p. 135-136).

It is, however, not true that mental images are descriptional. There is a strong parallel between mental images and pictures, which holds much less for photographs. One can take a photo from a certain angle and distance what causes some aspects te be more or less prominent, but the photo shows always certain details in which the photographer is not interested. But this is different from mental images and pictures. They may both be detailed or schematic (stick figures), more or less resembling what they represent. In imagining no attention need be paid to certain aspects of the imagined thing, so that one cannot answer some questions about the content of the image. But the same applies to pictures and the more so when they are more schematic. Details or what from another point of view would come first can be omitted.

Dennett admits that in eidetic (photographic) imagery the subject can read off or count the details (p. 137, n. 1.). Other subjects without such a kind of imagery can also often do this, but to a lesser extent. Of course most mental images are not fully determinate, but only in some respects.

Concerning the example of the hat, if I imagine the head of a man I can usually say whether he is wearing a hat, because that is something special these days. If I did not imagine a hat, I know there is none. What Dennett says, that some details are simply not 'mentioned' in the imagining, applies to other things, such as hair color.

But, as Block has shown, some kinds of pictorial representations also have this option Dennett reserves for descriptional representation, namely the option of not going into detail. For example, a stick figure need not go into the matter of clothing (1981, p. 13-14).

The example of the mental image of a striped tiger is also weak. Sometimes one is able to determine roughly the number of stripes, sometimes one is not. But of course, the same holds for many pictures, even for photographs, which may be blurred. Take the example of an out-of-focus photograph of a page of type. There is a definite answer to 'How many letters on the page?', but there need not be an answer to 'How many image letters on the photograph?' (Fodor, 1976, p. 189, n. 22). Pictures are, as everyone can know, not always determinate in all respects. In an impressionistic painting one cannot count the stripes either. So, the fact that one cannot always determine the details of mental images is no argument against their being pictorial. It is enough that they represent pictorially, by resembling it, some aspects of the imagined thing.

Dreams

Dreams provide a good example of mental images. On the traditional view dreams are mental, inner experiences that we sometimes remember when waking up. Dennett tries to undermine this idea (ibid., ch. 8). He points to dreams whose contents are influenced by a disturbance in the dreamer's environment that wakes him up. He thinks that the traditional view requires foreknowledge of the future to explain this phenomenon. This is not true, however. Other possible explanations which Dennett mentions are plausible. For instance, the incorporation of a disturbance in a dream may happen quickly during the incident.

He uses this phenomenon to claim that we have no conscious dream experiences that we remember afterwards. Instead certain processes take place in the brain during sleep which, when we wake up, make us think of what we regard as the content of a dream. He calls this the cassette theory of dreams. The brain is supposed to make these cassettes during sleep (or even while awake). They are played when we wake up. In the case of a disturbance during sleep the brain pulls out a cassette that fits the disturbance. According to this theory there was no dream experience. The production of the cassette is unconscious and without any experience (ibid., 138). When we think we remember a dream, this is an illusion. Dennett thinks that neither this theory nor the traditional theory can be proved. For this reason it is an open, theoretical question whether dreams are experiences.

His theory of dreams is, however, no better than the traditional theory at explaining the influence of external disturbances on the content of dreams. For we would have to suppose either that there is foreknowledge of the future when the cassettes are produced, or that so many are produced that there is always one that happens to fit a particular disturbance. This is very improbable.

The whole theory is unacceptable. In the first place it runs counter to certain empirical indications. For example, physiological processes that normally accompany fear, excitement and the like occur during dreams that contain these emotions. This corroborates the view that we had them at that time

Secondly, this theory denies the reliability of any claim that we remember our dreams. One could then extend this denial to the memory of events in our environment, as Dennett indeed does. Descartes invented a malicious demon who misleads us continually about the world. Dennett seems to think that we must believe in a demon who deceives us systematically about our mental states.

Next, his move does not entirely eliminate experiences of dream contents. He seems to admit this himself (p. 138). His strategy, if successful, would only show that we did not have experiences while sleeping. But the existence of experiences with the same contents after we wake up is unaffected. Dennett could then claim that those experiences are only extrapolations of what we want to say about our dreams, and that thus the waking experience of these contents is also not real. But in chapter 3 I have already shown this position to be untenable. We may add here that we often do not capture the content of our dreams in words. With this my refutation is complete.

TWO FORMS OF FUNCTIONALISM

Generally speaking functionalism consists in an approach which considers things with respect to their role in a larger whole. Functional analysis is a form of explanation. A whole is analyzed into parts, and the functioning of the whole is explained by the functioning of the parts and their relations. Thus there is a form of functionalism that analyzes the workings of the mind as computation with mental representations, on the model of the operation of a digital computer.

A functionalist does not have to be a materialist, but I will only discuss a philosophical form of functionalism which often is given more or less materialistic import. I say 'more or less,' because different versions are materialistic in different degrees.

According to functionalism, mental states are functional states. The basic idea is that mental states are characterized in terms of their causal role, that is, in terms of their causal relation to sensory stimuli, the production of behavior, and other mental states, which are also defined in terms of output. So mental states are treated as theoretical entities that we don't know but postulate as an explanation (Lewis, 1983, p. 212).

Some functionalists think that a particular case of pain—as opposed to pain in general—is something physical, a brain process. But the difference with the materialistic identity theory is that according to those functionalists pain in general cannot be identified with a physical state, because pain can correspond to different organic states in different animals. Instead of using the more neutral term 'correspond' a functionalist says that 'pain' is a functional state that is 'realized' by various kinds of physical states. It may be objected that sensations and other mental phenomena are not abstract, but I will reserve my criticisms for later.

Other functionalists model mental states on the states of a Turing machine. It is difficult to explain this idea in a few words. One could try to understand it by analogy with a coke machine, which is in a certain internal state such that when we insert two quarters it produces a can. If we insert one quarter it acquires a different state which produces a can when we add more coins. These states of the machine can then be identified with the desire for coins, and when this desire is satisfied the machine produces something (Block, ed., 1983, p. 173). A Turing machine does not produce cans but information. It works according to rules that produce the following sorts of results. When the machine is in a particular state, for instance when a switch is on or off and a certain symbol is under the reader, it acquires another state and a different symbol is specified. At the same time the direction of the tape—or something like that—is determined. The language of such a machine consists in symbols, for instance 0 and 1, and transformation rules. Such a machine can be completely described by specifying for each possible state of the machine and for each symbol that can be under its reader, which symbol it should write down, what state it must take on next and in what direction the tape must move. This is the principle by which computers operate (Weizenbaum, 1976, ch. 2).

Causal Role

Functionalists think that what makes a pain a pain is its causal role: 'Pain is what is caused by external stimuli like pin pricks and what causes worry.' 'Worry' is then defined as 'what causes brow wrinkling.' This description gives an idea of the view, although of course an adequate definition would have to be much more detailed (Block, ed. 1983, pp. 173-174). Pain is identified with the property 'being causal' that causally connects inputs and outputs—which belong to the observable world—and which for that reason can be regarded as something existing. So pain is a theoretical entity.

By its emphasis on input and output functionalism is related to behaviorism, but the latter view has two serious defects that functionalism does not share. a) According to behaviorism mental states are not causes of behavior. They are mere dispositions, which amount only to the probability that specific behavior will occur. Functionalists, on the other hand, hold that at least some mental processes are causes, and in fact are nothing but causes. b) Functionalism takes into account not only the relationship of the mental with its stimuli and the ensuing behavior, but also connections between a mental state and other internal states.

Functionalism is reductionistic. For it reduces the mental to an input-output structure. The meaning of terms for the internal states is derived entirely from input, output and logical expressions. But in the non-materialistic versions of functionalism terms for the mental are not replaced by terms for other things that are observable. Something internal is admitted, but it is not mental or at least it does not have to be mental; it is the theoretical property of being causal.

As mentioned before the relationship to materialism varies. According to some philosophers (Armstrong, Smart, Lewis) functionalism implies that materialism is correct. Others (Fodor, Putnam) think that it implies that materialism is incorrect. I will first consider the form of functionalism closest to materialism.

1.

It has been argued that analysis of the concept 'pain' shows that this sensation fulfills the causal role R. A certain state of the nervous system also fulfills that role. Thus it follows that the pain is that state of the nervous system (Lewis, 1983, p. 207). The functionalist aspect of this view is that the meaning of 'pain' is identified with a definite causal role. This claim relies on the topic-neutral analysis of the materialistic identity theory (Smart), according to which the mental is indefinite and needs to be determined. The mental is then determined in the way just specified.

Pain is a functionally specified state of the nerves and brain. Alternatively it is argued that the common notion of pain is inconsistent. Thus it is better to forget about the properties that we ordinarily regard as essential to pain and to accept the claim that pain is the brain state that causes the usual effects (Dennett, 1981, ch. 11, p. 228).

It is admitted that pain may be a different brain state in a species different from ours. The correlation and thus also the identity with a type of physical state is specific to each species (Kim, 1983, p. 235). Lewis has claimed that the denotation of 'pain' may vary but the concept of pain is the same for different species (1983b, p. 233).

2.

The proponents of the 'pure' form of functionalism have raised the following objection to the materialistic version of the view. Even when only one species is at issue, human beings, the same psychological function can be fulfilled by different brain states. Sometimes when one part of the brain is damaged, another part takes over its function after a while. In that case there is not even identity between a type of mental state and a type of brain state within one human being (Block-Fodor, 1983, p. 238).

According to the pure version of functionalism sensations like pain are functional states of the organism, and this hypothesis is regarded as compatible even with dualism. The functional states of the system and its inputs and outputs are in themselves neither mental nor physical (Putnam, 1982, p. 436). It is conceivable that a state that is not physical or chemical in nature plays a causal role that characterizes a certain mental state. Even if our actual pains are all physical it is conceivable that they are not physical in other beings. In short one might say functionalism in its purest form would be the view that the mental is a theoretical entity that must not be interpreted realistically. That is, we must not assume that it will at one point be observable. The less pure version that is at issue here is the view that we will be able to interpret this entity realistically but that at this point we are too ignorant to do so.

Despite this reservation many functionalists interpret the general principle that mental states are functional states to mean that they are identical with states of the table of a Turing machine. This table works with probabilities so that a particular kind of state can lead to different results (Putnam, ibid., p. 434).

If a mental state is a state of a machine table, it is not a brain state. Given a table of certain functions of a human being, we cannot identify the states on the table with brain states. For it is plausible that all kinds of machines without brains are described by that same table, since they can execute the same functions.

For this reason Putnam and Fodor argue that mental states are identical to functional states and that the latter are not physical states. Pain is not a thing but the *property* we have when we are in the state that is caused by something of type X and that is the cause of something of type Y. What cases of pain have in common and what makes them pain is their causal role R, which is not something physical. So this form of functionalism leaves open *what* fulfills these functional roles; it could be all kinds of things, although it is expected to be physical. But the fact that it is physical remains to be shown (cf. Fodor, 1968, pp. 112ff.).

CRITICISMS OF FUNCTIONALISM

Let me first make a comment about the materialistic version of functionalism. My criticism of the materialistic identity theory covers most but not all of this view.

The materialism that often comes with functionalism is known as token as opposed to type physicalism. Sometimes this seems to mean that qualitatively identical 'tokens', particular instances of a mental state, are identical with qualitatively different physical states or processes. According to functionalists a single mental state can be realized by a large variety of physical states that have no necessary and sufficient physical characterization (Block, 1983, p. 295). Qualitatively identical instances of pain in different individuals would then be identical with qualitatively different physical states. M1 would be identical with F1 in one case, with F2 in another case, where the M1's are qualitatively identical but F1, F2 etc. differ qualitatively.

This is an impossible view. For if M1 is identical with F1 and F2, then F1 and F2 are identical, whereas the idea is supposed to be that they are not identical.

Sometimes token identity means that qualitatively different instances of one mental type (or kind) are identical with instances of different physiological kinds. The question is then what feature of the physical events explains that the mental events belong to the same mental kind (cf. Block-Fodor, 1983, p. 239). Suppose that a particular instance of pain is identical with a physical process having properties a and b, and that another qualitatively different case of pain is identical with a physical process with properties c and d. Then it follows that the two cases of pain have nothing in common. But this is an unacceptable result. If one does not accept the view that different cases of pain, or of other kinds of sensations, have something in common, then one should abstain from studying them.

In addition the identification of a mental process and a physical process runs into the same problems that we have discussed before.

Let us now turn to the proper, pure form of functionalism. The view that a mental state is identical to a functional state is inspired by the model of the Turing machine. This model does not work, however. I will only discuss a few of the many objections that have been raised against this view.

The theory is not sufficiently abstract. If persons A and B differ only in that A's probable reaction to pain is 'ouch' and B's 'shoot,' it follows according to this theory that A's pain is different from B's pain. For in a Turing machine a different output implies that there is a different functional state, and thus according to functionalism it implies that in the present case there is a different pain. There is no need to argue that this result is undesirable.

Furthermore psychological states have structural relations, for instance, 'A beliefs that P and Q' implies 'A believes that P'. A machine that represents psychological states as an unstructured list cannot make or represent these connections. Consequently it cannot display the productivity of these states, which depends on these relations (Block-Fodor, 1983, pp. 243-248).

Functionalism aims to establish parallelism between mental states and other states, and it chooses, of course, to establish a parallel with functional states. Block argues (1983, pp. 275ff.) that functionalism is either too broad or too narrow to establish such a parallelism. It is clear that it is too broad because an example can be constructed in which the population of an entire country of significant size is the realization of one human mind according to the Turing model. For an example can be described in such a way that a population satisfies the input and output requirements for a machine, even if the individuals each execute only a small mechanical task. So it is necessary to add a restriction to functionalism that rules out that such a population or a swarm of bees feels pain. Putnam added such a restriction (1982, p. 434), but this move is unsatisfactory because ad hoc (Block, 1983, p. 279). I will return later to the question why functionalism is too narrow.

Block thinks that *any* physical description of inputs and outputs results in a version of functionalism that is too narrow or too broad. He uses an argument that functionalists themselves have used against materialism. The problem with materialism according to this argument, is that one mental state can be realized by an indefinitely large number of different physical states. These physical states cannot be characterized in a way that provides sufficient and necessary conditions for a realization of that mental state. But if this is correct, then it also applies to inputs and outputs. For the following example shows that the brain structure that is regarded as a physical realization of mental states can serve as an essential component of the in- and outputs. Suppose that someone is burnt so seriously that he can display no reactions, but his brain still works. Furthermore his brain constitutes an essential part of in- and outputs because the electro-encephalogram is translated into Morse code. If there are such cases there is no physical characterization that applies to the in- and outputs of all and only mental systems (Block 1983, p. 295). Such a characterization will include beings that don't have mental states and exclude ones that do. So the criticism that the functionalist directed against materialism applies to his own view as well.

A Turing machine is too simple to serve as a model for human behavior and mental life. Putnam also drew this conclusion. A psychological state cannot be a state of a table for a Turing machine. For the state of the machine determines what follows, whereas my pain does not.

A psychological state can also not be identified with a disjunction of machine states—that is, something of the form 'a or b or c.' For a mental state such as jealousy is not a momentary state; its identity depends on learning and memory. 'X is jealous of Y' implies that someone has learned that X and Y are persons and in addition it implies a lot about social relations. States of a Turing machine are, on the other hand, momentary and not dependent on learning and memory. The latter processes can produce a state in a machine, but the identity of the state of the machine does not depend on them, unlike jealousy.

One could try to meet this objection by claiming that this mental state is a disjunction each disjunct of which consists in a machine state and a tape that contains the recently acquired information. But this approach deprives the theory of its original content. For the idea was to use the machine table as a model for a psychological theory. It turns out that this is not possible (Putnam, 1982, pp. 291-299).

It might be possible to deal with certain criticisms by finding other analogies between humans and machines. There is less room to play with the description of machines, which are known completely, than with the description of human beings. So one could model the description of human beings as much as possible on the description of machines. This strategy is not unfruitful, but pushed too far it is vulnerable to fundamental objections, as we saw in discussing Dennett's views.

Spectrum Inversion

The idea of the inversion of the spectrum is the idea that for someone the spectrum of colors might be switched. The possibility of such an inversion suggests that different mental states can have the same function. Suppose that a person has always worn lenses that make him see red as green and green as red and that invert other colors as well. This inversion would probably have no effect on how that person functions. He would apply names to colors in the same way we do even though he has different color impressions. When he sees green he is taught to say red. Red plays the same role for him as green does for us. So red cannot be identical with the causal role R. For then green is also identical with R, and it would follow that red and green are identical (cf. Shoemaker, 1983, pp. 258, 263; Block, 1983, p. 302 fn. 21).

If this conception of spectrum inversion is correct, then it counts not only against functionalism, but also against the claim that we can know the mental states of others. For we would not notice anything about the person in question except for his hardware, the lenses. A functionalist can say then that there is a difference in input because of the lenses. But next we can leave out the lenses and suppose that different people under the same physical circumstances yet have different color impressions.

It is hard to assess the idea that this would make no difference to their functioning. It would make no difference to selecting objects, but maybe it would influence other sorts of (emotional) behavior. Furthermore it is striking that the idea of the interchangeability of mental contents is only plausible for colors. This fact makes colors a special case, one that is nevertheless worth mentioning.

THE INCORRECTNESS OF DEFINITIONS IN TERMS OF INPUT AND OUTPUT

It is incorrect to define something real and empirical in terms of its causes and effects. A definition of the mental along these lines presupposes that it is a theoretical entity. I have already argued against that view. But let us consider the implications of this kind of definition of the mental.

Like behaviorists, functionalists use output to define the mental. Some functionalists, for instance D. Lewis, take output to be behavior in the ordinary sense. This view is vulnerable to the same objections as behaviorism. When there is no behavior due to circumstances, as in the case of paralysis, these functionalists will have to say that there is no mental state, when in fact there is one. So the definition is too narrow (Block, 1983, p. 283).

Some functionalists define pain in terms of input (Putnam, 1982, p. 434). They use the fact that we feel pain when stimulated in certain ways as support for the claim that pain is the reception of those stimuli. But we can easily imagine that a person is in pain whereas there is no input or it is completely different from the normal input specified by the definition. In that case the functionalist must say about a person who is in pain that he is not. A functionalist cannot consistently ascribe pain to a sufferer who does not have the kind of input specified in the definition of pain in terms of its causal role. For pain is identical with causal role R as described for people in general, and the person in question does not have R (cf. Horgan, 1984, p. 459). Lewis has tried to solve this problem as follows (1983a, pp. 217-219). He claimed that a paralyzed person who displays no pain behavior is in pain, because he is in a physiological state which in human beings, but not in other species, is identical with pain. He wants to avoid the radical form of physicalism according to which pain is the same physiological state in all organisms. Owens (1986, pp. 60-61) has shown, however, that this view implies that a human being is in pain when he is in one physiological state, and a Martian when he is in an entirely different one. It is then completely unclear on what ground we can say that they are both in pain.

New and deviant inputs and outputs can be included in the definition. This results in a disjunctive list. The question arises then what different instances of pain have in common. A disjunctive definition can determine what makes something a case of pain, but it does so without showing why the different cases of pain are all instances of the same sensation. 'Deviant' can mean here that stimuli and reactions are familiar but that they do not normally accompany pain. The inclusion of deviant stimuli and responses in the definition of pain would make pain indistinguishable from other sensations, since there would be no stimuli and responses specific to pain.

Pain is not identical with the response to pain, as I have urged against behaviorism. Nor is it identical with the stimulus or cause, even if combined with a response.

Functionalism does admit internal states, but only insofar as they are implied by definitions in terms of in- and output. As a result when these in- and outputs are not there the internal state drops out as well. The problem with this approach is that in fact the internal states are logically independent from the in- and outputs. It is unlikely that a pain occurs without any cause or effect, but it is conceivable. Sometimes we don't know what caused a particular pain and merely suppose that there must be some cause or other. Consequently it is incorrect to include cause and effect in the definition of pain and other sensations. This is wrong regardless of whether one takes behavior or physiological processes to be the relevant causes and effects. If pain were by definition identical with what happens to someone when he cuts himself, burns himself and the like, then beings in another world would by definition feel what we call pain when they cut themselves. In fact, however, they might feel something completely different. The question whether someone feels pain when he cuts himself is an empirical, not a logical question.

We saw that many functionalists treat mental states as theoretical entities that we don't know but posit for explanatory purposes (Lewis, 1983, p. 212; Putnam, 1982, p. 330). I have already argued against this approach: we do know mental states, and we know them to have definite characteristics. For example, we know certain properties of pain such as its duration and intensity (Sussman, 1975, p. 281). This point is unaffected by the fact that there are problems with the notion of pain. Dennett claims that the normal use of the term 'pain' supports both the idea that for pain 'being' is the same as 'being perceived' and the idea that pain can exist unperceived (1981, p. 225). I have discussed this issue in chapter 1 and proposed a possible solution. But however interesting this question may be, it is of marginal importance for ordinary usage of the term 'pain,' since the cases at issue are quite unusual. Dennett uses these marginal cases to argue that we should ignore the nature of pain as experienced by us, which is in fact essential to pain. This move is arbitrary, however. (Dennett's own theories are much more problematic, as I have shown.) The essence of 'pain' is determined by the way it appears to us (Kripke, 1981, p. 152). Pain is not an unknown x about which we can say that it is identical with a functional property or a brain state. The essence of pain is revealed by our experience of it.

Functionalism defines a mental state as what fulfills a certain causal role. Physiological discoveries show a brain state fulfills that role. Some functionalists think it follows from this fact that the mental state is identical with that brain state (Lewis, 1983, p. 207). But a mental state is more than its causal role. Furthermore we need not speak of 'the' item that fulfills that role. If the mental state is defined as 'an' item that fulfills this role, then the argument no longer works and the identity with the brain state is not secured. It is possible that the mental state is a causal factor in addition to the brain state. I will argue for this view when I defend the theory of double causation.

The materialist functionalist thinks that the mental state is nothing other than its causal role, but that the physiological state is something in itself in addition to being what fulfills some causal role. But if both the mental state (M) and the brain state (B) are nothing other than what fulfills a causal role (CR), then one may substitute CR for both M and B in 'M=B'. The result is trivial: 'CR=CR'. This is not the functionalist's intention. Now a physiologist will not report that a brain state is identical with its causal role, but that it has a causal role. Reliance on that observation allows the functionalist to arrive at the non-trivial result that the mental state is identical with the brain state. This shows that he uses 'is' in 'M is CR' in a different way from 'is' in 'B is CR.' In the first statement 'is' states an identity, in the second it serves to ascribe a property to B. It is true of the mental state as well, however, that it is not identical with the functional role, but that it has this role. In any case the functionalist's formulation does not show that the contrary is true, he merely claims that it is.

The functionalist definition does not do justice to mental states, because apart from their causal role they have a nature in themselves. Pain is something that *has* a causal role, it is not identical with that role (cf. Margolis, 1978, p. 74). It may be possible to analyze this sensation into two elements, one of which is functional in nature, the other not. For after certain surgical operations people claim that they still feel pain, but that it no longer bothers them because they no longer feel the need to get rid of it (Trigg, 1970, p. 134). In the case of mental images it is even clearer that they are not identical with their causal role, which is often very hard to determine.

Terms for the mental do not only serve as explanations but also as descriptions and reports (Cornman, 1969, pp. 187ff.). If psychological concepts are introduced as theoretical entities they are introduced primarily as explanations, and their function as descriptions derives from their explanatory role. But the descriptive role of consciousness and other psychological concepts is in fact equally important (Margolis, 1984, p. 62). At least in our own case their descriptive role is in fact primary. Elimination of terms for the mental on the ground that they are not needed for explanatory purposes, would not be legitimate. We don't claim that we have a headache merely in order to explain our behavior. Our claim that we have one is a report even if it doesn't explain anything.

In response to the objection that functionalism cannot account for the content of sensations, for 'what it is like' to have them, Smith and Jones have proposed the following solution. They claim that no such account is necessary, because knowing what a sensation is like is not knowledge of a subjective *fact* (1986, pp. 218-219). They are forced to take recourse to this defense, but it is a completely implausible move. If a diabetic knows what kind of sensation precedes an oncoming attack, what it feels like, he does know a subjective *fact* that is very useful to him and that lets him know that he should take his medication. The same point applies to more common examples like pain, itches and dizziness, although the familarity of these phenomena may make the point less obvious in those cases.

Smith and Jones think that the claim that functionalism does not give sensations to a person causes no problems for the theory (ibid., p. 218). Of course this is true, but it is a problem that the theory does not and cannot give any *idea* of the nature of the sensations. Similarly it does not count against the theory that it does not enable someone to recognize a sensation at once. But it is a problem that according to functionalism we only infer the existence of a sensation indirectly on the basis of causes and behavior, whereas a subject in fact recognizes his own sensations directly. Thus the theory is in conflict with the facts.

Perhaps philosophical functionalism is a better theory than behaviorism and materialism, as Putnam has claimed. It is a broader theory which allows incorporation of elements of both behaviorism and materialism. But this does not imply that it is correct. We do not have to choose from these three theories.

Insofar as it is no more than an hypothesis that encourages research about mechanistic models for organisms (Putnam, 1982, p. 435) there is nothing wrong with it and it is even very interesting. But that is a scientific approach and not the philosophical theory that some philosophers want it to be.

Functionalists want to determine the essence of mental states on the basis of its causes and effects (Block, 1983, p. 286). Science studies these relations, but this does not mean that philosophical functionalism is a scientific theory. For science is not concerned with 'essences,' but tries to explain the existence of its objects and the changes they undergo. Sometimes it is concluded that a phenomenon or aspect thereof does not exist. But in science there is no attempt to eliminate the properties of phenomena by means of definitions.

HISTORICAL BACKGROUND:
THE PRINCIPLE OF VERIFICATION

In general I am not concerned with the historical background of the views I have discussed, but I want to make an exception for Carnap's influential article 'Psychology in Physical Language.' Carnap gave a simple argument. He claimed that the meaning of a statement does not go beyond what can be verified. This was a tenet of Viennese neo-positivism: the meaning of a statements is its method of verification. According to Carnap something that is publicly observable is verifiable, and only physical events can be so verified. He assumed—as almost everyone did—that statements about the mental have meaning. It follows on his view that they can be verified and that they have the same content as statements that only contain terms for the physical (1932, pp. 173-175 and passim). A similar position is found in Hempel (1935).

This is a dogmatic view. These philosophers did not consider the question what is the best way of verifying a particular statement, or whether all statements can be verified (publicly). They simply claimed that the same approach had to be followed everywhere, because it is— they believed—used in natural science. It has to be this way, therefore it is this way, and if it is not this way, so much the worse for the facts. It is not necessary to criticize this view here since this has been done enough elsewhere (Urmson, 1969, pp. 169ff.). I want to point out, however, that it is part of the background of several of the views I have discussed. It is quite clear that it is an important motive for behaviorism and materialism. As we saw, Ryle claims time and again that if behaviorism is not true, then we cannot know anything about the minds of others.

The view of the later Wittgenstein can also be understood against the background of Carnap's and Hempel's views, although the connection is not as direct as in the case of logical behaviorism. Suppose the conclusion that the mental states of others must be physical, because otherwise statements about them are not verifiable, strikes one as implausible, but one does not want to give up the principle of verification. What view should one adopt then? Wittgenstein's solution is roughly that statements about the mental states of others do not have meaning in the ordinary sense of being about those mental states. He did not accept Carnap's argument that statements about the mental have meaning in the ordinary sense and that they therefore are verifiable in the way in which statements about physical objects are. Rather he argued that they cannot be verified in that way and therefore they do not have meaning in the ordinary sense. The denial of Carnap's view—which was held by almost everyone—that statements about the mental have meaning in the ordinary way, allowed Wittgenstein to avoid the problem of verification and to save the principle of verification, which he accepted (1953, section 353).

Furthermore his view is that statements that are regarded as being about the mental states of others may be made on the basis of behavior. But they are not statements about that behavior, or about the mental states. This is Wittgenstein's linguistic behaviorism. He thinks that the statements in question cannot be verified, that is, we cannot determine whether they correspond to the other person's mental states. We can only determine whether these statements conform to the current use of the language, the ruling conventions.

There is also a connection between functionalism and the view that verifiability of statements about the mental requires that the mental is physical, although much has happened in the meanwhile. Functionalism comes somewhat closer to mentalism, but it refuses to acknowledge the empirical nature of the mental in our own case. Since the mental is regarded as a theoretical entity it is denied its essential nature. (This is a connection with Wittgenstein, who thought that this nature could not be expressed in language.) It does not follow that the mental is physical, although this possibility hovers in the background. On a realistic conception of theoretical entities, it is possible that at some time they will be observable and that their existence will be verified. If we are ever to be able to observe the mental in others, it must be physical. But this verification is put off until later. Functionalism is more sophisticated than Carnap and Hempel's view—in fact Hempel's views later developed in this direction. But it is also motivated by the desire that statements about the mental be verifiable in the way in which statements about the physical are. In fact, however, the existence of mental states in others is detected in a different, indirect way, as I have argued.

As Searle points out it is a mistake to exclude the subjectivity of mental states by definition. It is a given that mental states are not objective in the sense of being accessible to all in the same way in which they are accessible to their subject. If 'science' is the term for the objective and systematic truths that we can assert about the world, then subjectivity is an objective, scientific fact.

In conclusion I want to discuss Searle's view about the mind-body problem. He combines a functionalistic position with the mentalistic view that I want to defend in the next chapter. On the one hand Searle acknowledges the special nature of the mental, unlike functionalists. He admits not only its subjectivity, but also its intentionality and the fact that the mental causes behavior. Furthermore mental processes are supposed to be caused by brain states. But at the same time—and this is the functionalist side of his view—mental processes are features of the brain, realizations of the brain system at a higher level. He compares the mental with the solidity of physical objects, which is caused by their molecular microstructure and which is at the same time qua macro-structure a realization of this microstructure.

This view leads him to propose the following answer to the question as to how thoughts, which have no weight, can cause motion. Thoughts are not weightless, Searle suggests. For when we think there is activity in the brain. This activity causes corporeal movements, but is at the same time identical with the mental at the micro level. Since mental states are features of the brain, they can be described at two levels: at the higher

168

level they can be described in mental terms, at the lower level in physical terms. He thinks that the same causal forces can be described at both levels (1984, pp. 21, 26).

I disagree with Searle for reasons explained in my discussion of functionalism. In particular I do not see how a description of the mental could be a description of the macrostructure of the brain, and how a description of the brain could be a description of the microstructure of the mental. A description of the macrostructure of the brain is not phrased in mental terms, but in physiological terms. And a description of the mental uses mentalistic, and not physiological terms.

9. THE RELATION OF MIND AND BODY

The discussion of the previous two chapters leads to the conclusion that materialism and functionalism also do not provide a solution to the mind-body problem. Someone who thinks that the mental is something different from the physical is a dualist in some sense. This does not mean, however, that such a person is necessarily a metaphysical dualist in the Cartesian sense. A metaphysical dualist thinks that the material and the mental are two different kinds of substances, that is, things that can exist apart, without each other. Descartes argued in his *Méditations* (pp. 487-488) that these two 'things' are not only distinguishable but separable. Someone who rejects the separability but accepts the distinguishability of the mental and the physical as two different kinds of properties is also in some sense a dualist. Even materialists start with this view, but they try to get rid of it. Anyone who maintains that the mental and the physical are distinguishable and different can be called a mentalist.

Mentalism and dualism both run into the problem of the relation between mind and body. Ever since Descartes philosophers have labored over this problem. There is an abundance of views about the issue, but no satisfactory solution has yet been found. I will discuss several of these views and argue that one of them is more plausible than the others. This discussion will clarify various aspects of the problem. I will first discuss a theory which occupies an intermediate position. This theory is monistic, but does recognize that mental and physical properties are different.

DOUBLE ASPECT THEORY

According to double aspect theory (DAT) the mental and the physical are two aspects of one thing or substance, like the two sides of a coin. This is a kind of monism, although the one substance does have two aspects. It is not reductionistic. When the one thing or substance is omitted, on the ground that it cannot be known, the view can approach materialism (cf. Feigl, 1967, p. 82). But this move can also bring it close to idealism, as I will show.

DAT was first proposed by Spinoza. Descartes had claimed that the mind and the body are essentially different: bodies are extended, minds are not, their essence consisting in thought. He concludes from this that mind and body are different, separable entities. But this does not follow. Descartes assumed that mind and body are 'things.' Given this assumption it is plausible that they are in principle separable if distinguishable. But if extension and thought are properties they might well belong to the same thing. For a thing can have very different properties. For instance a statue can be old, beautiful, and made of marble. We distinguish the properties, but that does not mean that there are different things or substances.

In favor of the view that minds are substances it has been argued that unlike many properties minds are not subject to gradation, that is, qualitative or quantitative differentiation (Teichman, 1974, p. 20). But that is not clear. There is gradation among minds according to what they can contain or process. The activity of paying attention, which is an essential activity of the mind, does vary in intensity.

In his *Ethics* (1677, Part 1, P10, Sch.) Spinoza denied that the mind is a substance and claimed that not only human beings but everything has extension and consciousness (panpsychism). The corporeal and the mental are two aspects of human beings. This idea can be illustrated by the following image: a figure can be concave one side, convex on the other. It depends on one's point of view which aspect one mentions. A person can be conceived either as bodily or as thinking.

Only Two Aspects

Variations on Spinoza's basic idea have been developed by many philosophers. The substance of which the mental and the physical are supposed to be two aspects has often been eliminated, quite explicitly by Prince (1885, p. 191) and Feigl (1967, p. 82). What is a state of consciousness from the point of view of inner self-perception is a process in the nervous system or movement in the organism from the point of view of sense perception (Lewes, 1877, p. 155; Erdmann, 1907, pp. 203, 207). Forms of this view have been adopted by many philosophers. Usually they have abandoned Spinoza's panpsychism, restricting the view to human beings, or to the higher organisms generally.

When no substance is admitted, only the two aspects are left. DAT has sometimes turned into a form of materialism or idealism. This happens when it is claimed that one of the two aspects is more fundamental than the other one, and that the first one alone is real, while the other one is merely a way of conceiving of the first one. Thus according to Prince the mental alone is real. Corporeal motion is an impression that is caused by the way in which others perceive this reality. A philosopher who regards the mental as the primary reality will say that from the outside mental feelings or strivings appear as material, whereas reality is known directly in inner self-perception. For Schopenhauer the mental, which he identifies with the will, is reality as it is in itself. This reality appears to our senses—touch and vision—in the guise of material objects, but this is no more than an appearance (1818, pp. 152ff.). I have already mentioned Feigl's modern linguistic form of this view in chapter 7.

Materialistic versions of DAT are sometimes presented as forms of the materialistic identity theory. It is claimed that the material—the electrochemical operation of the brain—is experienced from the inside as thought or feeling. But that is no more than a subjective perception or appearance of the physical, which alone exists objectively (Wilson, 1979, p. 94).

On my view mental and physical phenomena are equally real. The view that one of them is primary or the only one that is real rests on personal preference and is philosophically arbitrary. I don't see how something of a particular nature can appear as something completely different. That view requires some conceptual connection between the mental and the physical. Nagel, who adopts the Spinozistic view, acknowledges that we have no notion of such a connection (1986, pp. 46-48).

This kind of monism presupposes that every mental event is parallelled by a physical event. This is denied by some philosophers, for instance Bergson (1896, pp. 83, 253) and Popper. In *The Self and its Brain* Popper assumes that consciousness is not a succession of often repeated elementary or atomic perceptions. It follows that there is no room for the idea of a one-one correspondence between mental states and brain states, since it is no longer clear what should correspond to what (1977, p. 90). Although there is something to this view, it is possible to distinguish different perceptions in the mind, which, although they may not be atomic, do often have more or less the same content. Secondly, brain processes often or always vary at least slightly. Thus even if all of a person's perceptions were slightly different, it would still be possible that they each correspond to slighty different physical processes. Popper sees this. He does not, however, consider the possibility that perceptions are atomic, in the sense of being unanalyzable and yet different, and that each is accompanied by a different physical process.

I don't think the kind of argument he gives can show that there is no correspondence. Such arguments do point out that it is hard to establish what mental entity, state or process corresponds to what physical one.

DAT as well as materialism would be untenable if it were shown that there were mental phenomena that didn't have physical correlates. There is no proof that there is a physical correlate for every mental state, but discoveries continue to be made in this area. If progress in this area lags it will not be concluded that there are no physical correlates. Research will continue or it will be assumed that given the current state of science we lack the techniques and instruments necessary to obtain further results. The idea that there are physical correlates for all mental states has become a kind of postulate like the postulate that everything has a cause. This postulate is supported by already established results.

What do proponents of DAT say about the interaction between mind and body? Consider the factors P(hysical) 10, 11, etc. and M(ental) 10, 11 etc. If we suppose that F's and M's with the same number occur simultaneously, they do not interact because they are aspects of the same. In addition it is often claimed that F's only cause other F's and M's other M's. Of course according to DAT an F in itself cannot cause an M or vice versa. But since F and M together represent the substratum, one could say that together they cause the next appearance of this substratum, F11 and M11. Since F10 and M10 are two appearances of the same item, FM10—the substratum of F10 and M10—is the cause of FM11. Empirically this amounts to the idea that F10 and M10 together cause F11 and M11, the thesis I will defend.

THE PERSON THEORY

Strawson (1971) has advocated a monistic theory of the person according to which the human being, the person, is a primary entity, and the mental and the physical are aspects that are abstracted from the person. He thinks that other theories cannot account for the notion of the 'I.' The notion of the person is irreducible, that is, it cannot be analyzed into components. A person is something that necessarily has both mental and physical characteristics (Strawson, ibid., p. 102). When we speak about people we assume such a unitary entity. We say 'when he fell through the air he wondered whether his parachute would open' and not 'when his body fell through the air his mind wondered whether his parachute whould open.' (Shaffer, 1968, p. 55).

Strawson thinks that we must take predicates that refer to human actions to be central (ibid., p. 111). Some actions indicate the unity of the human being particularly well, such as writing a letter, playing tennis, going for a walk. Those actions do not raise questions about mental states that correspond in another person to his perceptible movements. And when we ourselves perform these actions we don't have better knowledge than others about the mental states involved. In fact I do often know more about my motives and intentions, but others can know equally well what motivates me in these actions while performing them.

At least for actions that include a definite pattern of bodily movements and no distinctive mental states, the distinction between the mental and the physical seems artificial (ibid., p. 111).

One may be favorably struck by Strawson's view that the notion of a person cannot be analyzed, since that notion is notoriously difficult to dissect. Attempts at analysis of this notion are never quite satisfactory. I think that they are usually instructive, however, and I find them more interesting than Strawson's attempt to drop the whole controversy. His monism only concerns the 'I' which is neither physical, nor mental, nor a composite of the two. The concept of a pure individual consciousness that is the owner of particular kinds of states, and which the Cartesians identified with the 'I,' is supposed to be a secondary notion (ibid., p. 103). Strawson maintains, however, a dualism of physical and mental properties.

For this reason I will only comment on his attempt to emphasize the unity of the person as an empirical being. The distinction between the physical aspect of an action—the movement—and its mental aspect—the desire and the accompanying thought—is harder to draw for some actions than for others, but it can always be done. When going for a walk we have the intention to relax by calm bodily movements and appreciation of our environment, without which the movements would not constitute taking a walk. This intention can be distinguished from the movements. As Ayer observed in 'The Concept of a Person,' however close the relation between our mental states and their physical expression may be, there is a relation between distinguishable terms. We can sometimes observe in some sense what others think or feel, but this is always an interpretation, where the sign must be distinguished from what it signifies (Ayer, 1973, p. 97; cf. Williams, 1973, ch. 7).

These remarks lead back to an issue I have already discussed, however, in chapter 6. Strawson's monism is limited, since it primarily concerns the pure 'I' and does not seem to contain the claim that mental and physical properties are identical, but perceived from different perspectives.

NEUTRAL MONISM

Another form of monism is the neutral monism of Bertrand Russell (1921). It is based on 'the given' or 'experiences' which are neither physical nor mental. The physical and the mental are constructed from this. When the given is conceived of as physical it falls under physics, when it is considered as an impression it falls under psychology. Something can belong to both the physical and the mental or to just one of them. Insofar as something is considered to belong to both, this monism is a kind of parallellism.

The question is, however, whether this 'given' is really neutral. Since it is something like a sensation, it would seem to be mental (cf. Russell, 1921, p. 98). Thus the view resembles Berkeley's idealism, where the physical is a construction from mental impressions (Quinton, 1968, p. 216).

The problem with this view is furthermore that there are givens that are only mental, such as mental images and feelings. No doubt classification and abstraction by the intellect play a role in constructing notions like 'dream' and 'joy.' But if the given is sometimes only mental then the view that the mental is constructed from something more fundamental is untenable. It must be at least in part fundamental and thus we are again faced with the problems that were supposed to be avoided by monism.

DUALISM AND MENTALISM

As we saw, according to Descartes's dualism the mind can exist by itself. This implies that the soul is immortal. He thought that only thought necessarily belongs to the I. For we can doubt the existence of the body without doubting our own existence. So the body is not essential to our existence. Finally what a human being can distinguish clearly and distinctly can be separated by God, who is omnipotent (1631, pp. 487-488).

An appeal to an omnipotent God should not play a role in philosophy, however, since we don't know anything about Him, despite Descartes's attempt to prove His existence. Furthermore his 'thought experiment' does not result in a proof. Can we really doubt that our body exists? And if we can, is the idea of a self unaffected? This is doubtful. I think that when I doubt the existence of my body I doubt my own existence. All that is left is the existence of the thought, the doubt.

The question is whether what can be distinguished clearly and distinctly can therefore exist separately. As I have suggested, this is not true for properties. Consider the length of a line. It can be distinguished from its breadth, but this does not mean that the length can exist without the breadth, as Descartes's contemporary Arnauld remarked in the *Fourth Objections* to the *Méditations* (1643, p. 641). So if thought is not a thing, contrary to Descartes's assumption, but a property, his argument does not work. Furthermore from the fact that it is (logically) possible for thought to exist by itself, it does not follow that thought does exist by itself. Without the premise of an omnipotent God all that is left is the idea that thought and body are distinguishable and that the essence of my thought consists in my thought. It is not surprising that the idea that I form of myself consists only in my thought if I purposely confine myself to thought.

The idea that the soul is immortal is in conflict with the fact that during our life it does not exist continuously. It is temporarily absent during dreamless sleep. As is known we more often notice that we dreamt when awakened suddenly than when we slowly wake up by ourselves. In the latter case we frequently forget that we dreamt. But if we don't remember any dreams when awakened suddenly there is no reason to think that we dreamt the moment before. Locke argued that the soul does not always think (1690, Bk II, ch. 1) without concluding that it does not exist when not thinking. This conclusion is natural, however, when consciousness is the essence of the soul. One would expect, of something that is immortal, that it exists continuously. But this condition is not satisfied by our soul insofar we know.

One could argue that the soul when not functioning (i.e. not having conscious episodes) nevertheless exists. But what does this supposition mean? If it only means that normal bodily processes will make that soul function again (Swinburne, 1987, p. 177), the soul is, when not functioning, a mere disposition and nothing real. Or one might assume that someone who is in dreamless sleep has sensations that are connected to his vital functions, and which would cease if he died but which he has forgotten when he wakes up (Leibniz, 1765, II, 1 section 15). But it hardly seems plausible that such sensations, which animals may have as well, constitute the soul which is supposed to be something immortal.

It is harder than one might think to imagine incorporeal souls. It may be possible to imagine one such mind on the basis of one's own case by analogy with dreams in which we have mental images without any representation of our own body. But it would be egocentric to think that there is only one such mind. On the other hand, the idea that there is more than one such mind raises even more serious problems.

a) How could we identify such minds? Whenever we notice something in this life it is something physical. Contact with pure spirits seems impossible. At the very least a mind would need something like a voice in order to manifest itself, and then it would no longer be a pure mind. When someone thinks that he has contact with a mind while there is nothing physical, this contact would be indistinguishable from a hallucination, dream or fantasy. So even if minds existed, we would not know it (cf. Strawson, 1971, ch. 2).

b) Minds would be distinguished by differences in mental states, thoughts, feelings etc. But if they had the same mental states there would be a problem about the distinction between them. Physical objects can be distinguished merely by the fact that they are in different places (Campbell, 1974, pp. 44-45). The problem arises even for minds that are different. For they are in part similar if they have thoughts in common, for which this problem of distinction arises.

It might be suggested that the problem is solved by the fact that the memories of one mind are different from those of another mind. But what about minds that have lost their memory, as happens to people? Are they no longer minds? And if the mind of an insane person remembers Napoleon's life as his own, is this mind then Napoleon's? (Teichman, 1974, p. 17).

We can also not imagine how minds with completely different contents which exist at the same time can be distinguished if not on the basis of spatial location. A bodiless mind is everywhere and nowhere: how could the contents of different minds exist separately? If there are minds that are completely different from the physical they still need something physical to make themselves known and to distinguish themselves from one another.

When we speak about minds we assume that they are the bearers of states of consciousness. This is a difficult idea: the mind is something different from the states of consciousness and 'bears' them and unifies them. But we don't give it particular properties, since those belong to the states of consciousness. In itself this idea is no more obscure, however, than the idea of a material subject that is the bearer of material states. It is hard to answer the question what unifies these material or mental states to form an entity (Locke, 1690, Bk II, ch. 23). Consequently the idea of a material substance has been dropped. It has been replaced, roughly, by the idea of properties, processes and forces. And for this kind of reason the existence of a mental subject is sometimes also rejected.

The rejection of such a subject is compatible, however, with mentalism. It is possible to hold that there are mental states that differ fundamentally from physical states, while agreeing with Hume that they form a bundle without an underlying, single subject. The mentalist can hold, however, that there is a self, a mental organization, that gives the mental states of the individual a certain unity, but he thinks that the mental does not occur without the physical. I think it is unlikely that mental entities exist by themselves. Even if they did, we could not say anything about them (cf. Penelhum, 1970, ch. 6). This idea is the basis for a variety of views.

The mentalist is also confronted with the problem of the relationship between the physical and the mental. There are different views about this issue. a) There is causal interaction between the mental and the physical. b) There is no such interaction. Mental and physical processes run parallel. c) The physical acts on the mental but not vice versa. The mental is something separate, but it is a side effect (epiphenomenon). d) The view that I regard as most plausible is the view that the mental cannot by itself act as a cause, but can do so in combination with something physical. This is the theory of double causation, a modern form of interactionism.

Among these views epiphenomenalism is not compatible with the belief in a soul, the theory of double causation is hard to reconcile with that belief, and the other two views are compatible with it.

CAUSAL INTERACTION

The view that the mental and the physical act on each other is quite common. In ordinary language we often assume that there is such interaction. We say that the thought that it is late makes us get up and leave. A match that burns our hand causes us pain, and the pain causes us to withdraw our hand. The thought of future danger makes us break out in sweat. But there are various arguments against this common view.

1) (Un)intelligibility

A fundamental objection is that it is not intelligible how the mental and the physical could act on one another. According to this objection the mental and the physical are too different (Ryle, 1949, pp. 14, 65). One might reply that even in physics it happens that very different things act on each other. Yet the question remains how the thought that it is late causes an electrochemical process that sets our body in motion in order to leave. Mental states do not occupy any particular place. So how could they set into motion or change the movements of particles in the brain, which do occupy a particular place? In a letter to the princess Elizabeth (May 21, 1643) Descartes cited gravity as an illustration of the fact that no contact is required to set something in motion. The problem with this example is that it is still a case of a body acting on another body. Modern dualists do not seem to have made much progress when they rely on the observation that bodies don't act directly on each other but via electrical or gravitational fields (Popper-Eccles, 1977, pp. 181-182).

Alternatively the interactionist can admit that the interaction of mind and body is unintelligible and defend his view by claiming that we should simply resign ourselves to this fact. According to the modern conception of causality that is found in Hume and J.S. Mill, the connection between cause and effect is in general unintelligible. It is something that is observed empirically. We can call something a cause in the sense of a 'sufficient condition' when it is always followed by a certain effect. Such causal relations can be found, but there is nothing to understand about them.

This Humean view of causality is defensible provided that one adds that *ultimately* causality is not intelligible. Many causal connections are to some extent intelligible, because they can be explained by further lawlike connections, but ultimately there is nothing to understand. For example, we understand that fire makes water boil if we know the theory of heat and kinetic energy. But it is not intelligible why one particle makes another particle move. This might in turn become intelligible by virtue of a more fundamental law which is not intelligible. Ultimately the lawlike changes in the world are not understood but observed to be as they are (cf. Campbell, 1974, pp. 36-38).

This is not the place to devote more discussion to this conception of causality. But if it is correct, the unintelligibility of causal relations between the mental and the physical is not unusual. This interaction is a fundamental given and thus cannot be reduced to other laws. It makes no sense to ask how it takes place, for there is no further explanation, not even in physics (Richardson, 1982, pp. 25-26).

2) Is the Physical World a Causally Closed System?

There is a postulate in natural science that the physical world is a causally closed system. A physical process always has a physical cause. If this is true, then how could a mental state be the cause of a physical state? A physiologist will assume that a corporeal process is caused by another corporeal process, and will not accept any gaps in the chain.

A Cartesian interactionist will have to maintain that there are such gaps, however. This claim is sometimes defended on the ground that mental states can influence the movement of particles that are not causally determined by physical causes or for which one cannot, in any case, find such causes. But reliance on such considerations is risky, because they make the role of the mental depend on gaps in our knowledge of nature. The discovery of the relevant physical causes would then eliminate the role of the mental. I think, however, that even given such discoveries, the mental does act on the physical.

On the theory of double causation, which I will defend, the chain of physical causes and effects does not need to have gaps. On this view when the mental acts on the physical, the physical cause is not sufficient. So the continuity and causal activity of the physical world are preserved, although that world is not regarded as a causally closed system (Broad, 1980, p. 111).

The present objection to Cartesian interactionism is strengthened by an appeal to the law of conservation of energy. If a mental state changed something in the physical world, the energy of the physical system would increase, and if the physical acted on the mental there would be a loss of energy in the physical system. But this law is a very useful postulate in natural science. So there can be no interaction that is incompatible with this law.

Interactionists have pointed out, however, that according to the law in question, when energy leaves A it must get into B, but that the law does not require that A must lose energy in order to produce a change in B (Broad, 1980, p. 107). Such transfer of energy is probably necessary for causation within the physical world, but the interaction between the mental and the physical may not require energy. Although the interactionist can thus claim an exception for mind-body interaction, this is a weakness in his defense. Popper thinks that the law of the conservation of energy causes no serious problems for interaction. He suggests that the quantity of energy necessary for a change in direction of the body caused by the mind is very small. Furthermore one should consider not only the body but the entire physical system of the body and the earth (Popper-Eccles, 1977, p. 180). But even so it seems that the action of the mind on the body does add some energy, however little, to the total physical system.

The arguments against the interaction theory are not decisive. Nevertheless I think that the Cartesian conception of interaction is unacceptable because it requires that the mental can by itself cause physical movements, from which it follows that there are gaps in the sequence of physical processes. I will return to this point in my discussion of the theory of double causation.

PARALLELISM

One cannot rely on examples to show that there really is interaction. Such examples merely show that there is a correlation, that one process succeeds another one. Some philosophers who regard the objections against interaction as convincing have taken recourse to parallelism. This is not just the view that every mental event is parallelled by a physical event. That idea is also accepted by other theories, for instance, double aspect theory. Parallelism involves the further claim that there is no explanation for this parallel. Physical and mental processes do not cause one another. The cause of a physical process is always a physical process, and a mental process is always caused by a mental one. Leibniz (1686, pp. 66, 68) adhered to this view, and he did think that there is an explanation. He thought that the parallel is explained by the fact that God had ordained beforehand that the two series of events run parallel to each other, just as one could wind up two clocks and set them in such a way that they keep the same time. But now that the explanatory value of a divinity has been lost it seems impossible to find an explanation for the parallel between the mental and the physical.

A second, related, difficulty, is the following. For a physical event we can always find a physical cause, or at least an antecedent, physical event which could be its cause, but this is not so for the mental. When someone cuts himself and feels pain, it is not clear what mental event caused this pain. In the past one could appeal to God who had, as Leibniz thought, ordained that the pain occurs at the same time as the cut. But if one does not recognize the God of the pre-established harmony, the occurrence of pain becomes inexplicable for the parallelist, since there is no mental cause to be found. Even the assumption of unconscious representations that suddenly come to the surface cannot solve this problem. So I think that this theory has only historical significance, unless it is interpreted as the philosophical position that we cannot go beyond the conclusion that as a matter of empirical fact mental and physical processes run parallel to each other, since the correctness of any further philosophical interpretation of this fact cannot be proved. In contemporary philosophical discussions this is often all that is meant by parallelism. Thus Zamaria (1985) holds this view, following many earlier psychologists, on the ground that in contrast to materialism, this view recognizes a domain proper to the subject's consciousness, and creates room for introspection.

EPIPHENOMENALISM

Especially philosophers whose thought is influenced by a preoccupation with natural science often think that the corporeal can act on the mental but not vice versa. The mental is causally inert and a side effect (epiphenomenon). This view is inspired by the belief that natural science will eventually discover the causes for everything, and so far the causes it has found have all been physical. The epiphenomenalist does recognize the mental as a separate category, but it is as powerless as the steam from the whistle of a locomotive, as the nineteenth century biologist Th. Huxley put it (1874, p. 140). This is a dubious illustration, since the rest of the steam does push the engine and the steam from the whistle also has an effect.

Sometimes the mental seems to cause our behavior, for example when we execute a decision or when pain makes us wince. According to epiphenomenalism it is not our decision that makes us act, but the environment and/or a brain process. It is not the pain that causes us to wince, but only the injury, the damage to the skin and nerves. The physical universe is causally closed; there is no room for a causal role of mental events. The thoughts and the pain are no more than a reflection of physical processes. This theory is also accepted by Skinner, who is a methodological behaviorist in psychology. Our actions cannot be explained by our feelings, but only by factors in the environment that influence us, which he called 'reinforcers'. Our feelings are merely 'byproducts' of our behavior or of the operation of a 'reinforcer' (Skinner, 1972, pp. 88, 102, 108). Epiphenomenalism is combined with materialism in the view of K. Campbell: mental states are material states, but the mental experience of these states is not physical (1974, pp. 110-113).

Some of the arguments against interactionism also apply to this one-way version of it. For instance, the objection that interaction is unintelligible, and the objection that physical energy would be lost when a physical event causes a mental one. But these are precisely the objections that I do not regard as decisive, so that I cannot use them against epiphenomenalism.

Huxley relies on an experiment with frogs, in which the front part of their brain is removed. As a result they do hardly anything on their own initiative, and probably they no longer have consciousness. But they do still move in reaction to stimuli. For instance, when a hand on which they sit is slowly turned over so that they could fall off, they adjust their position. Huxley concludes that the mechanism that can produce this much without consciousness can probably produce everything a frog does without consciousness (1874, pp. 136-137). But this conclusion is entirely based on prejudice, for one might conclude as well that the animal can do everything without the most important part of its brain, which was removed. But in fact the experiment shows that without that part of its brain the animal no longer performs activities like looking for food, and that probably it is no longer able to perform them.

It has been argued that conditioned reflexes can be learned without consciousness, as in the case of Pavlov's famous dog whose saliva began to flow at the sound of a bell. It is supposed to follow that consciousness is also not necessary for deliberate learning, which is also supposed to be based on reflex arcs in the nervous system, but in a more complicated way. It is not at all clear, however, that the new stimulus—the sound of the bell—has its effect without the dog's consciousness. The dog must hear the bell and preferably be hungry. At least this is the way it works in a human being who reacts in this way to a bell announcing a meal. Such data also don't say anything about other forms of learning, such as the invention of *new* reactions to old stimuli (Wisdom, 1970, pp. 80-81).

182

We have the experience of mental events like sensations, feelings, sudden insights and decisions causing specific forms of behavior in us, but the epiphenomenalist must regard that experience as deceptive. He might try to support his view with an argument from Hume, who attacked the idea that a decision *must* be followed by an action. According to him we merely learn by experience that an action often follows a decision, and the idea of an internal force, from which the action must follow, is misleading. For someone who is suddenly paralyzed can execute the same decision without his limbs obeying him (1748, pp. 64ff.). But all that follows from this argument is that the decision is not a sufficient condition for the action; it may still be a necessary condition and thus part of the cause (Broad, 1980, pp. 101ff.).

I prefer to return to the simpler example of pain, however. Sometimes we have an irrepressible urge to withdraw our hand from a hot object, and we experience a connection between the sensation and the movement, which can be either involuntary or intentional. Hume points out that our consciousness does not tell us anything about the physiological events required to withdraw our hand (1748, p. 66). But I don't think this is a reason for denying that our consciousness acquaints us directly with the fact that we withdraw our hand because of pain. Hume's observation only implies that our consciousness does not inform us about the physiological explanation of the causal process. It is not relevant here whether we can deduce what we are about to do from the sensation of pain alone, without ever having observed our behavior. It is enough that we experience the sensation as compelling us to perform a particular action, which we then proceed to execute. I see no reason to regard such experiences as misleading.

The foregoing does imply that we must add something to the Humean conception of causality. We must add that we can experience something to be a causal factor for our mind. So there is more than the mere observation that something is always followed by a certain movement. This does not make the causal connection logically intelligible but it does make it somewhat intelligible in the sense that it gives us a feeling for it. So I want to add to the Humean view that the connection between cause and effect does not have to be intelligible, but that it can be.

The Implausibility of Epiphenomenalism

In the rest of this discussion we have to keep in mind that it is impossible to prove or disprove the epiphenomenalist view that only the physical is causally effective. One might think that it could be refuted by producing a situation in which the mental is eliminated. This elimination will have an effect on the physical world and thus it will be clear that the mental acts on the physical. For instance, one could anesthetize someone who is in pain so that he no longer displays pain behavior. But this approach does not work, since a change in the mental is always accompanied by a physical change. Anesthesia involves a physical change, and the epiphenomenalist can say that this physical change explains why the subject no longer behaves as if in pain, which was supposed to be due to the mental change. For the same reason it is impossible to prove this theory, however. This would require elimination of the mental which resulted in no physical change, but again a mental process cannot be eliminated without affecting the accompanying physical process.

Even if a theory can be neither proved nor disproved, one can make a judgment about its plausibility. One consideration that immediately suggests the implausibility of the theory in question is that it is unlikely that thought and sensation would have developed and continued to exist if they had no value for the survival of the human being. It follows from epiphenomenalism that the sensation of pain is dispensible, whereas in fact it is a warning sign that something is wrong in the organism. An organism that feels no pain does not survive for long. Popper (1977) emphasizes this conflict between epiphenomenalism and a widely accepted version of Darwinism (pp. 72-74). But is there such a conflict? A polar bear has a thick, warm coat, which is also heavy. The warmth of the coat contributes to his survival, but its weight does not. Its weight is an unavoidable byproduct of the thickness and warmth of the coat. Similarly the mental could be an unavoidable side effect of the complicated nature of the brain, without itself having survival value (Jackson, 1982, p. 134). So this argument is also not decisive.

According to epiphenomenalism the world would run the same way as it does now if there were no thoughts or desires. Immanuel Kant would have written the *Critique of Pure Reason*, his hand would have moved across the paper and written down the same signs, even if there had been no thoughts and no images in his head.

The epiphenomenalist himself would also have adhered to the same views he holds now if he had had no thoughts. He claims that there are mental events, although they have no causal efficacy. On his own view he would say the same thing if his mental contents suddenly ceased to exist. In that case his claim would be wrong, but since the existence of his mind makes no difference to the signs produced by his brain and mouth, these signs would be no different. So the epiphenomenalist cannot maintain that he posits the existence of mental processes because they exist. This seems paradoxical.

Let us consider a more ordinary example. Suppose that someone tells another person that there is war, and that the other person is frightened by this and gets heart palpitations. The statement 'there is war' is the cause of these palpitations. According to epiphenomenalism the statement must be analyzed into a physical component, the sounds or signs, and the mental component, its meaning. It is most natural to think that the meaning, which is the mental component, causes the heart palpitations. Thus something mental, in combination with something physical, causes a physical event. It makes no difference whether we say that the mental component first causes the fright, which is also mental, and only then the heart palpitations. In that case also the meaning of the sentence is the cause of the physical effect.

In principle the epiphenomenalist can always mantain that the phonetic sounds cause the physical effect. He can always take this stance, since it is impossible to assign a purely mental event as cause. Nevertheless this defense is not convincing since phonetic sounds in themselves are only sounds without meaning. Moreover, different sounds — in different languages — can carry the same meaning and have the same effect. So the meaning must be part of the cause.

One might think that the fact that a computer can play chess without having consciousness counts in favor of phenomenalism. I will only make a few remarks about this argument. It runs into trouble, since the mechanism of such a machine probably works very differently from the brain of a human being. So it does not follow from the fact that a machine can play chess, that a human being can do it without consciousness playing a role. Furthermore a computer can play chess only because it has been programmed by a human being who has thought about the game.

DOUBLE CAUSATION

The main problem with Cartesian interactionism is that it allows that the mental by itself can cause a physical event. This is problematic because it implies that the chain of physical events is sometimes interrupted by a mental factor. On my view when pain makes someone wince the cause of the wincing is not only the pain but also the damage to the skin that accompanies the pain. In Descartes's days one could think of thoughts as acting by themselves, independently of the physical, to cause us to move. But now we know that probably every thought is accompanied by an electrochemical process in the brain, and it has become unlikely that a thought alone can cause a movement. When we disturb the thought or the electrochemical process—when we disturb one of them we automatically disturb the other—the effect that would have occurred otherwise does not take place.

For this reason the most plausible view is that a mental event can cause something physical, but only because it is accompanied by a physical event (Becher, 1926, p. 222). The pain and the state of the nervous system together cause the movements of the person who is in pain. Sometimes it seems that a purely mental state causes another purely mental state, as when one thought leads to another thought, but in that case also a brain process is part of the cause.

For those who adhere to the Humean view of causation, and also recognize the mental as something real that is empirically given, it is natural to think that the mental has causal efficacy. Moreover our mental processes, fantasies and thoughts contain our perceptions of the world. To say that the mental has no causal efficacy implies that our perceptions lack causal efficacy, which is quite implausible.

The theory does not claim that for every mental event there is double causation. A physical event can by itself cause something physical and something mental, as when a pin prick causes pain and a process in the nervous system. But according to this theory a mental event always has a physical correlate, and its effect is also caused by its physical correlate. When someone decides to do something for some particular reason both the mental decision and the accompanying electrochemical brain process are necessary causal conditions for the movements of the body when this person acts.

The theory of double causation is taylored to the present state of our knowledge. Since we now know that mental states are probably always accompanied by physical states it has become impossible to prove and improbable that a mental state can cause a physical event by itself. Epiphenomalism is also an untestable hypothesis. According to that view bodily behavior could be caused by processes in the nervous system and brain alone, although those processes do not take place without sensation. There is no reason to believe that this is true. It is better to take into account whatever presents itself to us than to claim that half of it is dispensable. In a sense the double causation view is the least theoretical one. This is an advantage, since theoretical hypotheses about the relation between the mental and the physical cannot be tested.

Comparison with Epiphenomenalism

One might think that there is a significant connection between the theory of double causation and epiphenomenalism, whereas in fact they are profoundly different. The impression of similarity and the actual difference between these two views are most clearly brought out by consideration of the not uncommon, but erroneous claim that epiphenomenalism is really a kind of interactionism. Consider the physical factors P10, P11 and P12 and the mental factors M11 and M12, where the numbers indicate the order in time. So P11 and M11 are simultaneous, P11 comes after P10.

```
-    M11 M12
P10  P11 P12
```

According to epiphenomalism P10 is the cause of P11 and M11, and P11 is the cause of P12 and M12, but M11 has no effect. One might object to this view on the basis of the logical rule: if A always leads to B and there is no B then there is also no A. P10 is the cause of M11, that is, it always leads to M11. Thus if there were no M11 there would be no P10 and consequently also no P11 and P12. So it follows from epiphenomenalism that M11 is a cause of P12 on logical grounds. This kind or reasoning has led to the conclusion that epiphenomenalism is a form of interactionism.

This is a mistake which results from a failure to see, or to see clearly enough that the argument relies on 'logical grounds.' It is important to keep in mind that the connection between cause and effect is contingent. That means for our example that even if in the world as it is P10 causes M11, yet P10 could be the cause of P11 and P12 and not of M11. The epiphenomenalist supposes that even if P10 did not cause M11, it would still be sufficient to cause P12 via P11. There is no objection against this supposition on logical grounds.

It is clear for a further reason that the conclusion that M11 is a cause in epiphenomenalism relies on logical considerations. For according to the present argument M11 is also a necessary condition for P11 although M11 and P11 occur simultaneously and thus M11 cannot be causally necessary for P11.

On the other hand, according to the theory of double causation P11 is by itself not sufficient to cause P12; M11 is necessary as well and thus the mental does play a causal role.

This view of the mental's causal role fits our experience that mental events do play a part in determining our behavior. Feigl thinks that the epiphenomenalist can also explain this experience, because according to him behavior follows mental events regularly so that the mental can be causally effective (1969, pp. 36-37). But Feigl overlooks the fact that according to epiphenomenalism the mental is only logically necessary and it would be very strange if the experience that the mental moves us to act in certain ways is the 'translation' of a *logical* point. Hunger and sex are not logical matters. On the other hand it is plausible that we experience the kind of causal efficacy ascribed to the mental by the double causation theory.

The Acceptability of this Form of Interaction

On my view there is a certain kind of interaction between the mental and the physical. We need to consider now which of the objections against Cartesian interactionism also apply to the double causation theory. I have argued that the objection that interaction of mind and body is not intelligible does not cut much ice when one accepts the modern view that the connection between cause and effect is in general unintelligible. The fact that on my view there is no gap in the chain of physical events further undermines this objection. The question as to how the mental, which is not extended, can cause motion in the physical world no longer poses a problem.

The advantage of the double causation theory is that it conforms to the assumption made in natural science that the physical universe is continuous. An important reason for epiphenomenalism is the belief that a physical cause can be found for every physical phenomenon. This belief is also part of my view. There always is a physical cause, but it is not always the complete cause. Interactionism is consistent with there being no gap in physiological explanations and with causal determinism (Cornman & Lehrer, 1974, p. 277-278). The fact that a physical factor is not always the complete cause of a physical event has been regarded as a problem by the epiphenomenalist K. Campbell (1974, p. 52). But this view is compatible with physiology. For it does not require that we look for gaps in the physical system, as many dualists do in defending the causal efficacy of the mental (cf. Popper-Eccles, 1977, p. 476). Although the physical world is not a closed system, in natural science one can pretend that it is. The natural scientist is concerned with the physical only. If he has identified a physical cause he can proceed *as if* that is the only cause, even if there is in addition a mental factor. For the physical causal factor, which is a necessary but not a sufficient condition, is accompanied by a mental factor which is also necessary to produce the effect.

This approach short-circuits the following argument in favor of the materialistic identity theory. Some conscious processes are necessary conditions for the occurrence of certain physical events (actions), and in a complete neurophysiological theory these physical events will turn out to have physical causes. Therefore these states of consciousness are identical with physical states in the brain (Carruthers, 1986, p. 133). This argument has no force. It is to be expected that neurophysiology will find only neurophysiological causal conditions; it cannot discover other causal conditions. But the assumption that the causes this science discovers always constitute complete causes is unfounded. As the argument starts out by recognizing, there are other, mental causes in addition. Often the neurophysiological and mental conditions together provide complete causes.

Another objection against interactionism relied on the law of the conservation of energy; but it was unclear to what extent this law applies in the present context. The objection seems to have little force against my theory since it does not require that the mental by itself causes physical events. The question remains, however, whether the physical system loses energy when a physical state causes a mental state in addition to a physical one. I want to suggest that the energy required to cause, for instance, pain, is contained in the energy required to cause the process in the nervous system and brain that accompanies pain.

If one thinks that a physical event causes a mental one by itself, one must also accept that this does not take any energy. For if it did this energy would disappear completely from the physical system. At best it would return later when a mental process causes a physical process. There would be a solution to this problem if the law of the conservation of energy did not apply at every moment, but were only statistically valid. This is doubtful, however (Popper-Eccles, 1977, pp. 541-542).

It is better to assume that the production of a brain process plus the accompanying pain takes as much energy as it takes to produce the brain process. That is to say, the production of the pain takes no extra energy, which does not mean that it takes no energy, however. If we take this view then we need not say that the production of a mental state requires no transfer of energy. This transfer takes place within the physical world and could possibly be measured in the process in the nervous system and brain. I say 'possibly' since this discussion is rather theoretical. The amounts of energy are usually too small to be measured (Popper-Eccles, 1977, p. 565). It remains unclear what should be said about this issue. It may continue to be a problem for every form of interactionism, but I think that it is a less serious problem for the theory of double causation.

I do not want to suggest that my theory is the only possible one, but only that it is more plausible than the others, partly because I regard those as too problematic. So my preference for the theory of double causation is based in part on negative reasons. This is not uncommon in philosophy, however, and I have indicated at length what counts in favor of my theory.

Precise Formulation

I want to consider various questions about the precise formulation of the theory of double causation. This is important because incorrect answers to these questions can turn the theory into a different one.

1)

We saw that on the present theory a cut causes a process in the nervous system and pain, and that these two together cause pain behavior such as moaning. According to the old form of interactionism one could say that the cut causes pain and that the pain causes pain behavior. This requires a gap in the chain of physical events. My theory excludes the possibility of such gaps.

I don't think anyone will contest the claim that the cut causes the process in the nervous system. An other possible description must be distinguished from the one that I regard as correct. The correct one is:

a) The cut causes the neural process and the pain.

But if the pain arises only after the process in the nervous system we get:

b) The cut causes the process in the nervous system and this process causes the pain.

These statements differ with respect to their claims about the temporal order, assuming the principle that the effect comes after the cause. This principle is somewhat controversial, but I will assume here that it is correct for events.

If the pain occurs after the process in the nervous system we can say that the latter causes the former. But the pain is simultaneous with another physical process, namely a process in the brain or a part thereof, which follows the process in the nervous system. This results in the view that a physical process causes both the pain and a physical process. The second formulation, (b), is not so much incorrect as incomplete. It is in conflict with my view only if it is supposed to be a complete description. A complete description runs approximately as follows: the cut causes the process in the nervous system, which in turn causes the brain process and the pain. Or, if the pain occurs only after a part of the brain process has taken place: the cut causes the process in the nervous system and a part of the brain process and this causes the rest of the brain process and the pain.

The importance of a complete and correct formulation is that omission of the physical correlate of the pain opens the door to dualism. For when only the pain is mentioned as an effect there is a temptation to consider the pain as the only cause of the pain behavior which follows the pain.

2)

What is the best way to describe the causation of pain behavior, for instance moaning? The following description would be incorrect: 'the pain, which is caused by the process in the nervous system, causes the moaning.' This formulation suggests that there is a physical gap between the process in the nervous system and the behavior. This gap is probably not there. Even if the pain arises only after the process in the nervous system and after part of the brain process, then still the brain process continues and there is no physical gap. The following formulation is correct:

c) The brain process (or part thereof) and the pain cause the moaning.

It is possible, however, that the brain process starts before the mental state. It seems plausible that the early stage of the brain process causes the later stages of the process as well as the pain and the moaning. So maybe we could say:

d) The brain process causes the moaning, but it can do so only because it causes the pain.

(If it could cause moaning by itself, pain would be an epiphenomenon. I have argued against this possibility.)

The difference between (c) and (d) is that (d) does not *say* that pain is a necessary causal factor of the moaning. It does *follow* from (d) that pain is such a causal factor for the moaning. So far I have no objection to (d). But (d) must not be confused with the epiphenomenalist idea that the mental is only *logically* necessary for the production of the physical.

The fact that (c) is what we need is clear from the following considerations. Suppose there are the following mental (M) and physical (P) factors:

-    M9 M10 M11 -   -
P8   P9   P10 P11 P12 P13

M's and P 's with the same number are simultaneous and therefore cannot cause one another. P12 is the moaning and we assume that it is purely physical and that it is not coupled with a mental phenomenon. We can say now that P8 causes P12 because it also causes M9, M10 and M11. In addition, according to (c) P11 and M11 together cause P12. The explanation is not that P11 causes P12 by also causing something mental, namely M11. For P11 and M11 are simultaneous and so P11 does not cause M11. Since there is no M12 we cannot say that P11 causes P13 because it causes the mental state M12. So (c) cannot be translated into (d), which suggested epiphenomenalism. Sometimes (d) does not apply and it follows that (c) is more fundamental.

I have tried to explain the difference between double causation and epiphenomenalism, because the two views might be thought to be similar.

Furthermore my theory is compatible with what follows from the double aspect theory about the interaction between mind and body. A proponent of DAT will add that the M's and P's that are simultaneous are aspect of the same, but otherwise he can accept the theory of double causation as a description of what happens from an empirical point of view.

EPILOGUE

I have not discussed the relationship of my view to determinism. I want to make a few remarks about it now. On my view the freedom of the will cannot be based on an appeal to the mind. The mind continuously determines actions of the human being, but those are also determined by physical events. The mind cannot determine the course of events by itself. So if the physical is causally determined, then so is the mental.

It does not follow that human action must be determined. Since the development of quantum mechanics indeterminism has again become a respectable position. The course of an individual particle cannot be predicted, and the laws of quantum mechanics are statistical in nature. It is not clear, however, whether this indeterminacy is real or merely a result of the limits of human knowledge.

It is questionable that this kind of indeterminacy is of any use to the proponent of free will. For it is unlikely that human choice depends on the motion of a single particle. Making a choice is a complex process and probably depends on mass movement of particles, which is predictable (Blanshard, 1970, pp. 22-25).

So if one abandons the idea that the mind can direct the body by itself, as I propose, it is doubtful that there is freedom of the will. For this freedom is usually ascribed to the mind. But even if this freedom does not exist, the mind does have a function. It makes choices possible by displaying a variety of possibilities, even if the choise itself is determined. A determinist claims that a human being can often do what he wants but that he cannot want otherwise than he in fact does.

Another problem is the question of the origin of the mental. At the beginning of this book I briefly discussed panpsychism. The philosophical background of that view is explained clearly by Nagel (1980, ch. 13). This view does not seem plausible insofar as consciousness is concerned. Inanimate nature does not display any signs of consciousness, and so it probably does not have any. But if panpsychism is rejected and if consciousness is regarded as something different, one is faced with the question how it comes to be.

I have argued that the mental cannot be reduced to the physical. Theories based only on observation of the physical do not contain terms that imply consciousness. The mental is something different, and it must have come to be in the course of evolution. This is known as emergent evolution. Although the mental cannot be deduced from the properties of the physical it might be that once the correlations with the physical are discovered, the emergence of the mental can be explained as a development of the physical. The existence of beings with brains explains the origin of the mental. But the mental properties of an organism are not implied by the material composition of that organism and its brain. I will not elaborate on this theory about evolution. It is discussed extensively by a.o. Popper and Eccles (1977). But I mention it because it is presupposed by my view.

BIBLIOGRAPHY

For articles published in books I have specified the publication date of the book. For books I have usually given the date of the edition used; but for historical works I have given the original date of publication. So in many cases this date is useful only for purposes of quotation.

Addis, L. & Lewis, D. 1965 *Moore and Ryle: two ontologists*. Iowa City-The Hague.

Albritton, R. 1968 'On Wittgenstein's use of the term "criterion". In: Pitcher, ed. 1968.

Alston, W.P. 1972 'Emotion and feeling'. In: Edwards, ed. 1972.

Anscombe, G.E.M. 1968[5] *Intention*. Oxford.,

Anscombe, G.E.M. 1981 *Metaphysics and the philosophy of mind*. Collected philosophical papers, vol 2. Oxford.

Armstrong, D.M. 1967[2] *Bodily sensations*. London.

Armstrong, D.M.1971[3] *A materialist theory of the mind*. London.

Armstrong, D.M. & Malcolm, N. 1984 *Consciousness and causality. A debate on the nature of mind*. Oxford.

Aune, B. 1961 'The problem of other minds'. *The philosophical review*, vol. LXX.

Aune, B. 1963 'Feelings, moods, and introspection'. *Mind* 72.

Aune, B. 1965 'On the complexity of avowals'. *Philosophy in America, essays*, ed. M. Black. London.

Aune, B. 1967 *Knowledge, mind, and nature, an introduction to theory of knowledge and the philosophy of mind*. New York.

Austin, J.L. 1979[4] *Philosophical papers*. Oxford etc.

Ayer, A.J. 1971 'An honest ghost?'. In: Wood-Pitcher, eds. 1971.

Ayer, A.J. 1972[7] *Philosophical essays*. London.

Ayer, A.J. 1973[4] *The concept of a person and other essays*. London.

Ayer, A.J.1984[2] *Philosophy in the twentieth century*. London.

Baier, K. 1970 ' Smart on sensations'. In: Borst, ed. 1970.

Bailey, G.W.S. 1979 *Privacy and the mental*. Amsterdam.

Becher, E. 1926 *Einführung in die Philosophie*. München & Leipzig.

Bedford, E. 1964 'Emotions'. In: Gustafson, ed. 1964.

Bergson, H. 1896 *Matière et mémoire*. Paris, 1968, 92th ed.

Berkeley, G. 1709 *A new theory of vision and other select philosophical writings*. London etc. 1929

Blanshard, B. 1939 *The nature of thought*. 2 vol. London, 1969[5].

Blanshard, B. 1970[3] 'The case for determinism'. *Determinism and freedom in the age of modern science*, ed. S. Hook. New York.

Block, N. 1983 'Troubles with functionalism'. In: Block, ed. 1983

Block, N., ed. 1983² *Readings in philosophy of psychology*. Vol. I. Cambridge (Mass.).

Block, N., ed. 1981 *Readings in philosophy of psychology*. Vol. II. London.

Block, N., ed. 1981 (b) *Imagery*. Cambridge, (Mass.)

Block, N. & Fodor, J.A. 1983 'What psychological states are not'. In: Block, ed. 1983.

Bohman, S. 1977 *Analyses of consciousness as well as observation, volition and valuation*. Uppsala.

Borst, C.V., ed. 1970 *The mind/brain identity theory*. London.

Bowlby, J. 1981⁴ *Attachment and loss II. Separation: anxiety and anger*. Harmondsworth.

Brentano, F. 1874 *Psychologie vom empirischen Standpunkt*. 3 Bände. Hrsg. v. O. Kraus. Hamburg 1973.

Broad, C.D. 1980⁹ *The mind and its place in nature*. London.

Brown, J.A.C. 1976¹¹ *Freud and the Post-Freudians*. Harmondsworth.

Brzezinski, J., ed. 1985 *Consciousness: methodological and psychological approaches*. Amsterdam.

Bunge, M. 1980 *The mind-body problem, a psychobiological approach*. Oxford etc.

Burton, A. & Radford, J., eds. 1978 *Thinking in perspective, critical essays in the study of thought processes*. London.

Campbell, C.A. 1969 'Ryle on the intellect'. In: Lewis, ed. 1969

Campbell, K. 1974² *Body and mind*. London.

Campbell, K. 1986 'Can intuitive psychology survive the growth of neuroscience?'. *Inquiry* 29.

Candlish, S. 1980 'The real private language argument'. *Philosophy*, 55.

Carnap, R. 1932 'Psychology in physical language'. *Logical positivism*, ed. A.J. Ayer. New York 1959.

Carruthers, P. 1986 *Introducing persons, theories and arguments in the philosophy of mind*. London & Sydney.

Castañeda, H.-N. 1971 'The private language argument as a reductio ad absurdum' (i). In: Jones, ed. 1971.

Chihara, C.S. & Fodor, J.A. 1968 'Operationalism and ordinary language: A critique of Wittgenstein'. In: Pitcher, ed. 1968.

Chisholm, R. 1976 *Person and object, a metaphysical study*. London.

Chomsky, N. 1980 *Rules and representations*. New York.

Choy, V. 1982 'The philosophy of James W. Cornman'. *Philosophical studies* 41 (1982).

Churchland, P.M. 1985⁴ *Matter and consciousness. A contemporary introduction to the philosophy of mind*. Cambridge, (Mass.).

Churchland, P.S. 1986² *Neurophilosophy. Toward a unified science of the mind-brain*. Cambridge (Mass.) & London.

Cornman, J. 1969 'On the elimination of 'sensations' and sensations'. In: O'Connor, ed. 1969

Cornman, J.W. & Lehrer, K. 1974² *Philosophical problems and arguments: an introduction*. New York & London.

Davidson, D. 1980 *Essays on actions and events*. New York.

Dennett, D.C. 1969 *Content and consciousness*. London.

Dennett, D.C. 1981² *Brainstorms, philosophical essays on mind and psychology*. Hassocks.

196

Descartes, R. 1641 *Méditations touchant la première philosophie*. In: *Oeuvres philosophiques, II*, ed. F. Alquié. Paris 1975.
Dilman, I. 1984 *Freud and the mind*. Oxford.
Donagan, A. 1968 'Wittgenstein on sensation'. In: Pitcher, ed. 1968.
Ducasse, C.J. 1968 'Minds, matter and bodies'. In: Smythies, ed. 1968.

Ericsson, K.A. & Simon, H. 1980 'Verbal reports as data'. *Psychological Review* 87.
Edwards, P., ed. 1972² *The encyclopedia of philosophy*. 8 vol. New York-London.
Ellenberger, H.F. 1970 *The discovery of the unconscious. The history and evolution of dynamic psychiatry*. New York.
Erdmann, B. 1907 *Wissenschaftliche Hypothesen uber Leib und Seele*. Köln.
Evans, C.O. 1970 *The subject of consciousness*. London.

Feigl, H. 1967 *The "mental" and the "physical". The essay and a postscript*. Second ed., Minneapolis.
Feigl, H. 1969 'Mind-body, not a pseudoproblem'. In: Hook, ed. 1969.
Feyerabend, P. 1970 'Comment: 'Mental events and the brain''. In: Borst, ed. 1970.
Feyerabend, P. 1970b 'Materialism and the mind-body problem'. In: Borst, ed. 1970
Findlay, J.N. 1969 'Recommendations regarding the language of introspection'. In: Lewis, ed. 1969
Fingarette, H. 1969 *Self-deception*. London.
Flew, A. 1978 *A rational animal and other philosophical essays on the nature of man*. Oxford.
Fodor, J.A. 1968 *Psychological explanation, an introduction to the philosophy of psychology*. New York.
Fodor, J.A. 1975 *The language of thought*. Hassocks.
Fogelin, R.J. 1980² *Wittgenstein*. Boston etc.
Freud, S. 1900 *Die Traumdeutung*. Frankfurt am Main. 1982.
Freud, S. 1915 *Psychologie des Unbewussten*. Studienausgabe, Bnd III. Frankfurt am Main, 1982⁵.

Geach,P. 1971⁵ *Mental acts*. London.
Gregory, R.L. 1984² *Mind in science*. Harmondsworth.
Groot, A.D. de 1978² *Thought and choice in chess*. The Hague etc.
Gustafson, D.F., ed. 1964 *Essays in philosophical psychology*. New York.
Guttenplan, S., ed. 1977² *Mind and language, Wolfson College lectures 1974*. Oxford.

Hacker, P.S.M. 1986 *Insight and illusion. Themes in the philosophy of Wittgenstein*. Rev. ed., Oxford.
Hallett, G. 1977 *A companion to Wittgenstein's 'Philosophical Investigations'*. Ithaca.
Hampshire, S. 1970⁴ *Thought and action*. London.
Hampshire, S. 1971 *Freedom of mind and other essays*. Princeton N.J.
Heidelberger, H. 1965 'On characterizing the psychological'. *Philosophy and phenomenological research*, vol. XXVI.
Hempel, C.G. 1935 'The logical analysis of psychology'. In: Block, ed. 1983.
Hilgard, E.R. 1986 *Divided consciousness: multiple controls in human thought and action*. Second ed., New York etc.
Hofstadter, D.R. & Dennett, D.C. 1981 *The mind's I, fantasies and reflections on self and soul*. New York.

Hook, S., ed. 1969[4] *Dimensions of mind, a symposium*. London.
Horgan, T. 1984 'Functionalism, qualia and the inverted spectrum'. *Philosophy and phenomenological research*, XLIV.
Hume, D. 1738 *A treatise of human nature*. 2 vol. London 1956.
Hume, D. 1748 *Enquiries concerning the human understanding and concerning the principles of morals*. Introd. L.A. Selby-Bigge. Oxford 1972[2].
Humphrey, N. 1984[2] *Consciousness regained. Chapters in the development of mind*. Oxford.
Huxley, Th. 1874 'On the hypothesis that animals are automata, and its history'. In: Vesey, ed. 1970

Jackson, F. 1982 'Epiphenomenal qualia'. *The philosophical quarterly*, 32.
James, W. 1890 *The principles of psychology*. 2 vol. New York, 1950.
James, W. 1912 *Essays in radical empiricism*. Cambridge etc. 1976.
Jones, O.R., ed. 1971 *The private language argument*. London.

Kant, I. 1781 *Kritik der reinen Vernunft*. Hrsg. K. Vorländer. Halle a.d. S. 1900.
Kenny, A. 1968 'Cartesian privacy'. In: Pitcher, ed. 1968
Kenny, A. 1969[4] *Action, emotion and will*. London.
Kenny, A. 1976[3] *Wittgenstein*. Harmondsworth.
Kim, J. 1983 'Physicalism and the multiple realizability of mental states'. In: Block, ed. 1983.
Kosslyn, S.M. 1980 *Image and mind*. Cambridge (Mass.) & London.
Kripke, S.A. 1981 *Naming and necessity*. Second ed., Cambridge (Mass.).
Kripke, S.A. 1982 *Wittgenstein on rules and private language*. Oxford.

Leibniz, G.W. 1686 'The discourse on metaphysics' & 'Correspondence with Arnauld'. In: Vesey, ed. 1970.
Leibniz, G.W. 1765 *Neue Abhandlungen über den menschlichen Verstand*. Hamburg 1971.
Levin, M.E. 1979 *Metaphysics and the mind-body problem*. Oxford.
Levin, M.E. 1984 'Why we believe in other minds'. *Philosophy and phenomenological research*, XLIV.
Lewes, G.H. 1877 'The physical basis of mind'. In: Vesey, ed. 1970.
Lewis, C.I. 1941 'Some logical considerations concerning the mental'. In: Vesey, ed. 1970.
Lewis, D. 1983 'Psychophysical and theoretical identifications'. In: Block, ed. 1983.
Lewis, D. 1983a 'Mad pain and Martian pain'. In: Block, ed. 1983.
Lewis, D. 1983b 'Review of Putnam'. In Block, ed. 1983.
Lewis, H.D. 1969 *The elusive mind*. London-New York.
Lewis, H.D. 1982 *The elusive self*. London.
Lewis, H.D., ed. 1968[2] *Clarity is not enough*. London.
Locke, D. 1971[2] *Myself and others, a study in our knowledge of minds*. Oxford.
Locke, D. 1971b *Memory*. London.
Locke, J. 1690 *An essay concerning human understanding*. 2 vol. Ed. A.C. Fraser. Dover Books, 1959, London.
Lovejoy, A.O. 1960[2] *The revolt against dualism*. La Salle.
Lucas, J.R. a.o. 1972 *The nature of mind*. Edinburgh.
Lurie, Y. 1979 'Inner states'. *Mind LXXXVIII*.

198

Lycan, W.G. 1987 *Consciousness*. Cambridge (Mass.) & London.
Lyons, W. 1986 *The disappearance of introspection*. Cambridge (Mass.) & London.

MacIntyre, A.C. 1967[4] *The unconscious, a conceptual study*. London
MacIntyre, A.C. 1971 *Against the self-images of the age*. London.
Madell, G. 1986 'Neurophilosophy: a principled sceptic's response'. *Inquiry* 29.
Malcolm, N. 1972 *Problems of mind. Descartes to Wittgenstein*. London.
Malcolm, N. 1975 *Knowledge and certainty. Essays and lectures*. New York.
Margolis, J. 1978 *Persons and minds. The prospects of nonreductive materialism*. Dordrecht etc.
Margolis, J. 1984 *Philosophy of psychology*. Englewood Cliffs.
Marres, R. 1985 *Filosofie van de geest*. Muiderberg.
Matthews, G.B. 1971 'Mental copies'. In: Wood-Pitcher, eds. 1971
McGinn, C. 1982 *The character of mind*. Oxford.
McGinn, C. 1983 *The subjective view, secondary qualities and indexical thoughts*. Oxford.
McGinn, C. 1984 'What is the problem of other minds?'. *The Aristotelian Society. Suppl. vol. LVIII*. London.
Meehl, P.E. & Sellars, W. 1956 'The concept of emergence'. *Minnesota studies in the philosophy of science*, 1, eds. H. Feigl & M. Scriven. Minneapolis.
Mellor, D.H. 1978 'Conscious belief'. *Proceedings of the Aristotelian Society* 78 (1977/78). London.
Mill, J.S. 1865 *An examination of Sir William Hamilton's philosophy*. Coll. Works IX. London 1979.
Mill, J.S. 1865a *Auguste Comte and positivism*. Univ. of Michigan, 1968.
Moore, G.E. 1922 *Philosophical studies*. London 1970[7]
Morick, H., ed. 1967 *Wittgenstein and the problem of other minds*. New York etc.
Morris, C.W. 1932 *Six theories of mind*. Chicago & London 1966[5]

Nagel, Th. 1970 'Physicalism'. In: Borst, ed. 1970.
Nagel, Th. 1980[3] *Mortal questions*. Cambridge etc.
Nagel, Th. 1986 *The view from nowhere*. Oxford.
Nisbett, R. & Wilson, T. 1977 'Telling more than we can know: verbal reports on mental processes'. *Psychological Review* 84.

Oakley, D.A., ed. 1985 *Brain and mind*. London & New York.
Oakley, D.A. en Eames, L.C. 1985 'The plurality of consciousness'. In: Oakley, ed. 1985
O'Connor, J., ed. 1969 *Modern materialism: readings on mind-body identity*. New York etc.
Oswald, I. 1972[5] *Sleep*. Harmondsworth.
Owens, J. 1986 'The failure of Lewis' functionalism'. In: Stevenson a.o. (eds) 1986.

Palmer, D. 1975 'Unfelt pains'. *American philosophical quarterly*, 12.
Passmore, J. 1970[2] *Philosophical reasoning*. London.
Peacocke, C. 1984 'Consciousness and other minds I'. *The Aristotelian Society. Suppl. Vol. LVIII*. London.
Penelhum, T. 1964 'The logic of pleasure'. In: Gustafson, ed. 1964
Penelhum, T. 1970 *Survival and disembodied existence*. London.

199

Penfield, W. 1975 *The mystery of the mind, a critical study of consciousness and the human brain*. Princeton.
Pitcher, G. 1964 *The philosophy of Wittgenstein*. Englewood Cliffs.
Pitcher, G., ed. 1968 *Wittgenstein, the Philosophical Investigations*. London.
Place, U.T. 1964 'The concept of heed'. In: Gustafson, ed. 1964.
Place, U.T. 1970 'Is consciousness a brain process ?' In: Borst, ed. 1970
Plessner, H. 1953 'Die Deutung des mimischen Ausdrucks. Ein Beitrag zur Lehre vom Bewusstsein des anderen Ichs'. *Zwischen Philosophie und Gesellschaft*. Bern.
Polten, E.P. 1973 *Critique of the psycho-physical identity theory*. Pref. by John Eccles. The Hague.
Popper, K.R. & Eccles, J.C. 1977 *The self and its brain*. Berlin etc.
Price, H.H. 1969² *Thinking and experience*. London.
Price, H.H. 1969b 'Some objections to behaviorism'. In: Hook, ed. 1969.
Prince, M. 1885 'The nature of mind and human automatism'. In: Vesey, ed. 1970.
Putnam, H. 1982⁴ *Mind, language and reality*. Philosophical papers, vol. 2. Cambridge.

Quinton, A. 1968 'Mind and matter'. In: Smythies, ed. 1968.
Quinton, A. 1971 'Ryle on perception'. In: Wood-Pitcher, 1971.

Radford, C. 1972 'Pain and pain behaviour'. *Philosophy* XLVII.
Reeves, J.W. 1958 *Body and mind in Western thought*. Harmondsworth.
Reid, T. 1785 *Essays on the intellectual powers of man*. Introd. B. Brody. Cambridge (Mass.) & London 1969.
Rhees, R. 1968 'Can there be a private language?'. In Pitcher, ed. 1968.
Richardson, R.C. 1982 'The 'scandal' of Cartesian interactionism'. *Mind*, XCI.
Robinson, H. 1982 *Matter and sense, a critique of contemporary materialism*. Cambridge etc.
Rorty, R. 1970 'Mind-body identity, privacy and categories'. In: Borst, ed. 1970.
Rorty, R. 1980² *Philosophy and the mirror of nature*. Princeton.
Russell, B. 1921 *The analysis of mind*. London, 1971¹⁰.
Russell, B. 1927 *Outline of philosophy*. London 1979¹¹.
Ryle, G. 1949 *The concept of mind*. Harmondsworth 1970⁵.
Ryle, G. 1979 *On thinking*. Oxford.

Sartre, J.-P. 1939 *Esquisse d'une théorie des émotions*. Paris 1965.
Sartre, J.-P. 1943 *L'être et le néant*. Paris 1963.
Scheler, M. 1922 *Wesen und Formen der Sympathie*. Bern-München, 1973⁶.
Schopenhauer, A. 1818 *Die Welt als Wille und Vorstellung*. Sämtl. Werke, I Band. Inselverlag, Leipzig.
Scriven, M. 1956 'A study of radical behaviorism'. *Minnesota Studies in the philosophy of science*, eds. H. Feigl en M. Scriven. Vol. I. Minneapolis.
Searle, J.R. 1983 *Intentionality. An essay in the philosophy of mind*. Cambridge etc.
Searle, J. 1984 *Minds, brains and science*. Cambridge (Mass.).
Sellars, W.F. 1971⁴ *Science, perception and reality*. London.
Shaffer, J.A. 1968 *Philosophy of mind*. Englewood Cliffs.
Shaffer, J.A. 1970 'Could mental states be brain processes?'. In: Borst, ed. 1970
Shaffer, J.A. 1970a 'Mental events and the brain'. In: Borst, ed. 1970.
Shoemaker, S. 1970⁴ *Self-knowledge and self-identity*. Ithaca & London.
Shoemaker, S. 1983 'Functionalism and qualia'. In: Block, ed. 1983.

Shorter, J.M. 1971 'Imagination'. In: Wood-Pitcher, eds. 1971.
Skinner, B.F. 1964 'Behaviorism at fifty'. In: Wann, ed. 1970.
Skinner, B.F. 1965[2] *Science and human behavior*. New York.
Skinner, B.F. 1972[9] *Beyond freedom and dignity*. New York.
Smart, J.J.C. 1970 'Sensations and brain processes'. In: Borst, ed. 1970.
Smart, J.J.C. 1970a 'Materialism'. In: Borst, ed. 1970
Smith, P. en Jones, O.R. 1986 *The philosophy of mind. An introduction*. Cambridge etc.
Smythies, J.R., ed. 1968[2] *Brain and mind*. London.
Sperry, R. 1983 *Science and moral priority, merging mind, brain, and human values*. Oxford.
Spinoza, B. de 1677 *Ethica*. Transl. N. van Suchtelen. Amsterdam 1979.
Stevenson, L. a.o. (eds) 1986 *Mind, causation and action*. Oxford.
Strawson, P.F. 1968 'Review of Wittgenstein's Philosophical Investigations'. In: Pitcher, ed.1968.
Strawson, P.F. 1971[5] *Individuals, an essay in descriptive metaphysics*. London.
Strongman, K.T. 1973 *The psychology of emotion*. London.
Sussman, A.N. 1975 'Mental entities as theoretical entities'. *American philosophical quarterly*, vol. 12.
Swinburne, R. 1987[2] *The evolution of the soul*. Oxford.

Teichman, J. 1974 *The mind and the soul, an introduction to the philosophy of mind*. London.
Thomson, J.J. 1971 'The verification principle and the private language argument'(i). In: Jones, ed. 1971.
Thomson, R. 1963[3] *The psychology of thinking*. Harmondsworth.
Trigg, R. 1970 *Pain and emotion*. Oxford.

Urmson, J.O. 1969[3] *Philosophical analysis, its development between the two world wars'*. Oxford.

Valentine, E. 1978 'Perchings and flights: introspection'. In: Burton-Radford, eds. 1978.
Vendler, Z. 1972 *Res cogitans, an essay in rational psychology*. Ithaca & London.
Vendler, Z. 1984 *The matter of minds*. Oxford.
Vesey, G.N.A., ed. 1970[2] *Body and mind, readings in philosophy*. London.
Vesey, G.N.A. 1965 *The embodied mind*. London.

Wann, T.W., ed. 1970[6] *Behaviorism and phenomenology, contrasting bases for modern psychology*. Chicago & London.
Warnock, M. 1976 *Imagination*. London.
Weizenbaum, J. 1976 *Computer power and human reason*. San Francisco.
Wenzl, A. 1933 *Das Leib-Seele-Problem im Lichte der neueren Theorien der physischen und seelischen Wirklichkeit*. Leipzig.
White, A.R. 1968[2] *The philosophy of mind*. New York.
Whiteley, C.H. 1961 'Behaviourism'. *Mind* 70.
Whiteley, C.H. 1973 *Mind in action*. London etc.
Williams, B. 1973 *Problems of the self, philosophical papers 1956-1972*. Cambridge.
Williams, B. 1979[2] *Descartes: the project of pure enquiry*. Harmondsworth.

Wilson, E. 1979 *The mental as physical.* London etc.

Wisdom, J. 1970³ *Problems of mind and matter.* Cambridge.

Wisdom, J. 1965³ *Other minds.* Oxford.

Wisdom, J.O. 1972 'Psychoanalytic theories of the unconscious'. In: Edwards, ed. 1972, vol. 8

Wittgenstein, L. 1953 *Philosophical Investigations.* Eds. G.E.M. Anscombe en R. Rhees. Transl. G.E.M. Anscombe. Oxford 1958².

Wittgenstein, L. 1958 *The blue and brown books.* New York 1965.

Wittgenstein, L. 1967 *Zettel.* Eds. G.E.M. Anscombe en G.H. von Wright. Transl. G.E.M. Anscombe. Oxford, 1981³.

Wood, O.P. & Pitcher, G., eds. 1971² *Ryle.* London.

Wright, E. 1983 'Inspecting images'. *Philosophy* 58.

Zamiara, K. 1985 'In support of psycho-physical parallelism'. In: Brzezinski, ed. 1985.

NAME INDEX